Build Your Home Theater

Send Us Your Comments

To comment on this book or any other PRIMA TECH title, visit our reader response page on the Web at www.prima-tech.com/comments.

How to Order

For information on quantity discounts, contact the publisher: Prima Publishing, P.O. Box 1260BK, Rocklin, CA 95677-1260; (916) 787-7000. On your letterhead, include information concerning the intended use of the books and the number of books you wish to purchase.

Build Your Home Theater

Gareth M. de Bruyn
Cub Karabian

A DIVISION OF PRIMA PUBLISHING

A Division of Prima Publishing

Prima Publishing and colophon are registered trademarks of Prima Communications, Inc. PRIMA TECH and *In a Weekend* are trademarks of Prima Communications, Inc., Roseville, California 95661.

Publisher: Stacy L. Hiquet

Marketing Manager: Judi Taylor

Associate Marketing Manager: Jody Kennen

Managing Editor: Sandy Doell

Acquisitions Editor: Rebecca Fong

Project Editor: Heather Talbot

Technical Reviewer: Keith A. Davenport

Copy Editor: Andy Saff

Interior Layout: Shawn Morningstar

Cover Design: Prima Design Team

Indexer: Joy Dean Lee

Important: Prima Publishing cannot provide software support. Please contact the appropriate software manufacturer's technical support line or Web site for assistance.

Prima Publishing and the author have attempted throughout this book to distinguish proprietary trademarks from descriptive terms by following the capitalization style used by the manufacturer.

Information contained in this book has been obtained by Prima Publishing from sources believed to be reliable. However, because of the possibility of human or mechanical error by our sources, Prima Publishing, or others, the Publisher does not guarantee the accuracy, adequacy, or completeness of any information and is not responsible for any errors or omissions or the results obtained from use of such information. Readers should be particularly aware of the fact that the Internet is an ever-changing entity. Some facts may have changed since this book went to press.

ISBN: 0-7615-2744-3

Library of Congress Catalog Card Number: 00-100002

Printed in the United States of America

00 01 02 03 04 DD 10 9 8 7 6 5 4 3 2 1

To my father,
Who bought me my first stereo system,
And who taught me to always ask how things work…

—Cub Karabian

To my parents, who never quite understood what I was doing,
But encouraged, supported, and paid for it nonetheless.

—Gareth de Bruyn

CONTENTS AT A GLANCE

CONTENTS

SATURDAY MORNING
Accessories and Purchasing 71

SUNDAY EVENING
Remotes, Operating the System,
Plus Video and Acoustic Adjustments 291

ABOUT THE AUTHORS

John Thomas "Cub" Karabian, a California native, attended college at the University of California at Davis, majoring in perceptual psychology and rhetoric and communications, also earning a law degree from University of California at Hastings. Cub has been involved in the home theater industry since its inception, roughly 10 years ago—first as a hobbyist and later as the director of marketing and systems integration with California Audio Technology (CAT), the industry's only custom loudspeaker design firm. Cub's passion is home theater system design, second only to watching movies on these systems. His favorite DVDs to watch are *Dances with Wolves* and *Aliens*. This is his first book on the topic of home theater, with more to come.

Gareth Morgan de Bruyn, originally from South Africa, was an MIS consultant until recently, now joining the world's leading Linux Solutions company, Penguin Computing as the director of Information Technology. Gareth bought his first set of home theater speakers in 1988 and has enjoyed watching the industry grow to the level where home theater quality exceeds that of actual movie theaters. His favorite DVDs are *Ghost in the Shell* and *Saving Private Ryan*, and he looks forward to the release of *Braveheart* and, perhaps someday, *Star Wars* on DVD. Gareth is an author and the series editor for Prima's *SAP* series. This is his first book on the topic of home theater, but definitely not his last.

ACKNOWLEDGMENTS

The authors want to acknowledge and thank the following people for their help in writing this text. Thank you, Rebecca Fong, for having the courage to present this title and support us in our efforts despite people's skepticism that home theater was actually popular. We thank Heather Talbot for being flexible with our schedules and helping us stay focused on the work and keep it on schedule. Thank you, Keith Davenport, for ensuring technical accuracy. Thank you, Robert Lyfareff, for your contributions to the initial part of this book.

We thank the close and special people in our lives who supported us despite our rotten moods and the ridiculous hours spent on this project. Thank you for not abandoning us or trying to discourage us from participating in this endeavor.

We would like to thank the many generous industry professionals for their help in contributing product, giving advice, and providing general support for this endeavor. Thank you to Gordon Sell and Bill Kanner, awesome public relations men and our initial contacts, who put us in touch with a great many people in the industry. We thank Kevin Lee and Daniel Graham from Monster Cable for their generous donations and reference material. To Jerry Bashin at Lovan Audio Racks, thank you for supporting this endeavor 100 percent and believing in our project. Your enthusiasm and your company's help were incredible. Thank you, Richard Sturger of Audio Design Associates, for showing us what true audio excellence is. Thank you, Randy Dowis at NHT, for lending us and providing us with sets of incredible speakers and information, and for being patient with our changing requests.

Thank you to Dawn Matsuyama of DVDexpress.com, now Express.com, for believing in the success of this project and investing your company in it. Thank you Debi Sherwood and Crown Audio, for providing us with incredible amplifiers. To Pam Golden Loder, Tim McNamara, and Lisa Fasold, thank you for helping us find the right people to talk with. Thank you to the many people at Blanc & Otus (especially Courtney Jacobs) who helped us with our TiVo questions and provided us with a unit to test and try out. Believe us, after TiVo, there is no going back to regular television.

Thank you to the companies Atlantic Technology, TiVo, and Outlaw Audio, and to Mike May at Rane Corporation and Randy Bingham at Sunfire for use of their equipment and explanations of factors we did not understand.

Finally, the authors want to thank George Lucas and Steven Spielberg, whose early and current works inspired the authors to love the cinema, but we regret that we have not been able to enjoy your movies in the full audio and video experience of DVD.

INTRODUCTION

Welcome to the amazing and addicting world of home theater. If you love going to the movies and experiencing the silver screen, this is your guide to the incredibly rewarding endeavor of building your own home theater. All the mystery and confusing techno-speak are explained in everyday English so that you might enjoy not only the final product, but the process of building this room yourself.

With the advent of new technology in computers, processors, sound quality, and digital formats, the incredible experience of home theater can often surpass what you will hear and see at your local movie theater. This book will guide you through what comprises a home theater, and how to set up one. Our combined years of experience and know-how will be transferred to you and transform a once regular room in your house into a showpiece and topic of conversation.

What This Book Is About

You have just bought a DVD player, and you want to take advantage of all its features. Or perhaps you just spent an evening at the house of someone who has his or her very own home theater. The task to build your own looks ominous and daunting, but in actuality it is a very obtainable goal, from a technical and fiscal perspective.

This book explains home theater to you in simple, everyday language, as if we met you at a party and just spoke to you and explained how a home theater works. The book is intended to take the mystery out of home theater and to help you understand how to build an exquisite theater of your own, on your own.

Who Should Read This Book?

We are so glad that you are reading our book about home theater. It is a very exciting process to build your first home theater starting from scratch, or to upgrade to newer technology. This book gives you a great reference to what is current in today's home theater market, explains great resources on researching that information, and finally helps you connect all the pieces of equipment to make the whole that comprises your home theater.

Finally, we help you fine-tune your home theater to sound as if a professional installed it. The goal of this book is not only to help you build your home theater, but to give you enough information so that you understand your home theater and how it works.

What You Need to Begin

To start this book, you will need a note pad, access to the Web, and some home theater magazines. All these items will help you research the components that will make up your home theater. In addition, you will need the note pad to make sketches to help you figure out connections on paper before you actually make them.

- ✿ A note pad
- ✿ A pen
- ✿ Web access
- ✿ Home theater magazines

How This Book Is Organized

- ✿ **Friday Evening:** "Home Theater Basics." This session explains what makes up a home theater. It explains the features for each component, power source, speaker, and accessory, so that you are completely informed when you decide how to plan your home theater.

- ✿ **Saturday Morning:** "Accessories and Purchasing." This session explains how to plan what items will make up your home theater. It creates an attack plan on how you should build your home theater, which order to choose your components, and how to work within a budget. Then it reviews some good online resources that will help you decide what items to purchase. Finally, the chapter sends you off to make a shopping list and purchase all your new toys.

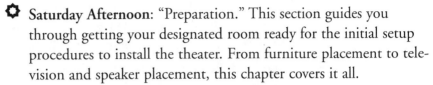

✪ **Saturday Afternoon**: "Preparation." This section guides you through getting your designated room ready for the initial setup procedures to install the theater. From furniture placement to television and speaker placement, this chapter covers it all.

✪ **Saturday Evening**: "Component Preparation." This section covers some research material in regard to handling video cable switching in your home theater. The home theater should be easy to use, and this chapter will make sure that even the uninformed will easily be able to turn on and run your home theater, or just the television. The chapter ends with you unpacking and prepping the components and cables for the tasks at hand tomorrow morning.

✪ **Sunday Morning**: "Bringing It All Together." It's time to connect your main components, that being the receiver to the speakers, or the processor/amplifier combination to the speakers. This is the heart of any home theater and must be done correctly so that the rest of the setup proceeds without a hitch.

✪ **Sunday Afternoon**: "Connecting Your Source Devices." Now that you have your rack set up, with your speakers powered and your receiver/processor ready to go, it's time to add all your source inputs. DVD players, tape decks, minidiscs, TiVos, laser disc players, CD players, CD jukeboxes, and televisions are all parts of the home theater that must interface with the central processor/receiver. This chapter brings all these components together.

✪ **Sunday Evening**: "Remotes, Operating the System, Plus Video and Acoustic Adjustments." It's time to sit back and enjoy your home theater. This chapter has some optional activities, from reviewing your system by testing it against some of our recommended DVDs to using some fine-tuning equipment to perfect the visual and audio experience.

✪ **Appendix A**: "The Future of Home Theater." This appendix details what is coming in the future for home theater, giving you a taste of what to look for in the upcoming months and years. This appendix should not stop you from starting your home theater now, but only help you decide what components will last for much longer and which ones will be replaced by newer technology.

✿ **Appendix B:** "Contact Details for Home Theater Products/ Companies." This appendix lists contact information for you to research and view the equipment that we have featured in this book.

✿ **Glossary:** A comprehensive guide to home theater terminology and verbiage, this feature will help you speak the lingo, and give you a good quick reference to any terms that you have not learned yet.

Conventions Used in This Book

CAUTION
Cautions generally tell you how to avoid problems.

NOTE
Notes provide additional helpful or interesting information.

TIP
Tips suggest techniques and shortcuts to make your life easier.

Let's Get Started

We hope that you enjoy this book as much as we did creating the content in it. This book is the culmination of Cub's and Gareth's experiences over the past 10 years in the home theater industry.

If you have any questions, please do not hesitate to contact each of the authors. You can contact them through Prima Communications, or you can write to Cub at **ckarabian@yahoo.com** or to Gareth at **gdebruyn@ ggsolutions.com**.

Home Theater Basics

- ✿ What is home theater?
- ✿ Receivers
- ✿ Processors
- ✿ Amplifiers
- ✿ Tuners
- ✿ Speakers
- ✿ Video monitors and televisions
- ✿ Sources

What Is Home Theater?

Home theater is built on the principle of simulating entertainment reality through audio and video products. Using equipment from several classes of home electronics, home theater owners can re-create the experience of an entertainment event as if they had actually attended the show, but they do so in the comfort and convenience of their own home.

Home theater gets its name from the movies. A movie theater is designed to give you an abundance of video and audio information to maximize your enjoyment and immersion into the movie you attend. When a fighter jet screams across the screen, the idea is to create the illusion that the F-15 actually flew by right in front of you. So, the speakers play the sound of a jet fighter loudly roaring from one side of the screen to the next, as you watch the image of an F-15 fly in the same direction as the sound travels. Home theater strives to give you that same realistic experience you had in the movie theater, but in your own home.

Although home theater's roots are in the experience of going to the movies, audio/video systems are not just designed to create the acoustic and visual reality of a movie theater. Instead, a home theater can enhance a wide variety of entertainment experiences. For example, when you turn on a football game, wouldn't you prefer to watch from the 50-yard line and hear the roar of the crowd around you as your team scores a touchdown—without ever leaving your house? Or wouldn't listening to a recorded concert be more entertaining if the sounds you hear made it appear that the artists are positioned across the stage as if you were seated in the concert hall front row center—even though you're sitting at home in your favorite easy chair?

This ability to simulate a visual and audio reality forms the cornerstone of a good home theater system. With each step you take in designing, buying, and setting up your home theater, your goal is ultimately to increase the realism of the program material and decrease the feeling that you are just "watching" it or just "listening" to it. Instead, you want to feel as if you are *experiencing* it.

What Types of Things Do I Play on My Home Theater?

You should design and build your home theater system to enhance your enjoyment of watching and listening to a wide variety of source material. *Source material* is the type of entertainment programming a home theater owner watches and listens to on his or her system.

The most basic types of source material used in home theater are widely known and used by the public today, including movies, recorded music, television shows, radio broadcasts, video games, and sporting events. Other kinds of source material that are less frequently associated with home theater include camcorder movies, Internet-based Web content, and educational programming.

Almost all types of source material benefit from treatment on a good home theater system. As you build and design a system, it is critical that you identify the primary types of source material that you want to enjoy on your home theater and tailor a system for the reproduction of these types of source material.

Remember that your home theater system is all about entertainment— have fun with your system and pick source material that you will enjoy.

How Do I Play the Source Material on My Home Theater?

After deciding the type of source material you want to enjoy on your home theater, you must design a system that can accept and process it. The source material is delivered to your home theater on its particular type of media. *Media* is the physical transfer device that gets source material into your home theater system for playback.

 NOTE Media is sometimes also referred to as software.

Chances are you already have much experience with many media types, including compact discs (CDs), videotapes (VHS), cassette tapes, and even cable television signals. Additional types of media that can be integrated into a home theater include DSS dish broadcasts, recorded events on camcorder, and computer information (using software, CD-ROMs, and modem lines for the Internet). The newest and perhaps most important media type that this book will discuss is the Digital Versatile Disc (DVD), which promises to be the primary media type for computers and audio/video systems for the next several years.

Each media type can transfer only certain kinds of data about source material. For example, a concert can be recorded on CD, which provides audio information only, whereas a DVD of a concert holds audio and video information. Likewise, some types of media are much better than others at reproducing the audio and video information of source material. A DVD is vastly superior to a VHS tape in reproducing audio and video from source material.

Don't worry yet about the types of media you will need and which ones are better than others. Throughout this book, you will learn about the wide variety of media available so that you can make an informed choice for your home theater. For now, just remember media's place in your home theater system.

How Does Source Material Get into My Home Theater?

Source material coded and stored on media is input into a home theater system through devices called *source components*. These are the pieces of electronic equipment that process and play each type of media and provide home theater owners with the sounds and pictures of their source material.

This section provides a brief introductory list of the most popular source components today. The next section analyzes them and their features, performance, and price level so you can choose the ones that are right for your home theater.

The source components for each type of media identified in this section vary in complexity, features, and performance from brand to brand and from model number to model number. As you design and budget for your system, you will need to decide which source components to buy based on which media types deliver the source material you want to see and hear on your home theater. Plus, your rank of the types of media important to you will also determine where you should invest in better source components to obtain the performance, features, and convenience that you want for a particular type of media.

CD Players

The compact disc has been the standard media for music over the past 10 years (see Figure 1.1). The CD player has been providing instant musical entertainment to millions of consumers, who can listen to almost every type of music ever produced. A compact disc holds roughly 70 minutes of high-quality audio on thin discs $4\frac{1}{2}$ inches in diameter. As the disc spins in the player, the data is read optically by a laser data pickup mechanism. Then the CD player translates this digital data into audio information to be used by the system.

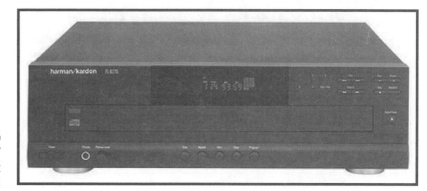

Figure 1.1

A Harman/
Kardon compact
disc player.

With convenient access features, such as the ability to jump around the disc to favorite songs instantaneously and the availability of hundreds of thousands of titles on the format, the CD player is a standard choice for most home theater owners.

CD Recorders

A new version of the CD player, a CD recorder enables you to record your own music onto compact discs for playback in other CD players (see Figure 1.2). These devices actually burn (or code) your music onto the CD with a tiny laser. CD recorders (with special compact disc media called *CD-R*s and *CD-RW*s) are available in both home theater source components and for your computer. Due to their popularity and increasing sophistication, they might deserve a place in your system.

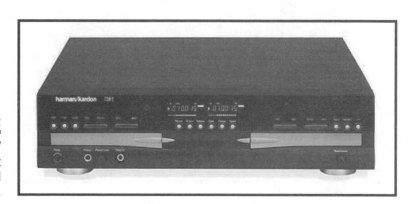

Figure 1.2

A Harman/
Kardon compact
disc recorder and
a CD-RW.

Videocassette Recorders (VCRs)

The venerable VCR stores and plays video and audio information recorded onto a magnetic tape media called a VHS cassette (see Figure 1.3). Like the CD player, the VCR has enjoyed tremendous success in the consumer electronics industry. The only drawback to VHS tape is the relatively low quality of the sound and images that can be recorded on the tape. However, with a massive video rental market and the ability to play and record both audio and video cheaply, the VCR remains an essential part of any home theater.

Cable Television

Although technically not a true source component, cable TV is a primary source for entertainment material. Its use is widespread—if you have a television, you probably have cable TV connected to it. Using a single wire, your TV or VCR receives audio and video information from cable networks and local television stations. Integration of cable with your home theater system is relatively easy. Cable does not demand much of your audio/visual (A/V) system because the signal that cable provides is limited in data. Recently, cable TV has upgraded its image—literally—by converting to new signals that improve the video and audio performance. This technology is called digital cable. Cable TV is also probably responsible for the phrase, "there's nothing on."

Figure 1.3

A Mitsubishi videocassette recorder (VCR) and a VHS tape.

DSS Dishes and Receivers

DSS dishes have emerged as the main competitor for cable TV in the television content marketplace. By mounting a small dish from 18 to about 36 inches wide on your home, you can receive signals broadcast by satellites in space. A decoding unit called a receiver then translates the satellite signals into TV signals and plays them on your television just like cable TV (see Figure 1.4). By offering many more programming options, a competitive price structure, and improved audio/video performance over cable TV, DSS manufacturers have forced home theater owners to decide which system will provide their broadcast television content.

Tuners

A tuner is the source component that enables you to play radio broadcasts on your home theater system (see Figure 1.5). Tuners can come as individual source components or can be integrated into other electronics equipment in your home theater.

Figure 1.4

A DSS dish and receiver.

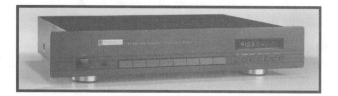

Figure 1.5

A tuner for radio broadcasts.

Phonographs (Record Players or Turntables)

In the past, the phonograph record (or just record or LP) was the only method for consumers to play back audio. A phono cartridge with a needle attached to a small arm on the turntable reads the pits and valleys of a spinning vinyl disc roughly 12 inches in diameter. This signal is then passed on to your speakers, emerging as music and other audio information. However, with advances in digital storage and tape technology (compact discs and cassette tapes), records have greatly diminished in use. Only a small group of enthusiasts and collectors continues to support the vinyl format.

Cassette Tape Players

Cassette tapes are a magnetic storage media that operates on the same general principle as a VCR, but does not provide video information. Cassette tapes reached the height of their popularity in the 1980s as a cheap and easy solution to provide transportable and recordable music to the masses. However, over the last several years, the cassette has declined drastically in use, especially as portable CD players have taken over for the first truly portable personal stereo—the Walkman cassette player. However, the cassette is still the cheapest and easiest method for recording music, so you may still want to consider a good tape deck for your system to make compilations of your audio library.

Minidisc Players

The minidisc player has slowly grown in acceptance since its lukewarm reception when introduced into the market in the mid-1990s. The minidisc is a small, nearly 3-inch-wide media based on a small magnetic disc, much like a floppy disk for a computer (see Figure 1.6). Using data compression, the minidisc player records up to 74 minutes of data and shrinks it onto the small disc. Copies made from CD to MD (as the disc is often called) are exact reproductions of the 1s and 0s bitstream of a CD, but some high and low sounds must be tossed out to compress the data to fit on such small media. Although never designed as a replacement for the

CD, due to its exceptionally tiny footprint (the discs are only a little over 2 inches square) and infinite read/write ability, the MD is a wise home theater investment if you want to create music mixes for an on-the-go lifestyle. Plus, they are a lot of fun.

Laserdisc Players

No other format discussed in this book pushed the envelope of home theater farther than the laserdisc (often abbreviated as LD). This 12-inch shiny disc dramatically upgraded the video and audio performance of a home theater system from VHS tape and drove the home theater marketplace quietly for nearly 10 years. Like compact discs, the laserdisc is an optical format—it reads information off the spinning disc with a laser (see Figure 1.7). The format was predominantly used for movies and live music performances, and no true home theater enthusiast was without one. However, due to inconvenience issues (such as the high price, the large size, and the multiple discs required to store a single movie) and because of the meteoric rise over the past two and a half years of DVD players, the laserdisc has been all but relegated to obscurity. However, in case you already have an LD collection and still want to use a laserdisc player in your home theater, you will find discussion of the format throughout this book.

Figure 1.6

A Sony minidisc player and an MD.

Figure 1.7

A Pioneer
laserdisc player
and an LD movie.

DVD Players

Since DVD's launch in March 1997, the format has doubtlessly generated more interest in home theater than any other consumer electronics product. Whereas the laserdisc is responsible for creating the original specialty home theater marketplace, DVD has expanded the market to the general public and is poised to deliver entertainment content for the next several years.

DVD is another optical format, with dual layers of information stored on a single side of a CD-sized disc. Because this disc has greater storage capacity than all other media available, the DVD can store large amounts of data (such as a full movie on one side of a disc) and can also integrate and hold computer data. Because of its ability to be used in both computers and home theater, DVD is called a cross-platform media and is quickly bridging the information gap between home electronics and computers. DVD could potentially be the content provider media for both home theaters and computers.

Additionally, DVD, which offers a razor-sharp picture and dynamic surround sound, can significantly increase the quality of audio and video available on your home theater. Movies, television content, and live musical performances are so far the primary source material on DVD, with many more titles added every week. For home theater builders designing their system, a DVD player is *the* hot ticket item and should be near the top of the list for purchasing.

Video Gaming Consoles

Companies such as Nintendo, Sony, and Sega have produced their newest video game machines to integrate easily with your home theater system (see Figure 1.8). Just as home theater enhances other source material, a home theater can dramatically enhance the fun from playing games on a video game console. The improved audio and video of these units can immerse you in the action and keep the children quiet for hours.

Computers

The use of computers with your home theater as a source component is only in its infancy, but already you can send computer output directly to your home theater, if you have the proper video device and computer hardware. By integrating an audio/video output card on your computer, you can play your computer's sounds and video through your home theater, including games, reference material, and Web content. Connecting your computer to your home theater opens up vast new amounts of data available from the World Wide Web, CD-ROM software, and downloadable content, creating a whole new set of entertainment opportunities enhanced by a home theater.

Figure 1.8

The Nintendo 64 game console.

Camcorder Recordings

The use of camcorders to capture events on video has also dramatically increased over the past years as these hand-held units have become less expensive and easier to use. As a source component, the camcorder acts similarly to a VCR, regardless of whether it records by the conventional tape system or the newer digital recording system. Camcorder recordings are easy to view on your home theater system and often have much greater impact. The use of large screens and dynamic sound systems enhances your audience's impression that they are actually experiencing the events presented in your own audio and video creations.

Digital Photography and Cameras

It used to be that to view a series of photographic images, you had to develop your film in slide format and then use a projector to show them on a screen. Now, with the proliferation of digital cameras that record onto a disc or in the memory in the camera, you can use your home theater as the projection system, displaying the images on the large screen in much the same manner, but with increased clarity and resolution.

You probably have several of these source components in your home already. If you do, you are already on your way to designing your home theater. Keep in mind what you have; you will need to purchase other equipment capable of integration with your existing source components.

Where Does the Information from Source Components Go Next?

When a source component plays a type of media, the information must be transferred to a new type of component, the *pre-amplifier* or *processor*. These interchangeable terms refer to the same device, which has several vital jobs in your home theater system.

Pre-amps/processors act as the central management device for all the source components in your home theater. Think of the pre-amp/processor as the brains of your system. It has *inputs* for each of your source components and enables you to decide which source component to play. The pre-amp/processor also handles the signal transfer when you are recording from one source component to another source component.

The next critical job for the pre-amp/processor is to process the audio and video signal and output it to each of the devices that enable you to see and hear the source material—the video display device and the speaker system. When a pre-amp/processor translates the source component's signal with high performance and accuracy, the audio and video appear and sound more lifelike and draw your perception directly into your source material.

The pre-amp/processor is also responsible for controlling your system's volume (which will be one of the most hotly debated topics in your household after you hook up your system).

How Do Source Components Send Data to the Pre-Amp/Processor?

Each source component is connected to the pre-amp/processor through *interconnect cables.* There are several types of interconnect cables; the one that is used for a connection depends on the kind of source component and the type of data (either audio or video) the component is sending to the pre-amp/processor.

There are two methods for transmitting data over cables from source components to your processor.

✿ *Analog.* This is the older of the two systems and is also the most widely used. Using electronic signals of various modulations, the electric current of an analog signal is analogous (hence the name) to the information it represents. A VCR is an example of analog information. The VCR sends out an electronic signal, which represents the sound it is producing to the processor; the processor then passes the signal along to the next device. Video signals are almost always transmitted to your pre-amp/processor by analog transmission, and information is passed to your speaker system by an analog signal as well.

✿   *Digital.* Once the new kid on the block, digital signal transmission now seems like the heavy favorite to totally replace analog electronic data transmission after almost 100 years of analog transmission. Rather than constantly changing in an attempt to represent data in analog, a digital signal captures data and translates it into a code created entirely from 1s and 0s. After a source material is captured digitally and coded, it can be kept and altered by computer as anyone sees fit. The compact disc is a perfect example of a digital media, where sounds on the disc are represented by 1s and 0s that your CD player or processor translates into information for your speakers to produce.

A key part of analog and digital signals in your home theater is a process called *digital-to-analog (D/A) conversion.* When a digital source component reads its digital signal from digital media, somewhere in your home theater system the digital signal has to be converted to an analog one. Usually this occurs either in the source component or in the pre-amp/processor. Because speakers are analog devices and generally accept only analog signals, any digital signal must eventually be translated into an analog one to be played by the system. However, the better the conversion, the better the system will reproduce the audio and video. CDs, DVDs, and DSS signals are all examples of digital media that require the conversion from digital information to an analog signal somewhere in a home theater system.

All the types of cables—including analog and digital cables and D/A conversion—are discussed extensively throughout this book.

What Does the Pre-Amp/Processor Do with the Video Signal?

The pre-amp/processor handles all the particular types of video interconnect cables and the different signals produced by all your source components independently of the audio signals. The video signal is sent from the source component to the processor, then on to the display device that is attached to the processor. A *display device* is any monitor or television that can output video signals. This includes TV sets and rear projection televisions, at least one of which you probably already have.

Therefore, when you select a particular source component that delivers video (such as VHS tape) to play on the home theater, the processor routes the images to the display device you are using. This process is called *video switching*.

What Type of Display Device Do I Need?

To be appropriate for home theater use, a display device must have a viewable picture of at least 36 inches. In a movie theater, the screen size is massive and designed to fill the audience's entire line of sight with the image so that the audience can see little else. This same principle should govern your decision on a home theater display device: The bigger the picture, the more it will dominate your vision and the greater it will immerse you in your entertainment presentation.

Also, it is important to have the proper video connections that match the particular media and source components you will be using on your home theater. Throughout this book, you will learn much about the types and characteristics of display devices. Just remember that bigger is usually better for a home theater display device.

What Does the Pre-Amp/Processor Do with the Audio Signal?

Unlike the video signal, the audio signal is actually processed by the pre-amp/processor through a series of mathematical calculations performed on microchips. This processing is the most important step in the audio portion of a home theater system, and it is critical in many of the decisions you will need to make regarding your home theater.

When a pre-amp/processor receives audio information, the entire signal is divided into as many as six separate audio signals, depending on how the information was encoded on the media and the settings on your pre-amp/processor. Each of these signals corresponds to the locations of the speakers in your home theater room. These separate speaker locations are called *channels,* and the number of speakers and the configuration of sound coming out of these speakers are referred to as the *processing mode* or *decoding mode.*

By steering sounds to each of these different channels, your pre-amp/processor can effectively place sound spatially throughout a room. This is the critical element in simulating the environment of your source material and creating a captivating presentation.

For example, imagine you are at a U2 concert—the sounds you hear come from multiple locations at the event as perceived by your ears. Bono is singing from dead center on the stage, while Larry Mullin, Jr., is behind him sitting at his drum kit. The Edge is on the right side playing lead guitar, while Adam Clayton, the bassist, strums away on the left side. But there are more sounds than just those of the artists. You hear the cheers of the crowd coming from behind you and on your sides. Plus, the music coming out of speakers around the arena is also reacting with the people, walls, and space in this environment, providing an echo that tells your senses that you are in a large open space with walls around you.

The goal of your pre-amp/processor is to take you out of your living room and place you at that U2 concert. Using speakers in the same locations as many of the places where your ears would perceive sound, the pre-amp/processor distributes the sounds spatially so that you hear the concert in your home as you would hear it in the arena.

Likewise, in a movie theater, sound is coming from all around you, depending on the on-screen action. If Captain Kirk is issuing orders from the bridge of the *Enterprise,* the center speaker should reproduce the dialog because Kirk is centered on the screen. When the *Starship Enterprise* flies at warp 10 from left to right across the screen, you hear the ship's flight noise from the left speaker, then the center speaker, and then the right speaker. This gives you the sense of both seeing and hearing the ship fly in that direction as if you were in space watching a mighty starship battle.

You accomplish the manipulation of sound in your home theater through the processing mode of your pre-amp/processor and the number of channels you have available in your speaker system. The more channels/speakers you have and the more adept your pre-amp/processor is at steering sound to the channels, the greater sense of reality your theater can simulate and the more immersing your presentation will be.

NOTE The processing modes available for source material generally depend on how the source material was originally recorded, and what kind of processing is encoded on the media. If a type of processing is not recorded on the media, then the processor cannot use that particular processing mode to decode the information and steer sound to the speakers. Conversely, if the pre-amp/processor does not accept a type of processing on a piece of media, then your system will be unable to present the source material in that processing mode either.

What Processing Modes Are There?

The number of processing modes has grown significantly in recent years, from mono and stereo systems to increasingly sophisticated and effective systems applying digital and other technological innovations.

Mono

Mono is the original sound system used in the early days of film, television, and music. No coding is necessary because only a single speaker is responsible for all the sound produced (see Figure 1.9). You hear mono when viewing old movies that were recorded with a soundtrack integrating voice, music, and sound effects on only a single channel. Mono remains in use in broadcast television, especially for comedy shows and dialog-heavy programming like the nightly news.

Figure 1.9

A Toshiba mono single-channel speaker system.

Because mono uses only one speaker for all sounds on a soundtrack, it is the least desirable processing mode and should be used only if no other mode is available. Almost all pre-amp/processors, however, are capable of producing mono soundtracks through a single speaker.

Stereo

Stereo processing was a huge advancement in sound after the single-speaker sounds of mono (see Figure 1.10). Acoustic engineers found that they could dramatically increase the realism of music if they recorded it with a left and a right microphone. By reproducing music with a corresponding left and right speaker, a stereo speaker system simulated the location of the sounds heard by each ear. These first spatial recordings revolutionized the way people listen to music today and have set the tone for multichannel music in the future.

Presently, stereo is the most widely used audio processing mode, especially for music. Your car undoubtedly has a stereo system with left and right speakers, or you have a basic stereo system at home for playing compact discs or cassette tapes. Television broadcasts are now reproduced in stereo over your TV speakers, and when you watch a VHS tape on your VCR over the same TV, you also get a stereo sound effect.

Figure 1.10

A stereo speaker system.

Because of its heavy use throughout the audio/video industry, stereo is an essential part of any home theater system. You will probably want to play compact discs over your system and watch television in this mode. Luckily, every pre-amp/processor on the market carries some capacity to play stereo sounds through a left and right speaker.

 NOTE Many pre-amp/processors take source material encoded in mono and play it with the left and right speaker, producing identical information for each speaker. This is not stereo, but remains mono processing.

Dolby Pro Logic Surround Sound

Designed by engineers at Dolby Labs in San Francisco, California, the Dolby Pro Logic processing mode is designed to increase artificially the number of channels processed from a regular two-channel stereo soundtrack (see Figure 1.11).

By summing the information of source materials' left and right stereo channels in a microchip performing instantaneous calculations, the system creates a center speaker. The effect on movies is a huge step forward from the two-channel stereo system. A large percentage of action

and dialog is centered directly on the screen during a movie, so placing a speaker there dedicated to such sounds makes a film or musical perform-ance much more realistic and enjoyable.

Likewise, the wizards at Dolby also mathematically extrapolated the information from the left and right stereo signal to create a new single rear channel of sound that surrounds the home theater audience. During movie scenes with heavy music and sound effects, the addition of this rear channel produces the sense that the sound is coming from all around and that you are right in the middle of the action.

However, there are limitations to the information rear speakers can provide in Dolby Pro Logic because the signal from the processor is restricted to the high and low ends of the sound spectrum and there is no distinction between the front and rear speakers. A left-rear and a right-rear speaker both play the exact same acoustic information (the surround channel in a Pro Logic system is considered mono because there is only one signal).

Many types of media today require Dolby Pro Logic for proper process-ing in a home theater system. Movies form the bulk of this source mate-rial, but some music has been recorded for Pro Logic processing as well. Also, television broadcasts often benefit from this type of processing mode to effectively re-create the atmosphere of sporting events and the impact of various kinds of programming.

In addition to offering the standard Dolby Pro Logic processing mode, many pre-amp/processors also have additional *sound fields* that adjust the Pro Logic calculations to simulate other environments for listening to sound programs.

For music, for example, by increasing the volume of the rear channel and electronically slowing down the sound coming out of the speaker, you can simulate the echo of a cathedral or the vastness of a sports arena. Although many such processing modes are merely novelties, on some pre-amp/processors they can be highly effective in enhancing a home theater presentation.

THX

The engineers at Lucasfilm are responsible for many of the advancements in surround sound technology in movie theaters (see Figure 1.12). They were the first to create a set of standards to ensure moviegoers that a theater sound system was properly calibrated and set up to provide the best possible movie theater experience. (*Star Wars* was the first movie that was broadcast in surround sound in the movie theaters.)

Lucasfilm's THX home system is designed with the same goal in mind for home theater. Using THX-approved equipment and media, the engineers want to provide the home theater owner with as close to a movie theater experience as possible in his or her home. The THX system employs two methods to this end. First, THX-equipped processors have a set of add-on enhancements to other sound systems (such as Dolby Pro Logic) that eliminate the brightness of your speaker system, match speakers' upper sounds more accurately, and increase the separation of the rear channels.

NOTE Remember that THX is not actually a processing mode like Dolby Pro Logic, but a series of additional circuits for enhancement of those processing modes.

Figure 1.12

The THX logo, which appears on both equipment and media as an assurance of audio and video quality.

Second, through its THX certification program, Lucasfilm has created a set of standards for audio and video components that ensure a high level of performance in your system. However, to gain all the benefits of a THX-certified system, you must have all THX-certified equipment, including speakers.

NOTE The THX program for home theater also approves media, such as videotapes, laserdiscs, and DVDs. The source material presented on these approved discs and tapes has audio and video performance of excellent quality. However, you do not need to have a THX-approved system to enjoy the benefits of media approved by THX.

Discrete Surround Sound Systems

In the past several years, movie theater surround sound systems have grown increasingly complex and highly effective in their ability to re-create the sonic characteristics of a presentation. Much of this technology has moved out of the movie theater and now is available on a slightly smaller scale in your own home.

The primary advancement in movie sound has come from the addition of new *discrete* surround sound systems. Whereas the Dolby Pro Logic surround sound system creates two additional channels mathematically from only two original discrete channels, the new sound systems are recorded with separately stored, individual channels that contain only the sound information for that specific channel. With these systems, as many as six totally independent discrete channels surround a room and create *very* specific sound placement.

Additionally, each of the discrete channels can produce the full range of sounds perceived by the human ear. The frequency limitations of Pro Logic no longer apply, and the result is a more realistic presentation.

These surround sound systems are usually called *5.1 channel systems*. This is because they incorporate the following channels in the system:

- *Center channel.* This channel places dialog and action-oriented sound dead center in the presentation. For movies, this speaker is the true workhorse of the system.

- *Left channel.* Placed directly to the left of the center speaker, this channel's speaker handles action that is oriented on the left side of the screen. This is your left stereo speaker as well for listening to music from compact discs, cassette tapes, and other stereo media.

- *Right channel.* Placed directly to the right of the center speaker the same distance as the left speaker is from the center speaker, this channel's speaker handles action that is oriented on the right side of the screen. This is also your right stereo speaker for stereo media.

- *Left-rear channel* (sometimes called *left surround channel*). The left-rear speaker generally sits behind the listening position and to the left. This speaker produces two kinds of sounds: ambient noises designed to emanate from all around the listener and provide atmosphere, and directional effects, such as a gunshot from behind the listening position in a gunfight.

- *Right-rear channel* (sometimes called *right surround channel*). The right-rear channel speaker handles the same two types of effects as the left-rear channel, but for the right side of the soundtrack and the action.

- *Low-frequency effects channel.* This is probably the most misunderstood channel in a 5.1 speaker system. Whereas the other five discrete channels are represented by the *5* in 5.1, the *.1* denotes a special channel that handles only low-frequency information, which is known as bass. Examples of bass sounds are the thumping and booming notes of a bass guitar or cello, or in the theater, the low, rumbling sounds of an explosion or gunshot. Such sounds come from a limited range of human hearing from about 60 Hz down to 19 Hz. In a discrete soundtrack, these sounds are given their own channel because the signals can be produced only from a special speaker, called a woofer, that is big enough to move the large amounts of air necessary to create these sounds.

The two competing processing modes that handle the six-channel sound of a source material soundtrack are Dolby Digital and Digital Theater Systems (DTS).

Dolby Digital

Dolby Digital (see Figure 1.13) represents the evolution of Dolby Pro Logic into a fully discrete six-channel surround mix. Five of the channels (Left, Center, Right, Left Surround, and Right Surround) are full range, so they can play the entire frequency range of the human ear in each channel to surround the listener with an acoustic environment. The sixth channel, Low Frequency Effects, produces all sound from 100 Hz to the lowest range of human perception, 20 Hz. The results are increased channel separation and a much more realistic soundstage where sound effects in a film come directly from the spatial location at which they would be located in the theater and on the screen.

Dolby Digital is currently available on DVDs, laserdiscs, and DSS broadcasts; only a handful of music CDs carry this type of coding.

Digital Theater Systems (DTS)

DTS has its origins in the movie theater industry, where it is the most popular system for producing sound in movie theaters throughout the world (see Figure 1.14). After falling behind to Dolby Digital in the home market, DTS has recently become an aggressive player, and most preamp/processors now can decode both Dolby Digital and DTS signals.

Figure 1.13

Look for the Dolby Digital logo to see whether equipment and media are compatible with this processing mode.

Figure 1.14

Look for the Digital Theater Systems logo to see whether equipment and media can decode this processing mode.

Like Dolby Digital, the DTS processing system has five discrete channels (Left, Center, Right, Left Surround, and Right Surround) that are also full range. The Low Frequency Effects channel produces sound from 100 Hz to 20 Hz.

Both Dolby Digital and DTS must use compression schemes to get the full six channels of information coded onto home theater media. However, the DTS compression technique requires much less compression than Dolby Digital. Some critics believe that the lower compression rates of DTS lead to a much more accurate and lifelike sound.

Regardless of which system you prefer and choose for your home theater processing, both Dolby Digital and DTS will provide you with an incredible entertainment experience. Of all the decisions you must make regarding your home theater, you should definitely choose to purchase and set up a system that can reproduce Dolby Digital and DTS soundtracks. These processing modes represent the pinnacle of home theater entertainment today.

Where Do Each Channel's Signals Go After Processing?

After a processing mode has been selected and the pre-amp/processor has sent sound information to each of the appropriate channels, the signal travels out of the pre-amp/processor through a second set of interconnect cables to the *amplifier*.

The amplifier is the power station of your home theater. It takes the output signals coming from the processor for each channel and amplifies them with the electrical power needed to make the speakers play. For each speaker in your home theater system, there must be a channel of amplification, enough power to enable the speaker to make sound, and enough steady power to play the sound accurately.

Therefore, amplifiers are grouped by how many channels of amplification they produce and by how much power they can output to each speaker. Don't concern yourself with the extensive and often confusing topic of amplifier power yet. You will learn much about the topic when you examine the features and characteristics of amplifiers later in this book.

Special Components: The Integrated Amplifier and Receiver

A popular home theater component is the *integrated amplifier,* which combines all the functions of a pre-amp/processor with power amplifiers for five of the channels in a home theater system. The left, right, center, left-rear, and right-rear speakers are all powered in this manner in a Dolby Digital or DTS processor, while the .1 channel is powered either by a separate amplifier or by an amplifier inside the speaker itself. Likewise, the *receiver* is an integrated amplifier that also contains a source component—the tuner—for listening to radio broadcasts.

By combining these two elements of a home theater into one chassis, you can save a large amount of money on your purchase and get into home theater with a much smaller initial investment. Generally, however, a separate combination of processor and amplifier offers better acoustic characteristics and features than an integrated amplifier or receiver.

After the Signal Is Amplified, Where Does It Go Next?

The final output device for the audio signal is your speaker system, which actually generates the sound that you hear when you play source material.

A single speaker corresponds to each channel from your processor and amplifier. The speakers must produce sound accurately and at the volume necessary for an effective presentation.

The signal from the amplifier reaches the speakers through *speaker cable*. This wire is designed to maintain the closest possible signal to the original output at the amplifier side. Without losing the detail of that signal, you can maximize the transmission as it travels to your speaker and not lose any of the power generated by the amplifier necessary to create sound in the speakers.

How Does a Speaker Create the Sounds?

After a speaker receives a signal from the amplifier, the speaker's components take over. This section provides a brief introduction to these components and to the basic workings of a speaker.

The *drivers* are the actual parts that produce the sound on a speaker (see Figure 1.15). They are the black circles attached to the front of the speaker box. When an electrical signal comes into the speaker and a particular sound must be generated, the analog current signal boosted from your amplifier for that sound instantly charges a magnet at the back of the driver. In close proximity to this magnet structure is a second magnet, which the signal has not charged. However, the magnets repel each other now because they have instantly become opposite charges. In between these magnets is a metal coil, which is pushed in and out between the two magnets as the charges shift back and forth from the incoming audio signals.

Connected to the coil is the cone, which, because of the sudden magnetic charge shift, now quickly pushes into the room and then returns to rest. The push of the cone's surface area into the room moves the air in front of the speaker. Thus, the sound is transmitted through the room as a movement of air called a soundwave.

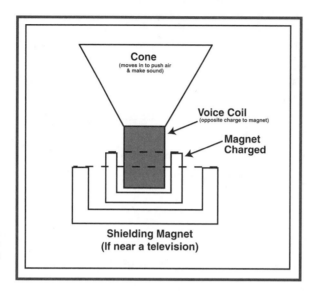

Figure 1.15

The basic layout of a speaker driver.

There are three types of drivers that you must know:

- *Tweeters.* A tweeter has the smallest surface area of the drivers (about 1 inch) because it is only responsible for the production of very high sounds on the frequency spectrum that do not require large amounts of air movement to produce. For example, the tweeter produces a woman's scream in a horror movie.

- *Midrange.* The midrange driver is usually 3 to 6 inches in cone diameter and handles all the sounds in the middle of the human auditory frequency range (see Figure 1.16). Most notably, the midrange driver must generate the sound of a human's voice. However, because the driver is physically larger than the tweeter, more amplifier power is required to charge the magnet structure and push the cone into the room to generate the sound.

- *Woofers.* The woofer is the largest of the three drivers and usually is 8 to 18 inches in diameter. Moving this large cone requires large amounts of amplifier power. The woofer is responsible for the production of low frequency information, called bass. Woofers are the drivers on a speaker that handle the Low Frequency Effects channels in Dolby Digital and DTS soundtracks. The soundwaves they

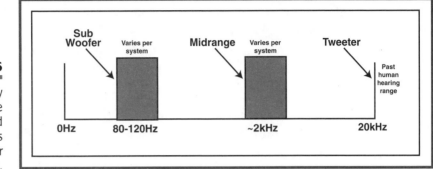

Figure 1.16

The frequency range of the human ear and the drivers responsible for parts of the range.

produce are large, generated from a huge push of air to create sounds such as explosions and gunshots.

Inside the speaker is the *crossover*, which acts as the gatekeeper for the electrical signals entering the speaker. After an amplifier sends a power signal down the speaker cable, the signal enters the speaker and hits the crossover. The crossover then routes the particular part of the signal that goes to each driver, enabling the speaker to use all three types of drivers at once and create the sounds that your home theater produces.

The drivers, speaker wire connectors, and crossover are contained in the speaker *enclosure*. The construction, material, and size of this box greatly affect the performance of the speaker.

How Do Speakers Differ?

The speaker system you ultimately select for your home theater depends on several factors that vary from speaker to speaker. This section summarizes these factors; you will learn more about these factors when you begin shopping for your speaker system.

- ✪ *Driver configuration.* Speakers vary by the number of tweeters, midranges, and woofers on each speaker and their location on the enclosure. Particular numbers of drivers and the ways in which the crossover is set up to route sounds significantly affect the performance of one speaker compared to the next.

- *Speaker component materials.* Speakers also vary in the materials used for their internal components. Certain types of materials make better cones, for example, that play louder or more accurately than speakers with driver cones made of other materials.

- *Enclosure size.* Some speakers are designed to operate with a very small box to house the drivers and therefore can be placed in many locations unobtrusively, whereas other speakers, called towers, can stand as tall as six feet.

- *Full-range or satellite and subwoofer.* Many speakers today no longer house all three types of drivers in one enclosure, as was traditionally the method. Instead, they split up the tweeter and midrange into one enclosure, called a *satellite*, that you can place more easily in your room, and another speaker enclosure designed specifically to house a woofer. This speaker enclosure, called a *subwoofer*, has become a cornerstone in low-frequency effects reproduction in home theater. You must identify which system you prefer.

- *Aesthetic considerations.* Remember that you will place several of these speaker boxes throughout your home theater room or living room. You should view them as pieces of furniture that should integrate attractively into your environment. However, this should be your final concern in relation to speakers, because performance is the most critical measure of a speaker. In this instance, you should sacrifice appearance for performance.

How Do I Control All the Parts of My System?

You might be wondering how you are going to operate all these components together and know which button to push for which function. Often, people buy electronics equipment without taking time to decide how they are going to control and interact with it. You should consider two levels of control in operating a home theater.

First, you must determine the effectiveness and intuitiveness of the remote control that accompanies the piece of equipment. This remote will operate that component, and you have to be comfortable using it. Most remotes for source components are relatively straightforward, whereas the remote controls for processors and integrated amps/receivers can be extraordinarily complex. Likewise, with just three or four source components, you must also be concerned with the sheer number of remote controls to operate all this equipment.

However, there is a cure for the complexity and number of remote controls. A secondary level of control is available, called the universal remote. This powerful remote control consolidates most of the functions of your components' remotes onto one larger remote for total system interaction on one device. Some pre-amp/processors and receivers come with universal remotes, and many more sophisticated controllers are available from makers of electronics equipment. This second level of control is critical in creating a system that is user-friendly because it will probably not be just you operating your home theater, but friends and family too. As you will see, many of these universal remotes offer sophisticated features designed to make it simple for even the least technologically inclined people to control the components of the home theater. These universal remotes should be high on your list for integration into your home theater.

Now that you have a good amount of background material on the pieces of a home theater and the method and sequence in which the components interact, it is time to examine each category in much greater detail to determine all the cool stuff you want in your system.

Receivers

An audio/video receiver is the center of any moderately priced home theater system (see Figure 1.17). The definition of a receiver is an audio component that combines in a single chassis a pre-amplifier, a surround sound processor, an amplifier, and a radio. The A/V receiver is further distinguished by the capability to route video signals in addition to the traditional audio signals.

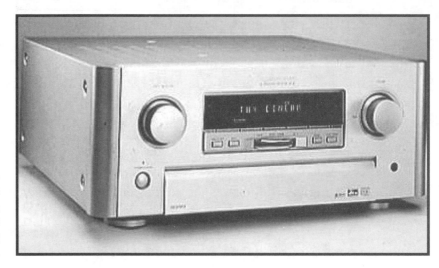

Figure 1.17

A receiver with DTS and Dolby Digital decoding capabilities.

If you want to build the best home theater possible and money is no object, you should purchase individual components rather than a receiver. For most people, though, a high-quality receiver is a much more cost-effective way to build a great home theater.

The role of the receiver is to accept inputs from multiple source components (such as a DVD or CD player), transform the signal, amplify the signal, and then pass the signal to the speakers.

Receiver Features

Because receivers perform multiple tasks, you might have trouble evaluating them properly. You need to look at each of the receiver's tasks, consider how important each task is to you, and then rate the receiver for that task.

When shopping for a receiver, you should look for the following features:

✪ Power output

✪ 5.1-channel digital processing

✪ Surround modes

- Composite video and S-video inputs
- Audio inputs
- Front-panel inputs
- THX certification
- Menus
- Remote control

Some of these features are less important than others, but you should consider each.

Power Output

Power output is the measure by which most people judge a receiver. It is an important quality for a receiver, but it should never be the only consideration. To judge a receiver's power output, you also need to understand how many output channels the receiver offers because its power will be distributed across those channels.

How to Measure Power Output

A receiver's power output is measured in watts. This power is used in the receiver's amplification function to drive your speakers. A receiver's power output has a large impact on how loud your theater sounds, but it is not the only factor. The speakers, the size of your room, and the shape of the room all affect your system's loudness. The power of your system is important even when you have the volume turned down low. A system with more power has more dynamic range—the low sounds will be lower and the high sounds higher. Just as in a movie theater, when the characters on the screen are simply speaking, the sound is not much louder than any ordinary conversation. However, when a building is exploding, the sound will swell to a level that shakes your teeth. Power output enables your home theater to duplicate the dynamic range found in a movie theater. If your system does not have enough power, then to get those room-shaking explosions, you will have to crank up the volume to a level where the conversation in the movie sounds like people screaming at each other. Also, if your receiver is underpowered, you will find that your speakers dangerously distort at higher volume level.

Power Output per Channel

A receiver is not measured in total watts but rather in watts per channel. This measurement is closely tied to the processor modes offered by the receiver. Six-channel processor modes (5.1), such as Dolby Digital or DTS, require each of the channels to have equal power. A receiver that supports 5.1 has its power reported as *watts*X5; for example, an 80-watt receiver is reported as 80X5 watts. The sixth channel refers to the sub-woofer and is not powered. The ".1" tells you the component is a true 5.1 receiver or Dolby Digital receiver.

Receivers that support the older Dolby Pro standard do not require all channels to have equal power. A Dolby Pro receiver usually has full-power front channels and half-power rear channels. This is acceptable because that is how the Dolby Pro standard was designed. As you learned earlier, there currently is no reason to settle for a Dolby Pro–only receiver; thus this book focuses on true five-channel receivers such as Dolby Digital.

CAUTION   Be careful of receivers that offer 5.1 support but do not offer true 5.1 channel power. For example, although such a receiver might be advertised as an 80-watt receiver, in the fine print you will see that only the front channels are 80 watts, whereas the rear channels are 40 watts. These receivers are usually older models or cheap manufactures. Avoid these types of components and make sure you are getting equal power across all channels for true 5.1 channel sound.

A Watt Is Not *Always a Watt*

If you have shopped for audio equipment in the past, you may have noticed something odd about the power output of different receivers. Often there is a huge difference in price for receivers with the same power output. You may have attributed this to other factors such as sound quality and processor features. But although many factors affect the price of a receiver, power output really is the predominant one. When you see a cheap receiver advertised as a 100-watt receiver, you need to understand that, in such advertisements, a watt is not always a watt. The dirty little secret of the audio industry is that power can be measured in different ways. What these ads for cheap receivers are really saying is that they offer 100 watts of *peak* power.

A receiver requires quite a bit of power—more power than an electrical outlet will drive. So the receiver actually stores up power before it begins playing music. A quality receiver that is rated at 100 watts stores enough power to use 100 watts and recharge itself before the power is needed again. On the other hand, a cheap receiver charges up those 100 watts and uses them, but must draw power again before it is fully recharged. The manufacturer's ads do not lie when they claim that the receiver outputs 100 watts of power; unfortunately, that output occurs for only brief periods.

The net result is that the speaker actually sounds like it has much less power output than its rating indicates. This is why a receiver from a quality manufacturer such as Dennon or Yamaha has only 60 watts but costs as much as a 100-watt receiver from a no-name manufacturer. Sixty watts of constant power definitely sounds much better than those phantom 100 watts. Unfortunately, there is no way to judge the accuracy of a manufacturer's power rating, so you have to depend on reviews from respected sources. Home audio is one area where you really do get what you pay for.

Processor Surround Modes

The processor function of a receiver supports a variety of surround sound modes. The most important are Dolby Digital, DTS, and Dolby Pro. Simply having support for one or more of these modes in your receiver is not enough. In addition, the audio source you are using must be encoded to work with the mode that your receiver supports. So to listen to a movie in Dolby Digital mode, you must use a DVD that is encoded in Dolby Digital.

Also available are surround modes that simulate the acoustics of different venues such as a concert hall, a club, or an amphitheater. These acoustic modes are used with audio sources such as CDs and do not require any special encoding of the source material. These modes don't add much to most music and should not be the basis of any buying decision.

Dolby Digital

Dolby Digital is the driving force behind the home theater movement. It is one of two 5.1-channel digital processing modes found in home audio. Dolby Digital enables you to have a movie theater experience in the comfort of your own home. As you learned earlier, the 5 indicates that the mode supports five full-power channels: right-front, left-front, center, right-rear, and left-rear. The .1 indicates that this mode has a separate subwoofer channel for bass.

You can get Dolby Digital from your receiver two ways. The easiest way is to get a receiver with built-in Dolby Digital. These receivers offer a 5.1 input that attaches to a DVD player, decodes the audio signal, and drives the six-channel speaker output.

The other option is to get a receiver that is Dolby Digital–ready. In this case, you need an external processor or, more likely, a DVD player with a Dolby Digital decoder. You can save a little money by getting a receiver that is Dolby Digital–ready if your DVD player has a decoder. However, in the long run, it is usually better to get a receiver with built-in Dolby Digital.

DVD and laserdisc players are the most common types of sources that are often Dolby Digital–encoded.

DTS

DTS is the second type of 5.1-channel digital processing mode available. Like Dolby Digital, it is a full-power six-channel mode that duplicates the movie theater experience. DTS actually began in movie theaters and is now moving into home audio. Most people believe DTS systems sound better than Dolby Digital systems, but the downside is that currently the only type of DTS-encoded sources are a few DVDs and CDs.

Dolby Pro

Before the current six-channel modes were developed, Dolby Pro was the standard for home audio. It is most commonly used with Dolby Pro–encoded videotapes. If you are still planning to rent the occasional video, you will make use of your receiver's Dolby Pro mode. Keep in mind, though, that as national chains such as Blockbuster and Hollywood Video expand their selection of DVD rentals, you may not be renting videos for much longer.

The good news is that any modern receiver with Dolby Digital support will have excellent Dolby Pro support, so you should not have to worry much about your receiver being capable of rendering excellent sound for Dolby Pro–encoded videotapes.

Inputs/Outputs

The A/V receiver is the heart of any home theater. Thus it accepts multiple audio and video signals from many sources and passes a single audio and single video signal on to the speakers and video monitor. These signals move into the receiver through inputs and leave the receiver through outputs. It is critical to understand how many inputs and outputs you need when choosing a receiver.

Inputs

A receiver can have several different types of inputs. These inputs can be classified as video or audio inputs. Unlike the traditional audio receiver, the A/V receiver used in home theater can accept video signals as well. Audio inputs can be classified further into different types of analog and digital inputs.

Composite Video and S-Video Inputs

Switching capabilities in an A/V receiver enable you to route video signals to your video monitor. Standard video inputs are called *composite* inputs. You have probably seen these many times before on the back of your VCR. A standard VCR has three composite inputs: one for video (usually colored yellow), one for right-channel audio (usually red), and one for left-channel audio (usually white). A composite video input handles video data only. This differs from the cable TV signal with which you are familiar, which uses a coaxial input and carries both video and audio data. A/V receivers do not usually accept coaxial signals. Make sure that the receiver you buy has inputs for all the video source components you plan to use (VCR, DVD player, and so on).

Many high-end source components can output video signals using S-video in addition to the standard composite inputs. S-video carries the brightness and color information of the video signal separately. Because of this separation, monitors that can display S-video offer a much sharper picture than a standard TV signal.

Figure 1.18 shows a receiver with yellow composite inputs stacked next to the black, round S-video inputs. The video inputs are under the column on the back of the receiver labeled Video.

To make use of S-video, you need a source component with S-video outputs. Such components include a DVD player, a digital satellite TV, an S-VHS VCR, and a video monitor with an S-video input. If you can use S-video, it may be worth looking for a receiver that has S-video outputs.

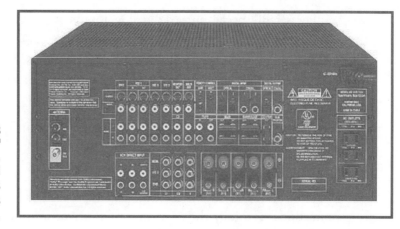

Figure 1.18

Composite,
S-video, and
analog inputs
on a receiver's
back panel.

NOTE   If you are on a budget, video inputs are one area where you might be able to save some money on a receiver. Many video monitors also accept multiple video inputs and can switch among them. If you already have this capability in your monitor, you do not need it in your receiver.

Analog and Digital Audio Inputs

Analog audio inputs are pretty straightforward. They are the traditional left/right composite inputs with which you may already be familiar. Make sure that your receiver has enough inputs for all your audio-only devices, such as CD players and cassette decks. A few special types of analog audio inputs may be useful and worth considering when choosing a receiver.

The analog inputs are the red and white inputs stacked horizontally along the bottom of the receiver's back panel.

If you still have a phonograph player, you should look for a receiver with a phono input. Phono signals are a much lower voltage than other audio signals, but a phono input lets you make the connection without a separate phono pre-amp.

Another set of special-purpose analog inputs is 5.1-channel inputs. As explained earlier, it is possible to get a receiver that is Dolby Digital–ready. In this case, an external Dolby Digital decoder is used to create the six channels of audio data, and the receiver simply acts as an amplifier.

The final type of analog inputs is front-panel inputs. These inputs are strictly for convenience. Using these inputs, you can quickly hook up devices such as video games or a camcorder.

Digital inputs are used with 5.1-channel sources and come in two types: optical and coaxial. You need a special type of cable for optical digital connections. Typically the only digital input you will need is the one for your DVD player.

Outputs

As you would expect, a receiver has the same types of outputs as inputs. The difference is that the receiver has fewer outputs than inputs because its purpose is to switch among many inputs for output to your speakers and video monitor.

Some other outputs you may consider are extra digital outputs for devices such as digital audiotape or minidisc players. By using digital inputs and digital outputs, you can record audio directly in digital format. Like digital inputs, digital outputs come in both optical and coaxial versions. Make sure that your receiver supports the same standard as your other components.

Other Features to Consider

You should consider several other features when shopping for a receiver, such as THX certification, on-screen menus, and remote controls.

THX Certification

As we explained previously, THX-equipped processors have a set of add-on enhancements to other sound systems (such as Dolby Pro Logic) that eliminate the brightness of your speaker system, match speakers' upper sounds more accurately, and increase the separation of the rear channels. If a receiver has been enhanced to meet THX standards, it will provide the highest-quality home theater experience when used with other THX-certified components and media such as THX-certified DVDs.

On-Screen Menus

Some A/V receivers enable you to control your receiver on your video monitor by using an on-screen menu. Others simply enable you to view status information on the screen. These features vary greatly. Another possibility is to have this information built into the receiver's remote control.

To use these on-screen menus, you must be using your video monitor, so these menus are not used with audio-only sources such as CDs or mini-discs. Also, the S-video output on many A/V receivers cannot be used with the receiver's on-screen menus. You can still connect the receiver's composite video output to your TV and view these menus by switching between the monitor's S-video input and composite input.

Remote Controls

A quality home theater will have many components, and each of them may have its own remote control. This can become a little confusing if you must sort through three or four remotes simply to play a movie. To solve this problem, many high-end receivers come with a *universal* remote. These remotes can control not only your receiver but also other components from the same manufacturer. The problem is that few people purchase all their components from one manufacturer. For this reason, it is better to invest in a quality programmable remote. Programmable remotes are discussed in detail on Sunday evening under the section "Secrets of Remote Controls."

Processors

A processor is the brains of the entire operation of a home theater, if you are using a separate processor and amplifier combination instead of just a receiver.

A processor essentially takes the signal in from a source, breaks down the signal into its respective parts, and then distributes the signals to the amplifier, which then pushes the signals through the speakers. If the source receiving the signal is a digital input, and if the processor is a Dolby Digital or DTS processor, it will further decode the signal and enhance your listening enjoyment.

The benefit of using a separate processor and amplifier is that each separate processor and amp has its own chassis and power supply so that each of these components can be optimized for different functions without introducing excess noise into each other's systems.

The processor controls the volume, does the A/V switching, provides surround processing modes, and essentially acts as the nerve center or brains for a good home theater system (see Figure 1.19).

Processor Features

All processors come with the same features as, if not more features than, the A/V receiver. From video switching, to digital inputs, to surround

Figure 1.19

The ADA Cinema Reference, a state-of-the-art processor.

processing, to different listening modes, each processor has pluses and minuses that you need to add up to equate to what you are looking for in a home theater.

Processors enable you to attach your source devices' video inputs into the back of the processor. Offering composite to S-video inputs and outputs, some processors (such as the Cinema Reference) now even have component switching capabilities for the new HDTV technology that is slowly creeping into the home theater world. Essentially, the processor controls what signal your television is receiving. Make sure that you have enough video inputs to accommodate all your video source components, plus more for future expansions.

The processor also takes in all the audio inputs from the CD players, DVD players, tuners, and tape decks, whether the signal is analog or digital (see Figure 1.20). The processor also includes analog outputs for recording devices such as tape players or minidisc players.

Digital inputs provide better sound because they bypass the D/A (digital to analog) converter process that often causes signal degradation. Also, the digital signals can carry DTS and Dolby Digital 5.1, which are much better surround sound processing modes for home theater viewing and listening.

Some processors provide front panel inputs for A/V devices. These inputs make it easy to hook up your video or digital camera. Essentially these inputs are for "temporary" components that you won't need to hook up permanently.

Figure 1.20

Analog inputs on a processor's back panel.

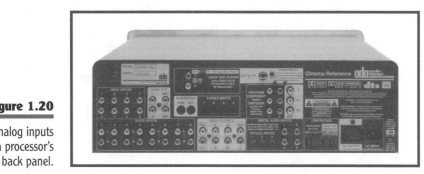

Another feature that some processors provide is THX certification. As mentioned previously, THX is a set of standards for audio and video components that ensure a high level of performance in your system. The crossovers for line levels are built-in, which makes it easy to hook up your subwoofer, and allows for all the different types of Dolby Digital surround modes.

Other processors have different listening modes. Some can cater to all your movie needs, taking into account room size, listening preferences, and so on. They can also take into account how you want to listen to music. For example, you can switch to a mode in which the processor emulates a jazz club for your favorite artist, even if the recording was made in a studio. These extra little features are fun and sometimes desirable. However, when selecting your processor, first make sure that it handles your home theater needs the best. You can add these fun features later.

Examples of good processors are the ADA Cinema Reference, the ADA Cinema Rhapsody, the Sunfire Theater Grand 2, and the Yamaha 450XX.

Amplifiers

An amplifier is a component that draws current from your wall, and then converts the current into raw power for your speakers. The amplifier transfers the power based on inputs that it receives from the processor for each individual speaker.

Amplifiers are generally large and quite heavy, because of the large coil inside of them. You will typically need at least five channels of power for your home theater, whether through your receiver or from your amplifier.

Amplifier Types and Features

First and foremost, what will your amplifier be powering? If it is the five speakers that comprise your home theater speakers (fronts, center, and surrounds), you need to purchase an amplifier completely different from one that would power, for example, a subwoofer.

There are different types of amps. A monoaural amplifier provides power to only one speaker, or one signal to multiple speakers if they are bridged together. A multichannel amplifier divides its power into a discrete number of channels, and then sends the power separately based on the signal input from the receiver/processor.

Many amps allow you to combine the output of two channels to drive a single speaker at multiple times the power of a single channel. Such amps are called *bridgeable*.

Other amps are defined by number of channels. Typically a five-channel amp is great for any home theater. Buy a six-channel amp only if you need to drive a subwoofer as well.

The one defining factor in an amplifier is power output. Each speaker requires a lot of power to drive its output. Although some people drive their speakers with 100 watts per channel, others need as much as 300 watts per channel, all the way up to 2,000 watts for subwoofers.

Your goal is to achieve 105 decibel peaks for each channel. Based on the power from your amplifier as well as the impedance rating of your speakers (measured in ohms), you should be able to determine what you need. Remember that raising power does not mean increasing the volume. For each factorial of 10 for your amp, you double your volume from your speakers. For example, a 10-watt output would be half of a 100-watt output, which would be only half of a 1,000-watt output. Make sure that your speakers can handle the power that you are delivering to them.

Also be sure that the amplifier you are using generates clean power. Some amplifiers might generate 400 watts per channel, but from the 200-watt range on up the power becomes erratic and bad for the health of your speakers. Be sure to read about your amplifier before investing in one.

Tuners

If you choose a separate amplifier and processor, generally your processor will lack a tuner capability. There are exceptions to the rule, such as Sunfire's Theater Grand 2 (see Figure 1.21).

However, most processors do not have this feature. So, if you listen to the radio, be sure to pick up a tuner. Tuners are quite simple products. They should have an AM antenna, an FM antenna, and possibly a coaxial cable input on the back panel so that you can receive digital stations, which you can subscribe to through your cable company.

You might think that a tuner has no place in a home theater system. However, most people like to incorporate their music needs into a home theater system, so we thought that we should mention it in the book.

You attach your tuner to your processor's analog inputs. A tuner is added via analog inputs to your processor and transmits signal once it receives its signal from the outside.

Simply put, find a tuner you like and just add it to your system. This is not an essential piece of a home theater system.

Speakers

Here lies the defining moment of your home theater system. Your speakers will define how good your home theater system can and will be. Your other choices may result in a lesser system, but cannot significantly

Figure 1.21

Bob Carver's Sunfire Theater Grand 2 processor with built-in tuner.

improve your system past the performance of your speakers; your choice of speakers sets your system's maximum potential.

In short, your speakers are not the place to scrimp and settle for a second-rate product. Here is where you should buy more than you can afford; you can upgrade the other parts of the system later.

Front Speakers

The speakers are divided into separate categories. First, you need two main speakers for the front of your home theater. These two speakers will be used for music as well as movies, and they should be the same model of speaker, just placed on the right and the left. The front speakers provide the main audio experience of the home theater, so be sure that they represent the highs and the midrange very well. You will leave the lows and the bass response to the subwoofer. If you are not going to purchase a subwoofer as you build your home theater this weekend, be sure that the main speakers have a good bass response as well.

NHT's Front Super One speakers (see Figure 1.22) are a great set of front speakers—so good, in fact, that we recommend them for all four speakers, front and rear. Atlantic Technology's speaker systems (see Figure 1.23) are sold in sets so that all the speakers are matched for that set of speakers.

Figure 1.22

NHT's Front Super One speaker.

Figure 1.23

Atlantic Technology's 370THX speaker system.

The Center Speaker

The center channel speaker is the speaker that provides all the dialog from your movies. This speaker will either be mounted above the television or rest on top of it. Make sure that this speaker is video-shielded so that its magnetic field does not affect picture quality.

The center channel should be matched with the two front speakers so that they all complement each other, creating a good "soundstage." A soundstage is an audio setup in which the audience cannot tell where one speaker starts and another one ends; essentially the sound you hear is a large wall in front of you that blends seamlessly, thus the definition of a soundstage.

The center channel should be from the same speaker manufacturer as the two front main speakers.

NHT's Audiocenter 1 (see Figure 1.24) is an awesome center channel—so good, in fact, that some audiophiles use a system consisting of five of these speakers.

Figure 1.24

NHT's
Audiocenter 1.

Figure 1.25

Atlantic
Technology's dipole
speaker system.

The Rear/Surround Speakers

The rear speakers can be the same size as the front speakers, although people often choose smaller speakers, which is perfectly fine. These speakers are sometimes also dipole speakers (see Figure 1.25). Dipole speakers diffuse the sound field so that the audience gets a more blended surround effect.

Again, the rear speakers should provide good highs and midrange while the front speakers provide the bass if the subwoofers do not.

Subwoofers

A subwoofer provides only bass for the system (see Figures 1.26 and 1.27). Some systems have as many as four to six subwoofers, whereas others have one or none. You should set up the subwoofer so that it begins where the other speakers end. You accomplish this through crossovers and the frequencies that are set there. Essentially, if the two front speakers stop their frequency response at 60 Hz, then the subwoofer should start at 60 Hz so that no gaps are heard. Likewise, the audience should not hear any duplication of sound where there might be overlap. This type of calibration is hard to achieve, but worth it in the end.

Subwoofers either come powered or unpowered. If they are unpowered, they are just like any other speaker and require an amplifier. If they are powered, they just need an input to provide the bass for the system.

Figure 1.26

Atlantic Technology's subwoofer with its 3500 system provides excellent bass.

Figure 1.27

NHT's dual Subtwos linked together provide directional bass— enough bass to make sure that you will not live in any apartment with these two pieces of equipment.

Video Monitors and Televisions

Whereas the speakers define your audio experience, your video monitor will define your video experience. To determine what size you need, measure diagonally on the television you want and you will see the size of the television. Determine what your room will hold, what your budget can withstand, and finally what features you need to make this television the one you really enjoy. Televisions have so many features these days that it can be very hard to sort through all of them to determine the right one, and which features are necessary.

Several types of televisions are available. First, there are the typical direct view televisions (see Figure 1.28).

This television is the one you were most likely brought up on. With today's technology, you want flatter screens and a digital comb filter. You also want a television set that can fit in your living room. The tubes range from 20 inches up to 40 inches.

Next, there are the rear projector televisions (see Figure 1.29). These screen sizes range from 40 to 80 inches. Three picture tubes are used: green, red, and blue. These tubes generate and reflect the image on the back of a special screen. The picture looks best when no bright lights are shining on it.

Figure 1.28

A direct view television.

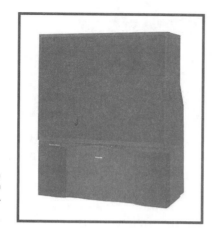

Figure 1.29

A rear projector
television.

Then there are the front projectors (see Figure 1.30). These projectors range from $4,000 to more than $90,000 for great projectors. The screen size ranges from 4 feet up to 8 feet, and you get a great picture. There are three types of front projectors: CRT, LCD, and DLP. The LCD and DLP projectors are very user-friendly, whereas the CRT picture requires professional installation.

Finally, there are flat screen televisions (see Figure 1.31). These televisions are quite incredible, but also quite expensive. They range from 34 inches to 60 inches, and generally are widescreens with a 16 by 9 aspect ratio (width to height). (Regular televisions have a 4 by 3 aspect ratio.)

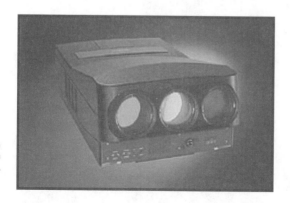

Figure 1.30

A front projector
television.

Figure 1.31

A flat panel display.

Video Monitor and Television Features

You need to consider quite a few features for your video source. First, there is the aspect ratio. Do you want the 16 by 9 ratio, or the regular familiar square-shaped 4 by 3 ratio? That is personal preference. The 16 by 9 ratio will handle letterbox movies better, and show movies as they would be shown in the theater.

Next, consider horizontal resolution. Resolution is measured in lines up and down the tube. HDTV offers the best resolutions. Most televisions have at least 500 lines of resolution.

Consider your inputs. You want multiple video inputs into the set. First, for expandability, make sure that the set has component video inputs. The set should come with the component and S-video inputs. Also, coaxial cable inputs and outputs are useful. Some televisions have front panel inputs so that you can easily plug in camcorders, digital cameras, and similar devices.

The picture-in-picture technology is also quite useful because you can watch several channels at once or check what is happening on one channel while staying at another.

The digital comb filter is important because it separates color and brightness information in the TV signal so that it can be displayed. Some newer sets have color temperature control. This temperature controls the hue of the background images of your video experience. Make sure that your desired settings are set properly when the system is set to medium.

Some televisions come with universal remotes. These remotes are important, but you will see later that incredible universal remotes are available separately that can control every aspect of your home theater.

Sources

With the speakers providing the sound, and the amplifier/receiver/processor providing the signal and power, you need to address the inner core of the home theater: the sources from which you will get your listening and viewing pleasure.

These sources range from products that are not specifically made for home theaters, such as tuners or CD players, to definitive home theater products such as DVD players, TiVo, or DSS dishes.

CD Players and Jukeboxes

In the 1980s, the CD player got everyone excited about music again. Since the advent of the CD, sound systems hadn't changed much until the advent of the DVD. Today's CD players play HDCD and the newer formats that Sony is putting out. Keep in mind, however, that all DVD players now play CDs, so it can be a waste to buy a CD player when one machine can meet all your needs.

CD Player Features

CD players have several common features. They can play CDs, pause them, and play them in random order; some can shuffle several CDs, and others can even record from other CDs.

Some CD players come in carousels, in which you can load five CDs at a time, while others enable you to load as many as 300 at a time in large jukeboxes. For home theater purposes, try to integrate your CD player and DVD player so that you do not "burn" a digital input on your receiver/processor. By burn, I mean use up or waste the input. We are finding these days that there are more and more components to add to our systems, and not enough inputs to handle them.

DVD Players and Jukeboxes

Chances are that if you bought this book, you bought it along with a DVD player. Never has the advent of an item encouraged people so much to get involved in home theater again.

The Digital Versatile Disc (DVD) offers unmatched standards and incredible quality over the VHS videotape. These discs carry encoded DTS and Dolby Digital soundtracks that allow for the full usage of the home theater, breaking down the sounds into five discrete channels and one extra channel for the subwoofer (bass).

The DVD player is the component that plays these discs. The discs are the size of a CD, and hold an entire movie on them, both audio and video, along with quite a few "extras" that are discussed later in this chapter.

The DVD player has a variety of features that can make your decision a hard one when purchasing this item. Most people start with this item, and then build their home theater outward. We hope that you are at a starting point at which you can build the theater in the proper order, from speakers to power source to components. However, even if you have just bought a DVD player, this section will explain all the features that come along with your player.

DVD players play Digital Versatile Discs, as well as CDs, and some even play MP3 files and video discs. Figure 1.32 shows the front of the DVD player.

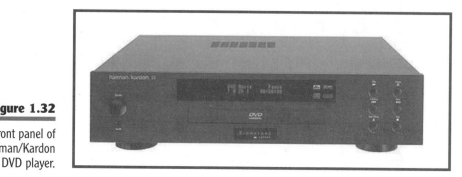

Figure 1.32

The front panel of a Harman/Kardon DVD player.

Notice that the front chassis and all its buttons look quite similar to that of a single-disc CD player. However, unlike a CD player, the DVD player offers digital outputs, either coaxial or optical, and video outputs on its back panel (see Figure 1.33).

Notice that the back panel not only has analog outputs for sound, but also two digital outputs. The square peg is the optical output, and the round peg is the coaxial digital output. These outputs carry the audio to the processor or the receiver, which decodes and separates the signal into its 5.1 discrete channels.

There also are three types of video outputs: composite output, S-video output, and component output. Composite output is the regular RCA jack–type output. This output offers the lowest quality out of a DVD player to your video monitor. All video outputs can either route through your receiver/processor to your video source, or directly to your video

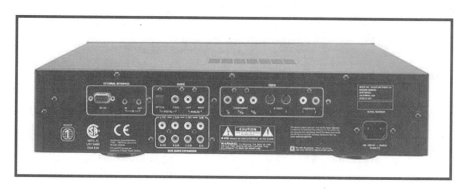

Figure 1.33

The back panel of a DVD player.

source. All audio must go through the processor/receiver if you want to take advantage of your home theater speakers.

The next grade up is S-video, which has been the standard for video for quite some time, starting with laserdiscs. S-video is now the first medium to be widely used on DVD players. This input requires a special cable (refer to the "Cable" section of the Saturday Morning chapter) called, appropriately, the S-video cable (see Figure 1.34).

The "Cable" section describes how the cable operates. For now, you simply need to know that S-video offers a superior way to display video on your television or screen. The difference between composite video and S-video is like night and day. Once you plug in your S-video cable to the back of your television, you will notice immediately how grainy your television looks when using your old VCR, or how your neighbors' television looks when they show you any type of video.

What, then, is the third cable, component output? The component video output divides the video signal into three separate pieces, and then sends that signal to your video monitor. Believe it or not (and you won't at first if you have experienced S-video), the difference between component video and S-video is drastic. You will now notice how grainy S-video is. Figure 1.35 shows a component video cable.

All three video outputs assume that your television has the correct inputs. Some older televisions have only RF cable inputs and no RCA jacks, and often do not include S-video or component inputs.

These are the external features that you will find on the DVD player itself. Now, let's look at what a DVD player can do functionally.

Figure 1.34

An S-video cable from Monster Cable.

Figure 1.35

Component
video cable from
Monster Cable.

DVD Player Features

All DVD players offer special effects features, such as freeze frame, slow
motion, and high-speed forward/reverse search, but some offer higher-
quality forward/reverse motion.

Dolby Digital/DTS Decoders

DVD players either send the Dolby Digital/DTS signal to the proces-
sor/receiver to be decoded, or they actually decode the signal for Dolby
Digital–ready processors/receivers. These receivers need a six-channel
direct input to make use of the DVD player's analog decoder output.
Some of the decoders in DVD players are good enough to manage bass,
sending the low bass frequencies only to your subwoofer rather than to
your surround speakers, which generally cannot handle these frequencies.

Digital Outputs

The analog outputs of the DVD player can output Dolby surround
signals to a Dolby Pro Logic receiver, whereas the new digital outputs can
send a full DTS or Dolby Digital 5.1 signal to the processor. These digital
outputs come in two forms: coaxial and fiber-optic.

A coaxial output uses a conventional wire cable whereas a fiber-optic
output uses what is called a Toslink fiber-optic link. Most DVD players
now have both types of outputs because most processors have a limited
number of digital inputs.

Multiple Angles

The DVD has so much storage room on the disc that directors can throw whatever they want onto the disc, including supplemental footage, character anthologies, and multiple angles.

Some DVDs allow you to switch your perspective to watch the scene as it is filmed from a director's other camera at the same time, giving you another perspective on the scene (see Figures 1.36 and 1.37). Although most movies that take advantage of this feature are adult in nature, some major motion pictures released on DVD, such as *Suicide Kings,* use this feature as well.

Figure 1.36

A movie scene from a regular angle.

Figure 1.37

A movie scene from another camera angle.

These other angles usually are offered at certain moments throughout the movie, not throughout the entire movie. Be sure to read the back of the DVD's packaging to see whether the DVD offers multiple angles.

You control the angling feature through the remote, by pressing the Angle button (see Figure 1.38).

Chapter Search

A convenient feature of DVDs and DVD players is that they break movies down into "chapters," similar to the tracks on a CD. However, because the DVD player is visually oriented, you can see these chapters on the television screen and choose the point at which you want to start the movie (see Figure 1.39).

To pick a chapter, just navigate using the directional controls on the remote control and press the Enter or Play button.

All DVD players have this feature.

Languages

DVDs have so much space to store information that they can even store separate language tracks, in addition to subtitles and closed captioning for the hearing impaired. Just go to the menu of any DVD and pick the language that you would like to hear or see (see Figure 1.40).

Every DVD player enables the user to utilize this feature, as long as it is offered on the disc (see Figure 1.41).

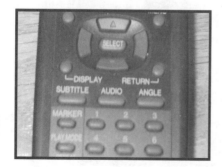

Figure 1.38

A DVD remote with the Angle button.

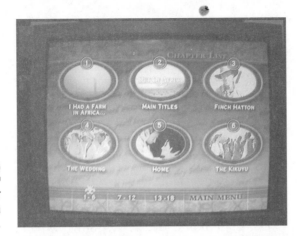

Figure 1.39

A chapter selection for a movie on DVD.

Figure 1.40

The language selection menu for a DVD.

Figure 1.41

A disc showing different language options.

Sound Encoding

Sound encoding comes in a variety of flavors. This book covers 2-channel Dolby Digital, the older Dolby Pro Logic, to the 5-channel plus sub-woofer (5.1) encoding which includes Dolby Digital 5.1 and DTS.

Widescreen/Letterbox Formatting

Ever notice the annoying black bars on the top and bottom of movies that use the letterbox format (see Figure 1.42)? Some people prefer that format, but others do not. Fortunately, the DVD has two sides and a lot of room, so both versions of the movie can be stored and chosen by discerning viewers. Letterbox is the movie shown as it was supposed to be shown and was shown in the movie theater. Because of the 4:3 ratio of the picture on most television sets, sides of the movie get "chopped" off for convenience sake. New 16:9 sets take advantage of the letterbox format and show it in its entirety without any black bars. When the picture is "chopped" this is called "Pan and Scan" format.

However, make sure that the DVD disc's packaging specifies the video format. A 4:3 ratio represents the regular aspect ratio for the Pan and Scan format, whereas 16:9 represents the widescreen/letterbox format.

Character Anthologies

Some DVD discs have enough room to give you a history of the movie's characters, as well as a story background. Some even go so far as to give you a director's track where the actors and directors talk while you watch the movie, commenting on how it was made.

Figure 1.42

When you view a DVD movie in letterbox format, you notice black bars on the top and bottom of your screen.

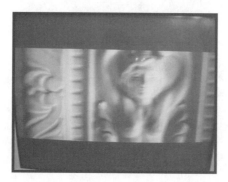

Progressive Scan

The best way to describe progressive scan is to compare the image you see on your TV, which uses a technology called interlacing to display an image, to what you see on a computer monitor, which uses progressive scanning.

Your TV displays the odd-numbered lines comprising a TV image every 1/60th of a second and *interlaces* these lines (or fields) with the even-numbered lines, which are displayed every other 1/60th of a second. These two interlaced fields create a complete image, or frame.

The problem with interlacing is that it leaves faint lines between the two fields, which can make the image flicker. Moving objects appear to lose definition, and *jaggies* are evident where curved lines overlap scan lines in two different fields.

A computer monitor, on the other hand, uses progressive scanning to display an image. That is, all the image lines are drawn sequentially 60 times a second, thereby eliminating interlace lines, flicker, and other imperfections caused by interlacing.

A DVD image consists of 480 lines. That's more than there are in any other video format—twice as many, in fact, as in VHS. That's why a DVD looks so good, with or without progressive scanning.

You may be surprised to learn that all DVDs are recorded with a 480-line progressive-scan (or 480p) image. But a standard TV cannot display this progressively scanned image. As a result, a regular DVD player must convert the progressive-scan data into a 480-line interlaced picture (480i) for display on your standard TV. A progressive-scan DVD player allows you to see the best DVD picture possible.

Movies and other DVD programs have a more filmlike quality when displayed in progressive scan.

A progressive-scan DVD improves image sharpness and eliminates the flicker seen in a broadcast TV image or a standard DVD picture. Also, moving objects appear to have more detail. Jaggies, the rough edges often seen in the borders of objects on a screen, and *moiré*, the dizzying movement that you see on a herringbone or checked pattern, are often reduced or may disappear entirely.

Jukeboxes

A single-disc player is never enough! At least that's what Sony and Pioneer thought, so they came out with the 200-disc and 301-disc DVD jukeboxes respectively (see Figure 1.43).

Many people enjoy going to the shelf and picking out a DVD to watch. However, as your collection grows, you might notice that you develop a "video archive" of favorite DVDs that you watch now and then. You might also discover that it's useful to maintain a "new releases" section of your collection, much like that of a video store. In either case, a jukebox is a useful feature, especially if it comes with cataloging software, as both of these players do. The Pioneer model can sort by movie and by movie category. These jukeboxes also play CDs, so if you feel like keeping half your music collection in them, they are capable.

The Pioneer model includes a slaving feature that allows you to connect another 301-disc changer to it so that you use only one digital input into your processor/receiver. However, it might be a while before you have more than 301 DVDs to fill your collection.

Figure 1.43

The Pioneer Elite DVF-07 can hold up to 301 DVDs.

Summarizing Your DVD Player

A DVD player will most likely be the hub of information for your home theater. Be sure to get all the features you want, but also try out a few DVD players at the store to find one that meets your needs. Also be sure to match the DVD player with your television for the best video performance.

Minidisc Players

Sony introduced the rerecordable magneto/optical digital disc in 1992. The company marketed these $2^1/_2$-inch-square discs mainly as a portable prerecorded format. Sony gave away more than one million prerecorded discs, expecting consumers to buy the players that went along with the discs.

Why didn't that happen? The units cost between $500 and $700 and that's in 1992 dollars. Blank discs cost almost $17 at the time. And the first generation of ATRAC (Adaptive Transform Acoustic Coding) encoding didn't sound very good. Many consumers and audio critics considered minidiscs a low-quality diversion to stop the introduction of a recordable audio CD format available to consumers.

The marketplace all but gave up the minidisc, but Sony did not give up and marketed it as a convenient recordable format and a replacement for the cassette tape. It lowered the price of the players, recorders, and blank discs and worked to improve the quality of the ATRAC encoding. These were all good moves on their part—and they eventually paid off. Today, the minidisc is alive and well in the home theater. It's available in portable, auto units, changers, and home recorders. Even some mini-systems have the minidisc.

Minidisc Player Features

The minidisc recorder and player offer an easy format to record and play. The features are as simple as those of a CD player.

Cassette Tape Players

People still enjoy cassette tapes. Fortunately, tape players still only work off analog outputs and inputs, so they do not steal any inputs from any new component you are getting. A tape player consists of either a dual or single cassette deck that connects to your receiver or processor. You can either play tapes to the speakers, or redirect another source to the tape player, which can then record the music.

Cassette Tape Player Features

Tape players often have auto-reverse features, which enable you to play a cassette tape continuously by switching to playing the other side of the tape when it reaches the end of one side.

Tape players also now have high-speed dubbing, which allows quick recording of another tape.

VCRs

A VCR is generally like a cassette deck, except that it records television or other video sources. A VCR has analog composite inputs and outputs, and also accepts and outputs coaxial cable input.

VCR Features

You can record on tapes for lengths of two, four, and six hours. Some VCRs have front inputs so that you can hook up camcorders and similar components. As the head count on a VCR increases, so does the picture quality. Some VCRs offer VCR Plus which is a way to easily record your favorite shows. We find that TiVo does a much better job at this, and VCR Plus does not work very well and has not been embraced by the home theater industry.

DSS Systems

A dish is definitely the new way to go when it comes to television and the news. Not only do you have access to many channels, but you get them invariably in a much better format than regular cable.

Also, via DSS, you soon will be able to receive HDTV signals, allowing for much better reception.

DSS Features

Multiplexers are a good feature to have in a DSS. They enable you to watch one channel while someone else watches another channel in another part of the house. Installing your DSS satellite dish is not that hard, and it even comes with instructions on how to do it yourself.

TiVo

The TiVo or PTVR (Personal Television Recorder) is a new technology consisting of a box containing a hard drive, a processor, and software to track and record the shows you like to watch.

TiVo Features

You can pause live television as TiVo tracks what you are watching currently, and then keeps recording as you have paused the screen.

For instance, TiVo lets you control live TV in the following manner:

- Pause live TV during interruptions—up to 30 minutes
- Fast forward and rewind with three speeds: 6x, 12x, and 60x
- Instant Replay button jumps you back 8 seconds
- Slow-motion at $1/4$x speed
- Create your own instant replays: rewind and play back in slow motion
- Frame forward and frame backward
- Jump button catches you back to real time
- Program status bar displays where you are in the show for cached and real time

TiVo also dials up and updates the current television schedule, displaying it on the screen to show you the show, as well as a current description, and expanding out a list of all the shows on the other channels and current shows on later that night on the same channel as the show you are watching.

TiVo's goal, it seems, is to make you forget about using your VCR. The interface is extremely user-friendly, and with 30 hours of recording time, is very amenable to your needs.

TiVo records your favorite shows on its hard drive so there's never any videotape to wear out, and it reminds you if you don't have enough room.

TiVo stores the shows like a CD stores its tracks, allowing you instant access to the show you want to watch, rather than having to scan through a VCR tape. You will find that a TiVo is to a VCR as a CD is to a cassette tape.

The technology TiVo uses is MPEG 2 encoding and is extremely good.

If you take a look at the back panel of a TiVo, you will see that it has not only component and coaxial inputs/outputs, but also S-video outputs that carry an extremely good signal to your set.

TiVo also makes it very easy to hook up to your home theater and television. The instructions included show how to hook up to a DSS dish, an antenna, or your cable provider.

You will see in our setup chapter a great overview of how to hook up your TiVo and integrate it into your home theater experience.

Conclusion

You should now have a good feel for the different capabilities of audio/video receivers, as well as all the other components of your home theater. You should start thinking about what features and components are important to you. The Saturday morning section "Planning Your System" will make some suggestions about what features are absolutely required and which ones you can skip to save some money. In addition, after you have thought about which components you need, we will discuss the cables you need to connect all these components, as well as accessories you want to use to integrate and expand your home theater.

Accessories and Purchasing

✪ Planning your system

✪ Cable

✪ Racks

✪ Speaker stands

✪ Accessories

✪ Hunting for bargains

✪ Making the purchase

Good morning! After reading the Friday night chapter, you should be well versed in what each component is, and all the features that are important to you and your home theater.

This morning you first will decide what you want to include in your system, shop for the best prices, and then finally purchase the system.

Planning Your System

Before we begin planning the schematics to your home theater, let's discuss some important topics we did not have time to discuss last night. These range from the cable you will need to connect all your components, to the racks you will store your components on, to the accessories you can add to your system for multi-room listening.

Cable

Although each component has its importance to the overall home theater system, the cabling of home theater systems is often overlooked. The cabling of a system is very important, from the speaker cable that everyone seems to be familiar with to the less familiar interconnects between components, amplifiers, and processors. Different types of cables are available for analog signals, digital signals, and video signals.

Monster Cable is a brand that we have grown to know and trust. This manufacturer provides a superior product, and has been in the home theater industry since the beginning.

Analog Interconnect Cable

The analog interconnect cable serves several purposes (see Figure 2.1). This cable carries your analog audio signals and video composite signals to their respective destinations. Analog interconnect cable also links the processor output signals to the different channels of your amplifier.

Everyone should be familiar with this type of cable. Whenever you buy a component, the package usually includes audio interconnect cable, although the cable provided is usually of very low quality. Be sure to purchase higher-quality interconnects for clearer and crisper signals.

You will learn more about the uses of this cable in later chapters when you determine what cable to buy and how to hook up certain components.

Digital Cables

Digital cables come in two varieties: the digital coaxial cable and the digital Toslink fiber-optic cable. The coaxial cable carries a digital signal over a regular cable to a processor. A Toslink fiber-optic cable has a laser signal outputted from the source and traveling all the way to the processor.

Figure 2.1

Analog interconnect cable.

Depending on your different components, you will need different quantities of these cables, and perhaps different types. Check how many components you have and how many digital inputs you have in the back of your processor/receiver. After you determine which components are inflexible (that is, which ones have only one digital output), see what inputs are left over on the processor and what cables you will use.

S-Video Cables

An S-video cable takes an S-video signal from a DVD player, TiVo, or perhaps a DSS and brings the signal to your video monitor in a sharp, crisp format. The S-video cable breaks down the brightness and color parts into separate signals and carries them to your video monitor.

Generally you want to connect your video sources directly to your video monitor so that you do not lose the signal anywhere. Just make sure that you use the optimum video signal available (use component input over S-video over RCA jacks).

Component Video Cable

Component video cable (see Figure 2.2) breaks down the color portion of the signal even further than the S-video cable, carrying the color on two separate wires to enhance color resolution even more. Some DVD players have component outputs, but most television sets with component inputs are fairly expensive. As mentioned before, however, the visible difference between the two formats is substantial.

Figure 2.2

Monster Cable's
component
video cable.

Speaker Cable

Speaker cable carries the power from your amplifier all the way to your speakers. If your system needs to drive a heavy load, make it easy on your system by using low-gauge wiring (thicker speaker cable) so that the cable itself offers no resistance.

You can use what is commonly called "lamp cord," which is 18-gauge wire that you can buy in any hardware store, all the way up to Monster Cable's incredible Z Series speaker wire, which costs as much as $10 per foot (see Figures 2.3 and 2.4).

If you are using high-power amplifiers and sensitive speakers, do not skimp on speaker cable. Although a beginning home theater builder might not notice the difference, cheap speaker cable can degrade your signal quite a bit.

Figure 2.3

Common lamp cord cable.

Figure 2.4

Monster Cable's high-end Z Series speaker cable.

At the end of each speaker cable, you generally attach binding posts, which make connections to your speakers and amps much easier. Although some amps allow you to connect raw copper wires, the fraying and potential for hazards and short circuits generally are just not worth it in the end.

A speaker cable generally consists of two copper wires, each covered in an insulating material to prevent shock or short circuits. Z Series wire goes even further to help you hide the speaker cable by covering both wires in a mesh covering so that they travel together looking as one cable.

Converters

Some cables convert signals from one to the other. One such cable is Monster Cable's S-video to component converter (see Figure 2.5). This converter is helpful especially when you want to connect your gaming console to the home theater or to the television after you have run out of composite video inputs. After you connect this cable to the gaming console's video cable, the converter can send signals in S-video format, allowing for dynamic switching through the home theater.

Another converter cable is the adapter that converts coaxial cable into an analog RCA input (see Figure 2.6). This becomes handy when you want to connect long runs of cable and do not have the RCA cables to do so.

Y-Cable

A Y-cable simply divides an analog signal into two separate signals (see Figure 2.7). The signal output degrades somewhat, so be sure not to divide the signal too much.

Figure 2.5

The S-video to component video converter from Monster Cable.

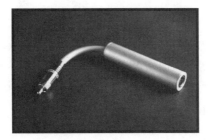

Figure 2.6

The coaxial cable to RCA jack converter plug.

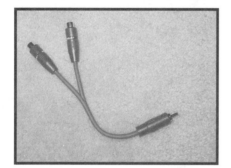

Figure 2.7

A Y-cable from Monster Cable.

Racks

After you have put together your entire component list for your home theater, you have to figure out where you can house all these nice little toys. One solution is to purchase a rack. Although some high-end equipment can actually be "racked" in computer server racks, aesthetic racks add to the ambience of your home theater.

Rack Types

There are generally two types of racks: the A/V rack and the component rack.

The A/V rack can hold your television as well as some components underneath. The base is generally much wider than a typical component rack because it must be able to accommodate a large television. Also, you cannot stack an A/V rack very high, because you do not want the rack's center of gravity to be too high. (Large televisions are heavy, so placing them too high on a rack is dangerous.)

Figure 2.8 shows a good A/V rack for placing a television set on top and still having shelves below for storing other components.

The component rack, on the other hand, stacks nicely to hold your components in their proper places. If you keep the back and sides of your racks open, installing components and changing wires is easier to do. Some people enjoy entertainment centers, but sometimes they can provide hours of headaches as you try to reach behind and move cables you cannot see.

The Lovan Sovereign series is a great example of a component rack (see Figure 2.9). It offers several shelving sizes so that you have the correct size shelf for different size components. A low-amp component rack sits close to the floor for a low center of gravity for the entire rack. The design also opens up some space in which you can work freely as you connect your home theater components.

A Lovan Sovereign rack has isolation points on the tips of each of its legs, essentially making the rack vibration-free, which is very important when you are working with signals and spinning DVDs.

Figure 2.8

The Sovereign A/V rack from Lovan Audio.

Figure 2.9

The Lovan Sovereign component rack.

Rack Features

Racks can have different features, but typically they are mostly aesthetic aside from the open/closed option that was previously mentioned (computer racks versus home racks). Racks come with a choice of different boards and designs so that they can match your home's décor.

Speaker Stands

Speaker stands (see Figure 2.10) can serve different purposes to your home theater. Not only do they raise your speakers up to listening level, but ideally they should reduce the vibration of the speakers to zero so that the only thing moving out of the speaker is the air that provides the great sound content for your surround sound.

Figure 2.10

Lovan's speaker stands for the surround and front speakers.

Lovan and other manufacturers attach isolation spikes to the bottom of the speaker stands. This stabilizes the speaker stands. If you have hardwood floors, you might prefer to use rubber isolation pads because they do the job very well (the spikes dig through carpet to find stability) and will not scratch up your floors.

Accessories

You need to consider a variety of accessories for your home theater, including universal remotes, sound level meters, audio/video tuning accessories, and power conditioners.

Universal Remotes

Universal remotes allow you to group all your remotes from all your different sources together in one remote control. Many remote controls are on the market today, some universal, some coming with your components, but none as advanced as the Philips Pronto (see Figure 2.11). This remote allows full integration with your computer, allowing you to program different codes, but also allowing for graphics and the programming of macros.

See the Sunday Evening chapter for a good setup of your universal remote. Universal remotes are awesome because they can control every component, regardless of brand.

Sound Level Meters

A sound level meter allows you to measure sound from different points in the room. You can purchase this accessory at any electronics store for less than $15. You will need this piece of equipment on Sunday evening when you test your configuration and setup of the home theater.

Audio/Video Tuning Accessories

Several accessories are available that can assist you in tuning your audio/video components. These accessories include Video Essentials and Avia.

Figure 2.11

The Philips
Pronto remote.

Video Essentials

Video Essentials is a disc that allows you to calibrate your home theater experience, especially the colors on your television (see Figure 2.12).

Avia

Avia is a generation ahead of Video Essentials, adding sound testing and video testing, as well as detailed explanations of home theater and how its components interact with each other (see Figure 2.13).

Figure 2.12

The Video Essentials disc.

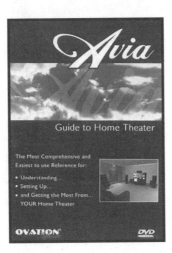

Figure 2.13

The Avia disc.

Power Conditioners

Monster Cable has a subsidiary called Monster Power. Monster Power makes a great set of products that takes your home's power and conditions and cleans it so that before it even reaches your components, there are no strange anomalies in the power signal.

Although you might think of this component as a giant surge protector, it actually goes far beyond that purpose. The power conditioning component controls all your components' on/off states through the power grid that it controls in the back of the unit. It provides special power filters for each different type of component, from high-current amps to sensitive video components. The power conditioner even provides extra inputs in the front of the chassis so that you can use a convenient power source when testing components.

Monster Power's HTS3500 and HTS5000 power conditioners even protect all your equipment through a special warranty that guarantees that power spikes will not destroy or damage any of your equipment as long as its power center is protecting it.

If you are investing in a serious home theater, this accessory is quite handy and provides some peace of mind. Also, you can connect its switching capability to your receiver so that your receiver/processor turns on the power center, which then activates all the other components one after another by providing power to them.

Digital-to-Analog Converters

After you have these wonderful new high-end toys, you will find that you want to experience the sound all over your house. Or, you might not have a receiver or processor that accepts digital inputs just yet. Anyhow, Entech, a division of Monster Cable, makes some great converters that make wiring a breeze in your house as you expand it. Note that these products are not necessary for a full working system right off the bat, but are great accessories for later as you build up your home theater into a complete home system.

The Number Cruncher by Entech takes a digital signal input, and outputs two analog signals (right and left). The conversion is very nice and the sound quality is very good. See below for the Number Cruncher module, and below that for the Number Cruncher back panel. (See Figures 2.14 and 2.15.)

A great use for this device is to run music to another part of the house. You can have the digital output of the receiver push signal to the Number Cruncher, and then have RCA jacks run to another processor somewhere else in the house to amplify the sound!

S-Video to Component to Composite to Component Converters

The video signals are getting better and better as time moves forward. A lot of signals from our old components might not have the quality, but it is nice to have them connect in a standard fashion to our new receivers or video monitors. There are several of these to choose from.

Figure 2.14

The Number Cruncher by Entech, a digital to analog converter.

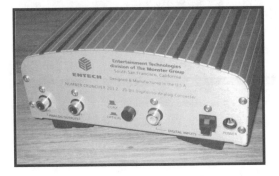

Figure 2.15

The back panel of the Number Cruncher, showing all the inputs and outputs.

First, there is the composite to S-video cable converter. This converts in both directions, from composite video cable to an S-video signal (see Figure 2.16).

This cable is great if you want to connect your video game console or your old VCR to your new S-video–enabled receiver.

Entech makes another all-around converter. It actually allows for multiple inputs and sends out a component output. Refer to Figures 2.14 and 2.15 for the front and back displays.

This unit is great if you want to run multiple signals to one box, and then let the box choose which signal is active and send that to the television.

Stabilizers

Several companies include stabilizer feet or cones on the bottom of their racks or speakers to reduce vibration. Vibration causes all sorts of impurities that then degrade the sound quality of your home theater.

Some companies make stabilizer platforms, made generally of MDF (medium density fiberboard), which sit on top of your rack and make sure the component is completely stable.

See Figure 2.17 for such a unit from Lovan.

These units are used ideally for amplifiers and DVD players.

Figure 2.16

S-video to composite converter.

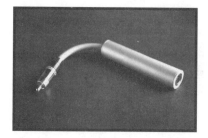

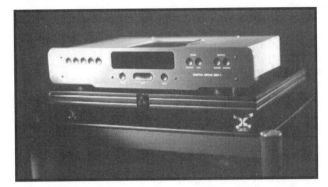

Figure 2.17

A stabilizer platform, the Triosilator by Lovan Audio.

DVD Racks

So, now that you have everything set up or worked out what you are going to buy, you need to think about storage. There are so many racks out there to store your CDs or DVDs. Remember, your home theater will show your personality, and you want a good quality product. Either find a nice cabinet to store the media in, or get a very nice rack. This does not mean go out there and spend thousands on a DVD storage rack, but look around. There are some great products that are also expandable and can grow with your collection.

One item the authors tried out are the racks by BOLTZ-USA. They can be found on the Web site www.boltz-usa.com. See Figure 2.18 for one of their racks.

The nice thing about the BOLTZ racks is that they are expandable and strong. See Figure 2.19.

The racks come in a variety of colors, from black to stainless, and they can accommodate more and more media as your collection grows. In addition, the racking can be stored into cabinetry if you do not want to display it. I think you can see from the theme of this entire book that the authors are embracing "expandable" technologies that allow your home theater to grow without replacing product!

Figure 2.18

Stainless steel
multimedia rack
(courtesy of
BOLTZ-USA).

The exciting part is about to begin. Now that you are well versed on all the options and components of home theater, it is time for you to plan what you will put into your personal home theater.

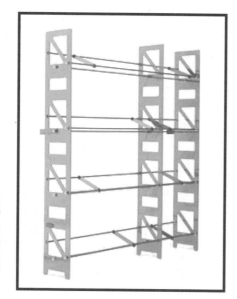

Figure 2.19

Expandable
features of the
multimedia rack
(courtesy of
BOLTZ-USA).

Size and Budget

Two variables influence what you will put into your home theater: the size of your room, and your budget. If you are building a nice "home" theater for your dorm room, you definitely do not need the same size and number of components as someone who is building a dedicated theater in the basement.

Also, to build a home theater, you can spend anywhere from $1,000 for a very small home theater setup to hundreds of thousands of dollars for a more state-of-the-art system.

We cannot help you track your spending item by item, but we can suggest the order in which you purchase the items. By purchasing certain key components in the suggested order, you can determine your home theater's makeup and ensure that it can grow steadily and easily into the future.

Order Counts!

This morning you need to purchase, at minimum, a video monitor (a television set), a video source (a DVD player or VCR), five speakers (with an optional subwoofer), and a receiver (or a processor/amplifier combination, depending on your choice). The subwoofer is actually a crucial part of a complete home theater; it is "optional" only in the sense that, of all the speakers, the subwoofer is the one that does not need to be connected immediately. Finally, you need cable to connect all these devices.

First, let's review how to plan this minimum architecture for your home theater. Then you can add extras to your system (such as TiVo players, DSS, multidisc CD players, and so on).

Step 1: Your Video Monitor (TVs or Screens)

First, how big do you want the picture to be? Based on your Friday night research, you should be able to determine whether you want a direct view, project, flat panel, or widescreen television. The size of your television is the measure of the distance between the top corner and the bottom opposite corner (see Figure 2.20).

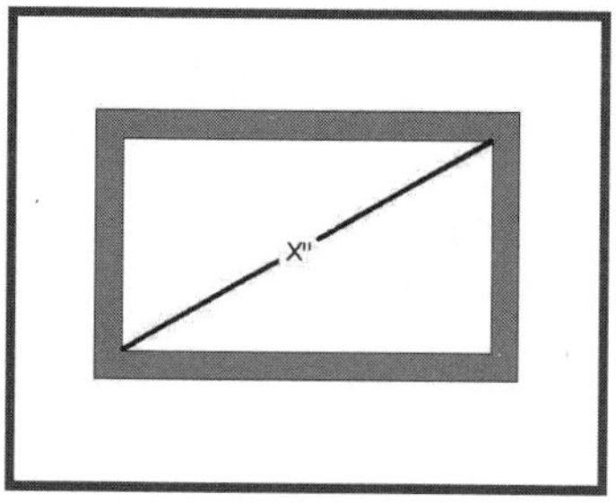

Figure 2.20

Measuring
television and
screen size.

Although size definitely matters, make sure that you do not pay for size only. Consider quality of picture as well. If you have bought a television of 26 inches or greater, make sure that you have an S-video port in the back of the set. Also, if your screen is 36 inches or greater, make sure that there is a component input in the back of the set. Both of these features are extremely important and will help you achieve a high-quality picture, especially when using your DVD player or an SVHS VCR as your video source.

After determining the size and quality of picture, consider all the other perks of the television. Does it have PIP (picture in picture), auto-volume control (which adjusts commercials and television programs to maintain a constant audio volume), channel lockout, or multiple video inputs? A multitude of options are available, but these are all secondary to size and quality of picture. These other options are discussed in detail in the section that you read last night while researching your home theater.

The size of your television also enables you to determine the size of your speakers. A 20-inch television with 6 feet tall main speakers will not provide a good balance of power, sound, and video. Make sure all your components complement each other.

Step 2: Your Video Source

It's time to determine what components you want to choose for audio and video output.

First, we highly recommend that you choose a DVD player. Not only are DVDs widely available, you can easily see a huge difference in picture quality between a grainy VHS tape and a crisp DVD image.

Also, most DVD players these days are quite affordable, ranging in price from $100 all the way up into the thousands. The $200 models are well equipped with features. To buy any model that provides a noticeable (but barely discernable) improvement in sound and picture quality than the $200 models offer, you will need to spend much more money. However, you must make one choice here.

Which component in your home theater will process the sound via DTS sound decoding or Dolby Digital? Will it be your actual DVD player, or your receiver/processor? We recommend that you choose the receiver/processor because the sound quality is noticeably better than if the processor is on-board the DVD player. However, if you already own a receiver that is "DTS-ready" or "Dolby Digital–ready", make sure that your DVD player has a processor on-board.

Also, if your television has component inputs, make sure that your DVD player has component outputs for the video out.

Step 3: Your Speakers

Why would you buy speakers before buying a receiver or amplifier? You want to determine the type of sound quality and volume to which you want to listen, and then pick the power source that will drive them.

You need to purchase two front main speakers, a center speaker to place on or above your television, two surround speakers, and possibly a subwoofer. If you choose not to buy a subwoofer, be sure that your two front main speakers have woofers capable of driving bass through them; otherwise, you will miss out on a wonderful aspect of most movies: the rumbling bass that you can actually feel. We recommend that you purchase a subwoofer. If you want to save some money, buy a subwoofer with a built-in amplifier so that you do not need to power it through your receiver or buy a separate amplifier for it.

The two front speakers should have good mid- and high-range drivers (tweeter and midrange) and possibly one woofer each for some directional bass. The center channel does not need to direct any bass, so concentrate on good midrange and tweeter drivers, something that can replicate the human voice well, because that is where all your on-screen dialog will be projected from. Finally, the two rear speakers should have diverse components capable of playing a variety of sounds, from dialog, to whistles blowing, to explosions, to anything that could happen behind you.

The size of the speakers does not always determine power and clarity. When you go shopping later today, be sure to listen to all your speakers in the store, and find out what the store is using to power the speakers. Some small BOSE speakers are very clear and crisp, whereas some larger speakers sound boomy and are not very good.

Also, try to stick with the same brand of speakers throughout. Speakers from the same manufacturer tend to complement each other. Although you can sometimes get multiple brands to work well together, they are often mismatched. One important note: Be sure to check that the frequency where the front main speakers stop (80 Hz or so) is where the subwoofer takes over (80 Hz and below). If the main speakers are pushing sound that the subwoofer is also pushing, they duplicate sound, which sounds bad. If the main speakers cut off at a frequency and the subwoofer picks up at a frequency below that, you will notice a "gap" in sound where those frequencies do not meet.

Some manufacturers, such as Atlantic Technology or NHT, make excellent speaker sets that match well together (see Figure 2.21). Atlantic's product tends to be more expensive than NHT's, but both sound incredibly good, especially for a beginning home theater.

Step 4: The Power and Brains of the Home Theater

Now it's time to choose the central hub of your system. First, should you buy a processor and an amplifier, or a receiver that combines these two technologies? From your research, you should be able to determine by now which you can afford, and which route you want to take.

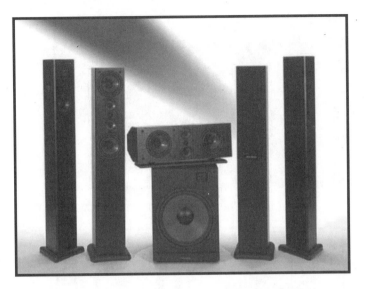

Figure 2.21

Some speaker
manufacturers
make matched
sets of speakers
that complement
each other,
such as Atlantic
Technology's
370 series.

This section addresses power and brains. If you bought the amplifier and processor separately, the power discussion should help you choose your amplifier, and the brains discussion should help you choose the processor. If you are buying a receiver, both discussions pertain to one unit.

Your speakers should have a minimum and perhaps a maximum rating. Make sure that your power source can produce clean power up to that maximum rating of the speaker. Although some power sources are rated up to, for example, 100 watts per channel, the power becomes unstable at 70 watts and produces a dirty signal to the speakers, which can permanently damage them. Good research on the Web or through catalogs will provide you with the information to make a good assessment of how much power you need. You will need five or six channels of power, depending on whether your subwoofer is self-powered (see Figures 2.22 and 2.23).

Notice that the binding posts on this amplifier are pretty sturdy and strong, and differ significantly from the RCA jacks that reside just above them. You will see the same difference on a receiver when looking at the back of it (see Figure 2.24). Here, however, all the input jacks from all the components reside right next to the power outputs for the speakers.

Figure 2.22

A good, affordable five-channel amp by Outlaw Audio on a Lovan audio/video rack (courtesy of Outlaw Audio, Inc. at www. outlawaudio.com).

Figure 2.23

The front view of the Outlaw Audio system shown in Figure 2.22 (courtesy of Outlaw Audio, Inc. at www. outlawaudio.com).

Figure 2.24

The back of a receiver, where audio/video inputs and power outputs to speakers share the same space.

If your receiver or amplifier has only five channels, like these two pieces, you might need to purchase a single-channel amplifier for your subwoofer or subwoofers. Crown Audio makes an incredible amplifier for just such a purpose, the K1 or the K2 (see Figures 2.25 and 2.26). Although this amplifier is a bit expensive, either this one or one from Sunfire Technologies will definitely drive your subwoofer with incredible power. Most subwoofer amplifiers are extremely powerful—much more powerful than your regular speakers.

Step 5: Cable

If any of the references in this section do not make sense, be sure to review the research notes on cable earlier in this chapter to differentiate among the types of cable that you should purchase.

Figure 2.25

Crown Audio's K2 amplifier to power your subwoofer.

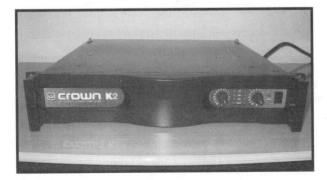

Figure 2.26

The front view of Crown Audio's K2 amplifier.

You should always connect your DVD player or VCR directly to your video source or television via the video connection. The audio connection goes to the processor section of your home theater. So, you will need, depending on the capabilities of your television, a component input cable (if your television is of the higher grade), an S-video cable (which most televisions now have), or one long composite (RCA-style) cable. Make sure that you purchase cables long enough to run from where you have positioned your DVD player (it probably sits on a rack somewhere in the same room).

Now let's move onto the next components of your home theater: the speakers. You will need speaker cables that run from your various speakers to the back of your receiver or amplifier. Some experts say that all these cables should be of equal length, so you will not hear any delay in signal. If you have such keen hearing that you can actually notice such a delay, you should simply buy equipment that can adjust for this discrepancy through delayed signals. Just make sure that you use nothing higher than 18-gauge speaker wire (commonly called lamp cord); you probably will not need anything thicker than 8-gauge speaker wire. You will need five lengths of this speaker wire. Make sure that all the ends of the wire have banana plugs on them. You can connect the bare wires on both ends to the speaker and power source, but for about $3 per wire, the banana plugs make it much easier to connect the cables and make the overall system much more presentable. If you have a subwoofer, you will need an additional run of speaker wire. Some subwoofers are "self-powered," which means that the amplifier is built into the subwoofer. If this is the case, you will need one composite RCA cord to link your processor stage with the subwoofer. Otherwise, if the amplifier or receiver is powering the subwoofer, you will need another strand of speaker wire to make that connection as well.

Now that you have what you need to connect your speakers to the amplifier or receiver, let's determine what you need for that component. Whether you purchased an amplifier/processor combination or a receiver by itself, you will need to connect your DVD player's and television's

audio outputs to this stage of your home theater. To connect the television, you need a pair of RCA composite cables. To connect your DVD player to the stage, you need a digital coaxial or a digital fiber-optic cable or another pair of RCA composite cables. That is why it is important to determine which set of components you are buying first, and then determine how you will cable them. Digital cables provide better sound than analog (RCA) cables. If you bought an amplifier/processor combination, you will need five RCA cables to send signals from the processor to the amplifier for the five channels (representing the five speakers).

Finally, did you buy a receiver or processor that is listed as DTS-ready or Dolby Digital–ready, and your DVD player has a processor on board? If so, you need one additional set of cables. This set will consist of six RCA-type cables that will go from your DVD player to your receiver. These cables are for front-right, front-left, center, subwoofer, right-surround, and left-surround channels.

Step 6: Extras

You now have your basic needs list, but what else do you want to add or should you add to your home theater? One good addition is a rack on which to place all your equipment. This rack could either hold your television or all your components. Refer to Figure 2.8 earlier in this chapter and Figure 2.27 show two of these types of racks, both made by Lovan Audio, a manufacturer of specialty racks.

Determine the number of components you need to stack, and then determine the number of shelves you need to purchase for the rack.

Besides adding your rack, now you need to determine what other sources of enjoyment you want to connect to your system. These include the sources that you considered in the research that you did last night, such as a TiVo player, a DSS dish and box, a universal remote control, a VCR, a CD player or jukebox, or perhaps even a tape or phonograph player.

Make a list of all these components, and then proceed to the next step, the fun part of determining where you will buy these items.

Figure 2.27

A rack, made by
Lovan Audio,
designed to stack
home theater
components.

Step 7: Media

Be sure to buy some DVDs (as in discs, not players) to play after everything is set up. Later you will definitely want to test your new system, and
without this media, you might find yourself a little frustrated. Refer to the
section "Top 10 DVDs to Try with Your System" in the Sunday Evening
chapter to determine what DVDs might be good to start out with.

You can review all these items at www.audioreview.com, which is a great
site to visit and read other visitors' comments about products in the home
theater industry.

NOTE   Go to www.audioreview.com to get the latest feedback from other consumers on the
products that you are interested in purchasing.

Hunting for Bargains

Now it is time to find the best price—unless, of course, you would like to go to your home audio/video store and simply purchase the system. If that is the case, skip this section, but we enjoy trying to find a good price for our components. Most stores, if they can, will charge you full price. The difference between full price and what you can find in some stores is quite substantial—at least the price of an extra component. The other benefit is that when you bargain hunt, you tend to learn more about the products, and may find that you want a cheaper or more expensive version of the component you are looking for.

Online Shopping

We highly recommend that you search the Internet for your new pieces of equipment, not just to research features, but most of all to find very good deals. We use the following Web sites to research and find good prices; you can use them as resources in your search:

www.etown.com

www.800.com

www.crutchfield.com

www.cameraworld.com

www.audioreview.com

www.onecall.com

www.mysimon.com

www.mercata.com

www.stereo411.com

www.dvdexpress.com

www.audioreview.com does not sell items, but you will find in many of the reviews a list of places where consumers found excellent deals.

The nice thing about etown.com, mercata.com, and mysimon.com is that they either give you the lowest price (which mercata.com seems to do on a regular basis) or show you the retailer with the cheapest price. www.etown.com lists the lowest retail prices, which is very useful.

www.mercata.com has sales called "powerbuys," during which the site essentially takes orders from consumers such as yourself, and as the number of consumers increases, the price of the product drops.

www.etown.com is a great resource for information on different systems, including reviews, and provides a fairly good low price search for the components that you seek.

If you would like to just find out information on the manufacturer of the components that you are interested in, go to www.stereo411.com to find a listing of all home theater manufacturers and ways to contact them, along with dealer listings.

www.crutchfield.com has a great resource library to explain all the little details about different components, along with term glossaries for the components that it sells. The site also provides easy-to-read comparison charts that you can use to make an educated decision about what is important to you, and determine which company offers all the features that you want.

Don't forget to log on to www.dvdexpress.com. That is where you will find great deals on all the new DVDs or VHS tapes that you will be purchasing for your home theater system. If you would like to rent DVDs first, try the Web site www.netflix.com.

Calling

If you do not have an Internet connection, you will need to resort to the old-fashioned telephone. That is quite alright; sometimes you can receive a great deal of information over the phone. Crutchfield and Onecall.com stores not only are extremely helpful, but are interested in participating in your home theater experience.

Catalogs

Catalogs are helpful too; however, there are fewer and fewer out there. If possible, check the Crutchfield catalog because it not only offers good products, but provides good definitions and explanations of all the features.

Manufacturers' Prices

Finally, make sure that you get the manufacturer's price on all these items before you buy. The worst thing you could possibly do is buy an item that is completely overpriced and then find out later that you paid more than the MSRP (manufacturer's suggested retail price). That should not happen at all. A good suggestion is to log on to the manufacturer's Web site, which usually lists all suggested retail prices for the product. As a rule of thumb, most products sell for below MSRP.

While you are on the site, be sure to see what warranties are offered with the products. High-quality products have lengthy warranties.

Online Auctions

Quite a few people sell through eBay on a regular basis. Quite a few people buy as well. Remember, there are two types of transactions that occur on eBay. First, you might buy a used product from someone who legitimately bought the product and then is reselling it after some use, or you could be buying from a person who actually sells new or refurbished products that you are interested in. Either way, you are most likely getting a good product. However, the most important question is whether the product's warranty is still valid. Some of these products are very expensive, and it is unwise to save a couple of hundred dollars by buying such a product with no warranty. It is also something we highly recommend that you do not do.

Remember that you should check online stores and retail stores before you get caught up in the hype of buying equipment on the auction block. Sometimes it is easy to get swept up in the excitement of auctioning, and you end up paying more than you normally would in a store or at another reseller.

If you choose this means to purchase your system, also remember that auctions take three to ten days to close, and then another two weeks for the transaction to finish. Auctions are not the most efficient way to purchase equipment, and thus aren't ideal if you want to build your home theater in a weekend.

Retail Stores

After you have done research on the Internet and the auction sites, you should have a good idea of how much these products you are looking for should cost. Amazingly, despite the Internet, you can still buy products in retail stores these days.

Go down to your local big brand audio/video superstore and see what it offers. Try to choose one that has good salespeople who are actually educated about their products, because after reading the first few chapters you will have quite a few questions about requirements.

Do not be afraid to barter. Some stores will match Internet ads, others will not. But even those stores that will not match Internet ads usually will negotiate price with you, especially if you purchase your entire home theater at the store. Remember, most salespeople get paid in commission. X percent of zero is zero, so these salespeople are motivated and encouraged to make the sale, even if they have to discount the merchandise.

One benefit of buying from a retail store is that if the merchandise does not work, you can walk in and take it back. Returning Internet purchases is much more difficult for the buyer.

If extended warranties (discussed in the next section) interest you, the retail stores are the place to go. Be sure to barter on these warranties because they are most certainly negotiable.

Extended Warranties

Retailers offer extended warranties that state that if your product fails to function or has problems after the manufacturer's warranty expires, the retailer will cover the cost of repair or give you a brand new model.

These warranties can be expensive. We usually do not buy them at all. If you are interested in them, however, make sure that the price of the component plus the price of the warranty do not add up to more than a higher-end component that you could buy instead. Higher-end components usually have fewer problems and offer much better warranties. In this business, you truly get what you pay for. Extended warranties are good for high-end components where you are protecting your investment. The low-end components will last long enough where you would rather take the money you spent on the warranty and use it toward a new component.

A retailer once gave me a free extended warranty for a CD player. When the player broke (after five years), the retailer replaced the laser in the CD player, which is still working to this day. This retailer lived up to the bargain of paying for the repair. In this case, the extended warranty proved to be quite valuable. Just consider whether the extended warranty is worth the added expense, and whether you plan to use the component long enough to make such a warranty worthwhile.

Making the Purchase

This is the easy part. However, we have a few tips for you. Buy the components using a credit card that has "lemon insurance." If you have this insurance and the purchased item is lost, stolen, damaged, or determined to be defective in the first 90 days, the credit card company will pay for replacing the item.

Credit card companies are strong advocates for you when you want to return something or make an exchange. If you write a check or pay cash, you give the merchant all the power, and if the merchant is not a reputable one, you might find yourself in a frustrating situation.

With that warning noted, you are ready to purchase the equipment. Make sure you have all the components, your video monitor, and your speakers on the list. Also be sure to have accessories, such as a universal remote, cables for every connection you plan on making (very important), and cable ties (to make the back of your system look neat and tidy). And don't forget to buy your binder and the plastic page inserts to store the warranties and manuals!

These pieces of equipment are fairly bulky, so be sure to take a car that can accommodate all your purchases. Some of the components (such as the amplifiers) are very heavy, so be sure you can carry the item out of your car after the store personnel puts it there, or make arrangements for someone to help you.

Conclusion

Go forth and purchase, and when you come back and have had lunch, we can move forward and start setting up your room, arranging your components and the television, so that tomorrow you will be ready to build the entire system.

SATURDAY AFTERNOON
Preparation

- ✿ Clear the room
- ✿ Placement of your video monitor
- ✿ Placement of your speaker system
- ✿ Room arrangement and furniture placement

We know you would love to jump in and open those boxes you just bought this morning, but before you do that, you must complete some preparation tasks. No one enjoys prep work, but it is probably the most important part of the home theater setup. If you take care of these initial steps correctly, the complete setup and finalizing of your home theater will progress on schedule and you will not need to revisit this chapter after you have assembled everything.

Keep in mind that you want to build a good home theater and have it ready by tomorrow evening. If you complete the steps in the correct order, tomorrow evening you will be enjoying the complete home theater experience.

Clear the Room

The first step is an easy one: Clear the room. Yes, we mean clear everything. All right, you may be able to leave the couch and whatever seats you have in the room if you can negotiate these obstacles, but leave nothing else. Home theaters involve a lot of cable (which you will deal with tomorrow morning when you connect everything) and much equipment that you must move around the room. After you clear the room, this equipment will be much easier to move, and you will be less likely to curse, because you will not trip over anything.

Also, anything besides the seats in the room will serve later to camouflage the home theater system. You ultimately want the home theater to blend in to the room. So, by putting the home theater components in first, you allow the other objects in the room to dominate it when you put them back in the room Sunday afternoon.

Now you are really ready to do some moving.

Placement of Your Video Monitor

◀ ◀
Video Monitor: The component in your home theater that produces the video. Three types of video monitors are available: direct view television, rear projection television, or front projector.
◀ ◀

As you begin setting up the components in your home theater, the biggest box is usually the best place to start. After all, your video source is generally the largest physical component in your system and also the one that will govern the location of many other items in your home theater.

General Home Theater Principles

The primary location for your video monitor is going to be centered in the home theater room with the back of the unit roughly 3 inches from the wall. The three inches will allow the cables that connect to the rear of the set to rest comfortably instead of being mashed up against the back wall and potentially damaging the video source's inputs.

The wall in which your video monitor is centered should also be free of major obstructions and structures such as doors and fireplaces because you will place most of the home theater elements in the front of the room around the video monitor.

The wall used for the video monitor should also be the shorter of the two walls in a rectangular room. This gives the maximum number of home

theater viewers a direct line of sight to the video monitor and the largest amount of light to reach the viewers from the picture. Likewise, center placement will produce the best brightness level for your viewers and result in an easy-to-watch picture that is the goal of a good home theater. Figures 3.1 and 3.2 show some sample rectangular room setups.

In addition, with a longer amount of room in front of the video monitor, you will have a wide variety of seating choices available without having to place any seating close to or right up against the back wall. Thus, you can preserve a sense of open space in the room without giving the audience a sense of being cramped against the back wall.

NOTE Even more important, seating against the back wall of the room will drastically affect your audio performance, which we will discuss when we place the speaker system.

In a square room, there is no shorter wall, so it is best to choose the least encumbered wall for placement of the video monitor and the rest of your audio/video gear.

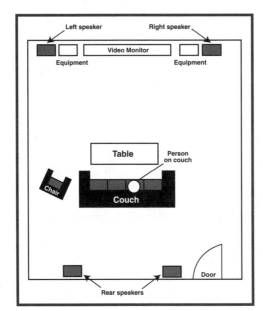

Figure 3.1

A sample rectangular room setup.

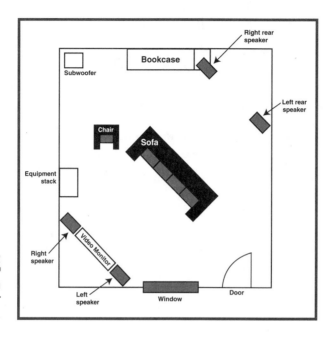

Figure 3.2

Another option for a rectangular room setup.

NOTE

Remember: Throughout our placement and setup tasks, think of your room as a kind of mini-movie theater. In a theater, the visual focus is the screen. This principle should govern your home theater and your screen's location.

From now on, we'll call the wall used for the video monitor the *front* location for both our video and audio setup.

Hey...My Room Doesn't Work Like That!

Perhaps the room that you have chosen for your home theater does not conform to the general principle of a centered video monitor against the

short wall in a rectangular room. Chances are that you will have one or more of these potential problems in your room already:

- A centrally located fireplace exactly where the video source would be properly located
- Built-in cabinetry that would be covered by a large direct-view television set or a rear projection television
- A window that the video monitor would block
- A door directly behind or too close to the video monitor

All these problems lead to the same two conclusions: Either pick another room for your home theater (argh!) or move the video source to another location.

If you don't have another wall suitable for a centered video source, you need to use a corner. Although this is definitely a less desirable choice than the rectangular setup, you can still enjoy a first-rate home theater presentation in this configuration. As you place the remainder of your equipment, we will address this rather unique setup option.

Light Levels

Although you may think of your home theater as an entertainment option primarily for the nighttime, when you're all done, you'll want to see and hear just about everything on the system. Trust us. Therefore, it is critical to keep the video monitor out of direct sunlight for the times when you will be watching. Light, especially sunlight, can affect the brightness of the video image that is produced and decrease the overall impact of the presentation.

Although this effect is not nearly as noticeable with a direct view television, which has a very bright picture, a large-screen rear projection television requires a lower degree of ambient light to get maximum image quality. Therefore, the introduction of strong sunlight will cause image washout.

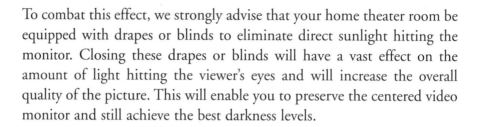

To combat this effect, we strongly advise that your home theater room be equipped with drapes or blinds to eliminate direct sunlight hitting the monitor. Closing these drapes or blinds will have a vast effect on the amount of light hitting the viewer's eyes and will increase the overall quality of the picture. This will enable you to preserve the centered video monitor and still achieve the best darkness levels.

NOTE It is also critical to have drapes in the room for acoustic principles, which we will discuss in the section "Placement of Your Speaker System."

If your room does not have drapes over the windows, you will need to compromise between center wall placement and putting your video monitor in a dark area of the room. The best way to evaluate these alternatives is to actually get your video monitor in the center location and check the brightness of the picture throughout the day. If you are getting washout at a particular time period during which you will probably use the home theater heavily, this might be enough of a consideration to reevaluate your setup. However, if the video image appears bright and vibrant throughout the day or during your peak daylight usage hours, you should leave the monitor centered on the shortest wall, as before.

Otherwise, if presetup evaluation of the monitor is not an option, take a quick visual test of the amount of light coming into a room just by sight. If at the point of your peak viewing habits the sunlight is directly on the place where your video source should be, it's back to the drawing board with the layout.

Also, it is important to avoid house lighting or spot/track lighting shining directly onto or above the video monitor. If strong enough, this overhead lighting can also cause image washout and produce a softer, less defined image.

How High Should My Screen Be?

To achieve a proper home theater effect, it is also important to have the screen at the right height for all your viewers. During a two-hour movie or a three-hour Super Bowl broadcast, you will not want to focus on a video monitor that is too high, which after prolonged periods will cause neck strain.

For a rear projection television, the proper screen height is not a critical element. The RPTV unit will have a base containing the internal projection components that places the bottom edge of the screen roughly 3 to 3 1/2 feet from the floor. This space should be roughly the height necessary for the screen to be at a comfortable eye level for a sitting viewer. Whether the RPTV sits out from the wall or is enclosed by cabinetry, it will be at an acceptable viewing height.

However, a direct view television usually does not have the base unit required by an RPTV and must rely on a secondary structure for the required 3 to 3 1/2 feet of height. There are generally two solutions to provide this necessary lift.

The first is any preexisting cabinetry or shelving built into the house designed specifically to accommodate a video monitor. Usually, such cabinetry includes a shelf at roughly the height needed and large enough to accommodate a 27-, 32-, or 36-inch television. However, the location of the cabinetry is fixed. So, if your home has a provision for a monitor in cabinets, but it is not in an optimal position, you must choose the alternative. …

The second option is to purchase a TV stand or entertainment center. These attractive pieces of furniture are ideal for solving this problem (see Friday Night's research period for more information). It will provide the adequate height and also serve as an attractive housing for the direct-view television plus other components and media. An attractive cabinet can make the difference between a home theater looking obtrusive and distracting in the room to having a polished system that integrates seamlessly

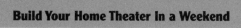
into the room. Plus, the acceptance factor with other members of the family will increase drastically if you can frame your technical marvel of a home theater in a refined, furniture-like package.

Now that you have a good idea of where your video monitor should sit, let's get that big box into its spot and start deciding where to put the speakers. After you finish this task, you can rest for a bit and then tackle components and a little background research later this evening.

Placement of Your Speaker System

After placing your video monitor in the home theater room, you now must unpack and set up your speaker system, which will provide the full acoustic benefits of your surround sound package.

For the initial speaker setup, you place all the speakers in your system at their general locations. After you have all your equipment totally connected on Sunday afternoon, you will get much more specific as to the angle and location of each individual speaker and even a few problems that must be dealt with.

For the purposes of this preliminary setup, we are going to prepare the system as if you have the following speakers: left, right, center, left surround, right surround, and subwoofer. This number and configuration of speakers corresponds to a full Dolby Digital or DTS sound system. However, it is also the basic system for Dolby Pro Logic and Stereo, which are the only other true processing modes you need to concern yourself with.

The key to proper front speaker placement is two diagrams that will serve as guidelines for the left and right speaker locations. These two speakers will be placed first, in accord with the diagrams, and then we will address the center channel. Next, we will place our rear speakers depending on which type of rear speakers you purchased. Finally, you will place the subwoofer, which is often the most difficult speaker to address.

Materials You'll Need

Of course, you will need to remove all your speakers from their boxes so that they are ready to be placed in the general spot that they need to be. In many cases, these speakers are very heavy (watch out for that subwoofer) or oblong (such as tower speakers); if so, find a friend who can help you with them. Plus, as we determined on Friday night and with your speaker purchase on Saturday morning, if you need speaker stands, they will also be required at this time. Finally, you will need a tape measure and a couple of pieces of masking tape to mark your locations.

Step 1: Measurements for Front Speakers

The front speakers include the center speaker and the left and right channel speakers. As mentioned before, two critical layout diagrams will help us place these speakers. You will work through each distance measurement on the following two figures to determine your speaker setup locations.

Figure 3.3 takes a piece of information you can obtain quickly—the video monitor's screen size—and extrapolates the exact distance that your seating should be away from the video monitor so that your eyes can comfortably watch that size screen with maximum visual impact.

• •

 The distance that you are about to calculate will also be used in the next task on planning your room layout and placing your seating. So don't throw away the piece of paper on which you do the calculation! Instead, put a piece of tape down on the carpet or flooring to mark the basic couch/seating position for later.

• •

Now it's time for a little geometry. (Ahhh!!! No, it's not that bad.) Start by measuring the width of the screen in inches with a tape measure.

S = screen width (of the viewable area).

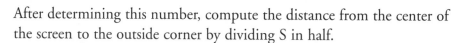

After determining this number, compute the distance from the center of the screen to the outside corner by dividing S in half.

C = ¹⁄₂ S, or the distance from the center of the screen to the outside edge of the viewable area.

We will need C for our first diagram.

Figure 3.3 shows us the 30 Degree Rule for screen size and seating distance. We will place our seating location so that your eyes do not have to strain outside of the 30 degree viewing angle to see. That way, you will be comfortable watching the presentation, but still get a large screen size for optimal viewing.

Our key variable here is D, or the distance from the center of the screen to the center of the seating location, our ultimate answer.

Therefore, to compute D, we are going to now use the formula that D (distance to screen) = C (¹⁄₂ the screen width) divided by the tangent of 15 degrees. The tangent of 15 degrees is 0.2679. Or more simply:

D = C/.2679

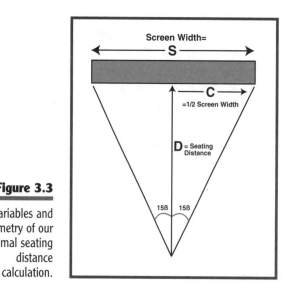

Figure 3.3

The variables and geometry of our optimal seating distance calculation.

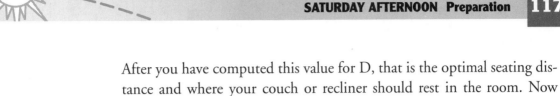

After you have computed this value for D, that is the optimal seating distance and where your couch or recliner should rest in the room. Now mark that area with a piece of tape.

NOTE The true distance here is to a person's eyes sitting comfortably in the seating. Therefore, your couch or chair will actually be about 6 inches *closer* to the video monitor.

Now take a look at the distance. Does a couch seated in this location make sense in the room? If you are watching a smaller monitor, does the distance feel too close and screw up the dynamics of the room? If so, it is acceptable to move the seating back somewhat to better match your room layout. This will decrease the impact of the screen, but you must decide whether you are interested in the best possible picture or a room that works aesthetically.

However, don't start moving the seating forward unless you really have to! Generally, this is the worst option and will hinder video resolution (you can start to see the pixels on the screen), cripple audio response as you'll see in a minute, and compress the room's overall look and feel. Only on very large screens of 60" diagonal and up do you have some play to move the seating slightly forward because you already have such a large image. If you have to, try it out first, and see whether you can tell the difference. If so, try not to move the seating up.

If you cannot place seating at D and have moved the seating from the optimal distance, you will need to measure your new seating distance, after adjustment. Use this distance for the computations shown in Figure 3.4, which indicates the location of the left and right speakers. This is your new value for D.

Now, using D, you determine the location of your left and right speakers and their distance apart. To compute the distance between the left and right speakers, you divide D by 1.25. This new distance is how far apart

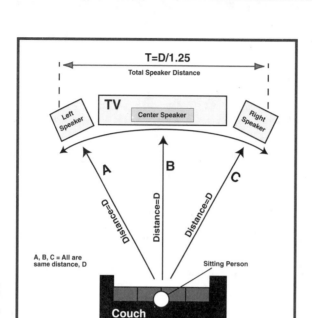

Figure 3.4

The prime locations for your left, center, and right speakers.

the *center* of the left and right speakers should be from each other. We'll call this new measurement T, for total distance.

> **T = D divided by 1.25, or the total distance between the left and right speakers based on screen size and distance to seating.**

This is the critical distance that you will need for placing the left and right speakers.

Step 2: Placing the Left Speaker

The left speaker is critical in two areas of the home theater experience. It will provide all the sound for movie soundtracks on the left side of the video screen to correspond with action on the left side of the movie. Also, the left speaker is responsible for the left channel in stereo music listening, also called two-channel audio.

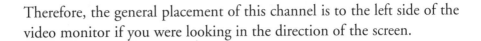

Therefore, the general placement of this channel is to the left side of the video monitor if you were looking in the direction of the screen.

Left Speaker Placement Step 1

Taking your earlier calculations of the variable C, you must start at the center point of the video monitor. If you already have a small piece of masking tape in that location, you're ahead of the game and can go to the next step. Otherwise, put one there now.

Left Speaker Placement Step 2

Let's divide T, or the total optimal distance between the left and right speakers, by 2. This new number is the distance from the center of the video monitor (your point marked with masking tape) to the center of the left speaker. Write this distance down because you will need it for first the left and then the right speakers.

Left Speaker Placement Step 3

With the tape measure, measure the half distance of T straight toward the left side of the room, away from the front piece of tape that shows the center of the video monitor, and mark it with another piece of tape.

Left Speaker Placement Step 4

Now that you have marked your speaker at the proper width away from the video monitor, you need to get the speaker to the proper depth. Start at the seating location's tape on the floor and measure D toward the left speaker width location that you just marked with a piece of tape. You will want to place the speaker at the intersection of the two lines you are creating, while trying to get as close as possible to the mark for width. After you have found the point of intersection, mark that as the location for the speaker (see Figure 3.5).

Then pick up your speaker (and stand) and place it in that spot. The middle of the piece of tape should correspond to the middle of the speaker.

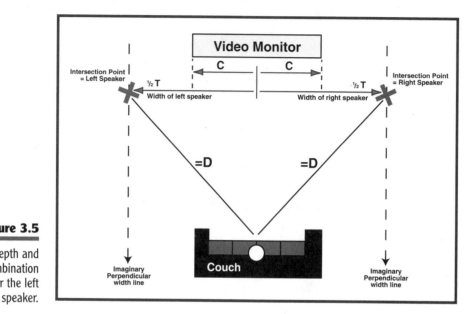

Figure 3.5

The depth and width combination view for the left speaker.

Left Speaker Placement Step 5

This step is not necessary if you have purchased tower speakers that have a base (such as a pedestal) or that come with stands that put the speaker drivers at ear height. Otherwise, however, you now need to unpack your stands or assemble them. (See the manual that came with the stands; there are too many different types of speaker stands to discuss here. Plus, these kits tend to be relatively self-explanatory.)

 NOTE Remember that if you have adjustable height stands or aren't sure whether the ones that you received are correct, the speaker's tweeter driver should sit directly at the same height as a seated person's ear when the speaker is on the stand.

Now place the stand down dead-center in the middle of the piece of masking tape that you used to mark the left speaker location. Then place the speaker on the top of the stand and center it on the stand to remain consistent with the piece of tape.

Now that the left speaker is placed, let's move over to the other side of the video monitor and handle the right speaker location.

Step 3: Placing the Right Speaker

Like the left speaker, the right speaker is vital for half of the sound for movie soundtracks. The right speaker carries all the sound on the right side of the video screen to correspond with action on the right side of the movie, and it is responsible for the right channel in stereo music listening.

The general placement of this channel is to the right side of the video monitor, at a distance from the video monitor equal to that of the left speaker.

You already have all the calculations you need from the left speaker, so let's dive right in.

Right Speaker Placement Step 1

Starting at the point on the video monitor that you marked as C with masking tape, take the tape measure and measure half the distance of T to the right of the video monitor (if you were looking at the screen). Then mark this down with another piece of tape as the width position for the center point of the right speaker.

Right Speaker Placement Step 2

Let's go to depth. Start at the seating location's tape on the floor and measure the exact distance of D in a direction toward the right speaker width location that you just marked. After you fully measure D and get as close as possible to the right speaker width location on the intersection of a perpendicular line for the width and a line for the distance (D), mark that as the new location for the speaker. Now pick up your speaker (and stand) and place it in that spot.

Right Speaker Placement Step 3

Finally, it is time to place your right speaker on its stand to get the speaker drivers up at ear height. You now need to unpack your stands or assemble them if necessary.

After you are done with the stands, place the stand or the entire speaker down in the middle of the piece of masking tape that you used to mark the width and depth of the right speaker location. Then, if needed, place the speaker on the top of the stand and center it on the stand to remain consistent with the piece of tape.

That's it. Your left and right speakers are placed. Let's move on to the most important channel for home theater operations: the center channel speaker.

Step 4: Placing the Center Speaker

Your center speaker is the most important speaker for a home theater system because approximately 85 percent of all sounds from a movie have some center speaker information. From dialog to gunshots, most action occurs on the center of the screen, and its corresponding speaker will therefore be put to the test.

Part of the key to a good center channel presentation is proper placement. This requires getting the center channel at the middle of the video monitor and as close as possible to ear height. Therefore, the best place for the center channel is on top of or below the video monitor. Remember that this will also correspond to the distance (D) that we found earlier for the left and right speakers.

On a rear projection television, this is a relatively easy affair. Often you just put the center speaker right on top of the cabinet of the rear projection television. The center channel speaker is almost always either built in an identical fashion as the left and right speakers but tilted sideways, or it is a version of the left and right speakers designed to sit horizontally.

Remember that center channel speakers are designed to sit sideways for two reasons. The first is to keep the vertical height down so that you don't have an extremely tall structure sitting on top of the RPTV or direct view monitor, making the structure 7 feet tall. The second is that with the customary twin midrange driver design with a center tweeter, you get the same dispersion pattern of the sound as you sit off-center, to the left and right sides of the video monitor (see Figure 3.6).

It is also critical to confirm that the center channel is a shielded speaker to prevent magnetic interference with the video monitor.

Center Channel Speaker Placement Step 1

You need to consider several factors before you actually put the center channel in its place.

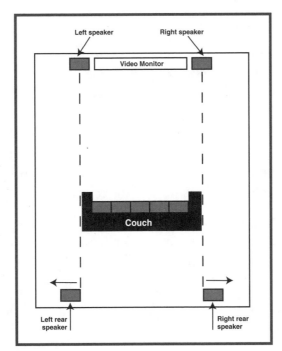

Figure 3.6

A center channel with the twin midrange driver and central tweeter, sitting in the proper horizontal configuration.

Entertainment Center/Cabinetry

If you have an entertainment center piece of furniture or prebuilt cabinetry, there will often be a shelf above the place where the rear projection television or the direct view television sits. This shelf is designed to hold artwork or even specifically the center channel. If such a shelf exists, it is a fabulous place for the center channel to sit horizontally.

However, if the shelf is too high above the screen, it will in fact detract from the presentation because the sound will be disjointed and unnatural to your ears. The optimal place for the shelf is directly above the video monitor, as close as you can get. If the shelf is adjustable, bring it down to rest almost directly above the top of the video monitor.

Get some rubber feet for the top of the monitor or to attach directly to the bottom of the speaker. These feet will minimize the vibrations from the speaker as the drivers move, and prevent scratches on the top of the video monitor or on the bottom of the center channel.

Entertainment Center/Cabinetry with a Shelf Under the Direct View Monitor

Another possible place for the center channel is on a shelf underneath a direct view television on a stand or on a shelf in an entertainment center. This is also a good place for the center speaker with rubber feet, as long as it is not too low. If you have more than one row of seats, your center channel's sound will hit the first row, but often the people in front will block the row behind from hearing the center channel.

A coffee table can also obstruct the direct audio line from the center speaker below to the ears of the audience. Such placement is totally unacceptable and should be avoided at all costs.

Take a look, and if the low placement of the center channel appears obstructed or too low, switch to the top of the entertainment center or to the next location.

No Furniture——Video Monitor Only

If you do not have a piece of furniture that is holding the video monitor and the A/V equipment, it is best to rest the center channel speaker directly on top of the video monitor (see Figure 3.7). This will provide a very close match to the sound coming directly from the center of the screen.

Also, as with the entertainment center shelf, remember to put rubber feet on the bottom of the center channel or on the top of the video monitor to minimize vibration as the drivers move in the speaker cabinet, and to prevent any scratching on both pieces.

Center Channel Speaker Placement Step 2

Now that the center channel is in the spot at the center of the video monitor, take a look at its angle. Undoubtedly, the center channel is not directly at ear height. Therefore, we strongly encourage you to prop up the center channel in the back (or the front in the case of a placement under the screen) so that there is a much more direct line from the drivers to the ears of the audience. This one small, minute-long operation can do wonders for the sound.

 NOTE Some center channel speakers come with a bracketing system that enables you to adjust the angle. If you are considering such a center channel placement, this is an excellent purchasing feature.

Figure 3.7

A center channel speaker resting on top of the video monitor.

It is not critical to prop up the center channel with any special material. Just make it something that you don't mind looking at and that achieves the proper angle you need. It is better if the material is somewhat dense, like wood, but make sure that it doesn't scratch the bottom of the speaker, the top of the shelf, or the video monitor. We have had great success with a piece of wood angle-cut with rubber feet on the top and bottom.

To determine the necessary angle, have a friend hold your tape measure in the center seat. Then take the tape to the center speaker. You should be able to see the general angle for the speaker to get the front placed correctly. Then prop accordingly.

The center channel is now in place and angled correctly, so let's move on to the rear speakers.

Step 5: Placing the Rear Speakers

As you now know, the ideal tasks for a rear speaker are twofold. The first is to provide a sort of diffuse soundfield that envelops the audience with sounds that appear to come from all around. A good example of this type of rear speaker presentation is the ambient sounds of a jungle as the main characters are charting their way through the Amazon. Birds chirp, the wind rustles the branches, and the bugs buzz. Also, the rear speakers are for producing specific noises, such as a gunshot behind the actors or the sound of a jet screaming from behind the action to the foreground.

In your research on Friday evening, you learned about the two major types of rear loudspeakers: dipoles and direct radiating. Therefore, the location of the rear speakers will depend almost exclusively on which type of speakers you have decided to buy. We will analyze the two rear speaker types and make suggestions for their location.

Identical Rear Speakers as the Front Channels

This type of speaker system is relatively obvious and makes perfect sense. It is also becoming a standard for upper-level speaker systems. After all, if you are seeking virtually the same acoustic characteristics as the front

speakers, why not buy two more of the same speakers for the left and right rear channels too? We are strong believers in this type of system.

If you have decided that you can afford this rear speaker choice and want the identical sonic characteristics, the optimal position is to have the speakers behind you, close to the same distance away from the listening position as the front speakers (remember variable D).

NOTE However, in most rooms, the rear speakers will be closer to the center seating position than the front speakers. To account for this, you will adjust the time that the rear speakers produce their sound through the receiver/processor (on Sunday evening).

Therefore, if the rear speakers are identical to the left and right front speakers, it is best to keep them at a distance slightly wider apart from each other than the left and right front speakers, and *behind* the seating position (see Figure 3.8). It is best not to place them directly in a corner but try to keep them at least a foot from both sidewalls on each side and about 3 inches from the back wall.

Remember that the least desirable setup for a home theater seating is with the back of the seating directly touching the back wall. If this is your

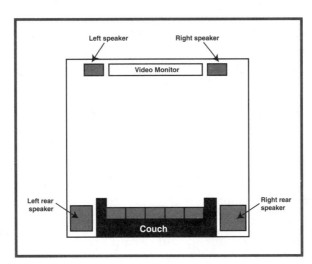

Figure 3.8

The matched rear speaker locations.

setup, you must place the identical rear speakers at the sides of the room at the very back corner.

Regardless of your room setup, it is important that you place the rear speakers roughly 1–2 feet above the listening position of an average size person sitting in the home theater seats. This placement provides a good surround soundfield that is both directional for very specific sounds and not so directional for more diffuse sounds that are supposed to be all around you.

However, this setup may be difficult for most home theater builders because getting speakers roughly 5 feet high requires large stands. Therefore, you'll need to locate and purchase stands that are tall enough, or you will have to mount the rear speakers on the wall. You can accomplish this with mounting brackets available at most electronics retailers or with shelves available at your local hardware retailer. Such a system will get the speakers up on the wall at the level you need.

Smaller Rear Speakers Than the Front Channels

This rear speaker configuration requires the same general placement as with identically sized front and rear speakers. They belong roughly 5–6 feet from the floor and 1 foot on each side from the front speakers.

The principle advantage of this type of speaker system is that the speakers tend to be smaller and more easily mounted or have stands that extend the required height. The principle deficiency is the sound characteristics, which are often of lower performance than the front speakers.

Identical or Small Speakers with No Rear Wall Space

As we discussed before, the optimal place for both types of direct-radiating speakers is behind the seating position. However, if you cannot place the speakers on the back wall, they must go on the side walls.

The best location for these speakers remains behind the seating position and at nearly a 5–6 foot height from the floor (see Figure 3.9). They should be tilted slightly inward toward the seating locations.

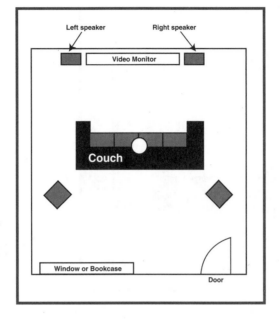

Figure 3.9

The proper location for rear speakers with no room against the back wall.

Specialty Speakers—The Dipole

As we discussed on Friday night during your research period, the dipole is another surround sound option that is used in many home theaters.

The idea behind a dipole speaker is that it creates sound around the listener by playing from both sides of the speaker mounted directly to the side of the listening position. Therefore, to place these rear speakers, you must have them roughly 6–7 feet high and exactly on a plane perpendicular to the seating location (see Figure 3.10).

Almost all dipole speakers have a mounting system to get them into the proper configuration for a home theater. Refer to the manufacturer for details. If no such bracketing system is available from the speaker manufacturer, you may also use thin shelving that is not larger than the profile of the dipole speaker, or use another commercially available mounting bracket.

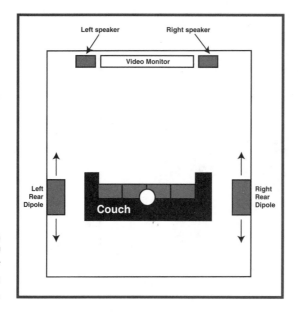

Figure 3.10

Proper locations for left and right dipole surround speakers.

The principle disadvantage of the dipole system is that when you have multiple rows of seating, you must pick one seating spot to make the perpendicular location of the dipole speaker (see Figure 3.11). However, if you choose the front row for the dipole to be even with the seating, the back row has the rear speakers firing in front of them. If you choose the back row for rear locations, the front row hears only the front portion of the dipole making sound. Then, all spatial sound is lost and you might as well use a direct–radiating (or forward-playing-only) speaker.

In addition, with today's Dolby Digital and DTS soundtracks, the sounds coming from the rear speakers are becoming more and more directed in a rear-firing or side-firing speaker array pointed toward the listening position. The dipole does not have this type of specificity of sound and can often delocalize sounds that should come very specifically from the left-rear area or right-rear area of the room.

Now that the rear speakers are in their spots, we move on to the most difficult speaker to place: the subwoofer.

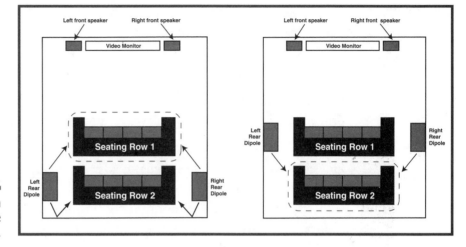

Figure 3.11

The two problem situations for dipole speakers.

Step 6: Placing the Subwoofers

The subwoofer is a special speaker designed for a specific task—to produce sounds that are low bass information, from 80 Hz down to less than 20 Hz. However, no other speaker in your system will be affected more by the room in which it is located. Sound waves of that frequency tend to behave differently from the rest of the frequency spectrum and tend to produce a phenomenon called bass hotspotting.

◄ ◄

Bass Hotspotting: An acoustic effect that occurs when at certain places in the room the bass is at very high volumes, but a step to the side yields almost no bass. This is due to the room's bass response and, more importantly, to the location of the subwoofer or subwoofers.

◄ ◄

Therefore, the location of the subwoofer or subwoofers must be very specific to achieve the proper bass response for the listening position. The result is a presentation for your audience that is uniform across the entire frequency spectrum, including low bass. Without such a pinpointed placement, you would have one family member complaining that the

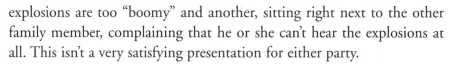

explosions are too "boomy" and another, sitting right next to the other family member, complaining that he or she can't hear the explosions at all. This isn't a very satisfying presentation for either party.

You will get a full idea of the placement of the subwoofers on Sunday evening when you actually test the system for the first time. As a general principle, it is best to actually play the subwoofer to determine its proper location.

However, you should follow some basic principles for the positioning of subwoofers, especially in a somewhat rectangular room. In other rooms, with strange shapes, dimensions, and even furniture, you can place the subwoofer in one of these locations, but it is unlikely that the following scenarios will be applicable.

Your ultimate goal is to achieve bass balance in the home theater room.

BUZZ WORD

◄ ◄

Bass Balance: An acoustic term that refers to the optimal bass response in a room; if you achieve bass balance, no matter where you stand in the home theater room, you get the same level of bass information at the same volume.

◄ ◄

Bass balance is generally achieved through multiple subwoofers placed in symmetrical locations in a room (see Figure 3.12). It is best to start with two subwoofers, one in the right-front corner of the home theater and the other in the left-front corner. This tends to even out the response as you move from left to right and creates a good front soundstage that includes bass information. Often, it is then a good idea to place subwoofers near the sides of the seating positions so that there is also bass balance through the depth of the room.

However, placing the four subwoofers symmetrically all around the room might not be enough to balance out the room's response and produce proper bass levels. You still need to make adjustments when you play the subwoofers for the first time to achieve uniformity.

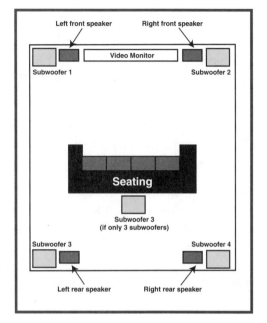

Figure 3.12

A general guideline for getting proper bass balance.

NOTE

Remember that the more subwoofers you have, the more bass response you can obtain and the less each woofer has to play to get the right levels, thus reducing distortion and tightening up your sounds.

Therefore, for the immediate speaker placement task, let's go through the most likely candidates for subwoofer placement according to the number of subwoofers in your system.

If you have one subwoofer, your best bet for placement is in one corner at the front of the room, by the left or right speaker. Corners tend to amplify the response of a subwoofer quite well, and only one subwoofer in a large room yields a limited bass response that will lose much of the impact that was the intention of the filmmakers or musicians. That is why it is critical to increase the number of subwoofers in a home theater system played in a large room. You will be able to provide a solid bass level for all your viewers and listeners.

If you have two subwoofers, the probable location for best performance is flanking the left and right speakers at the front of the room, slightly out from the corners. As mentioned before, this tends to create uniformity of bass response as you move from the left to right in seating.

If you have three subwoofers, the optimal location is with two subwoofers at the left and right corners by the main speakers and the third subwoofer behind the couch. This proximity tends to provide a better response to viewers who are sitting near the subwoofer.

Finally, if you have four subwoofers, it is best to place them near (but not wedged into) the corners of the room. This will theoretically produce an even response throughout the room with left/right and front/back balance.

Room Arrangement and Furniture Placement

Now it's time to start returning your furniture back to the room.

Some people are fortunate enough to have a room dedicated to home theater, but most people must share the home theater room with the functional living room. So, somewhere between the functions of the living room and the home theater room, you must find a compromise that gives you the best of both worlds. Also, to set up the ideal home theater, you need to consider the interests of others in your household. Although you might like to sit on what looks like the bridge of an attack submarine, with all your equipment in full view, light meters going off left and right while the movie plays, such a setup will not win you any points with the other people in the house who might not be as enthusiastic about home theater as you are.

Because you are trying to win these people over as fans of the home theater, and a good home theater is very understated in its physical presence in the room, you need to take steps not to conceal the home theater, but to make it blend in as a part of the room. That way, the audience will continually be amazed by a system that, while unobtrusive in the room, still astounds them with visual and audio experiences every time.

If you are fortunate enough to afford high-quality in-wall speakers (speakers that actually are built into the walls of the home) and are comfortable cutting holes in your walls to install them, you can achieve this effect rather easily. (Remember that in-wall loudspeakers are usually inferior to their freestanding cousins.)

NOTE The installation of in-wall speakers is beyond the scope of this book and is a procedure best performed by your local audio/video retailer who specializes in wiring and sheetrock work.

However, if your system will include actual boxes as speakers and television sets as video monitors, you must take some steps to ensure that your components are not distracting features in the room.

Arrange the Furniture

Now that the room is clear, and you are left with only the couch or seats in the room, it is time to arrange those so that the room has a normal seating arrangement, but does not interfere with people watching a movie or listening to a musical performance on compact disc.

As stated before, the rectangular room will aid most in creating a good "look and feel" to the room. In addition it is the best possible acoustic scenario available.

Now is the critical point to place the center of the couch on the piece of tape you marked earlier as the distance, D, that is optimal for viewing a screen of that particular size. If you make some adjustment by moving that distance a little further away, place the couch centered on that point. Remember that your front three speakers' placement is based on that very specific measurement.

Now let's work through some furniture placement scenarios that could create havoc for our perfectly distanced couch location that is centered on the video monitor (see Figure 3.13).

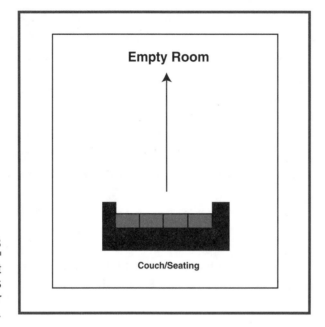

Figure 3.13

Ideal arrangement of a couch or seats in a rectangular room.

You will definitely want to avoid several other arrangements. Figure 3.14, for example, shows the couch at an angle in the corner of the room. This arrangement isolates the audience to one end of the room. The surround speakers can accommodate this arrangement, but the main front speakers will be arranged awkwardly and your measured distances will not correspond properly. Figure 3.15 is similar, but favors every speaker but the right surround speaker. In Figure 3.16, the arrangement of Figure 3.15 is adjusted to better accommodate the home theater.

The arrangement in Figure 3.17 creates a great talking area, but is not ideal for home theater. First, wherever you put the main speakers, the one set of chairs is blocking the transmission. Second, two people in the audience are facing the wrong way from the video source.

Remember that when your home theater is in a corner location, directing the couch toward the video monitor will leave it at an awkward angle and location in the room. However, this is the proper place for seating in a corner-oriented home theater and all your distance measurements will be attainable.

Figure 3.14

A seating arrangement that creates awkward speaker placement and poor acoustics.

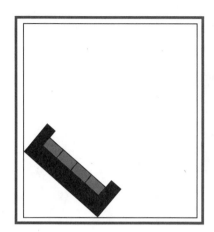

Figure 3.15

A similar but less awkward arrangement that favors every speaker except the right surround speaker.

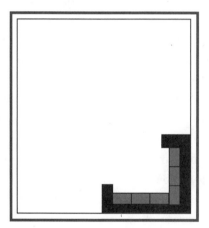

Figure 3.16

This arrangement shows how you can make Figure 3.15 a friendly setup to the home theater system.

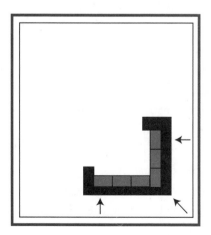

Figure 3.17

An arrangement that fails to seat viewers facing the video source.

The consistent theme here is that the entire audience should be facing the direction of the video source, and that there should be space on all sides for the speakers to bring all the sounds to the audience. The key to obtaining a high level of sound and video under this principle remains the distance calculations you performed earlier and keeping the seating close to those tolerances. Make sure that you have a comfortable couch that will be a joy to sit on for any presentation. Remember, if you truly love home theater, you will be spending many hours, days, and months on that couch, so do not skimp on that purchase. It is as important as each of the components of the home theater.

Conclusion

So you now have a good idea of the locations of the five monitor speakers and a *very* rough idea of the location of your subwoofers. Plus, you have the room looking like a room again, with your furniture in its proper place. Now, chances are that you are very tired from shopping, unpacking your purchases, and placing the first pieces of your home theater. Take a break. Next, it's back to the research as we discuss some important video concepts and then move on to constructing your rack and actually placing your components in the home theater room.

Component Preparation

- ✿ Video switching
- ✿ Video cables you will use
- ✿ Component placement—cables, racks, and components

Video Switching

Each source device in your home theater will send two types of signals to your video monitor and your A/V receiver or pre-amplifier/processor. The first type of signal is the audio signal, which we will discuss in the chapter on setting up your audio/video receiver or pre-amplifier/processor on Sunday morning.

The second type of signal is the video signal, which will provide the images that you see on your video monitor. Before you begin connecting the individual source devices, you must analyze the route that this video signal will take to output on the video monitor. Specifically, you will determine how during operation you select one video source or another to watch. This selection process is called *video switching*.

◄ ◄
Video Switching: Your home theater system's ability to switch between two video sources (such as a VCR and a DVD player) and the method that your system uses to do so.
◄ ◄

Two methods are available for video switching in a home theater: Your audio/video receiver or pre-amplifier/processor can switch the video from the source devices and then send it to your video monitor, or you can connect the source devices directly to the video monitor and have it do the video switching. Let's take a look at the benefits and problems of both systems.

Direct Connection to the Video Monitor

Direct connection to your video monitor offers the highest video performance and the simplest hookup method, but is also the least flexible connection to operate and probably will not accommodate all the source devices in your system.

When you connect a source device and an output device such as your video monitor, any additional components that the signal must pass through degrade the signal in some manner, usually in the form of noise and distortion, which will lead to poor picture quality. You also have at least one additional run of cable, which might also affect the signal, especially if you have poor quality cable.

Therefore, by connecting directly into each of the video monitor's inputs for each source device, you optimize your picture and ensure a solid connection. Also, you are only concerned about hooking up a single cable for the video of each source, which can save you from a serious headache if you have a fairly extensive system.

Problems with Direct Connections to a Video Monitor

The first problem, however, with the direct connection method is that chances are your video monitor does not have enough inputs to accommodate all the devices that you want to hook to it. Suppose that you have a DVD player, a DSS system, a VCR, and a video game system. That's four separate inputs required for the video monitor. And although many rear projection and direct view televisions have multiple inputs, they may not have the right number of the cable *types* you need. Because some types of video cables are better than others and particular source devices have only certain types of cables for outputs, your video monitor may not be able to handle all these wires.

Also, unless you have a relatively sophisticated remote control (we'll talk about this later in the chapter), to select one of the source devices in your system hooked directly to the video monitor, you must set the audio to the right source device on your A/V receiver or pre-amplifier and *then* select the video on the video monitor for the same source. This two-step process and inconvenience can often be the deciding factor to give up any performance benefits of the direct connect method.

Connection with the Receiver or Pre-Amp, and Then to the Video Monitor

The alternative to direct connection to the video source is to connect everything to the receiver or processor and then send a single video cable to your video monitor. This one cable will transmit all your video information to the video monitor. Whatever signal is active on your receiver or pre-amp/processor will also be the signal that is active on the video screen. This enables easy one-remote button touch of video and audio connections. All you need to do is press the source selection button on your receiver or processor remote for the VCR, DVD, and so on.

Disadvantages of the Receiver/Pre-Amp Connection Method

As we discussed before, the principal problem with this connection is the video noise and decreased resolution caused by going through a receiver/processor. Some receivers and processors are excellent video switching units that cause no visible loss of signal. However, the bulk of lower-priced receivers and processors (especially the receivers) will exhibit a noticeable decrease in sharpness, color, and overall image quality.

Alternatives to Consider Regarding Video Switching

You need to consider two more alternative factors in video switching that can also make the difference in the connection method you use.

Use an Advanced Learning Remote Control

We've talked about the vast benefits of learning remote controls on Saturday morning. The use of an advanced remote control can overcome the complexities of a direct-to-video monitor connection and make this combination an ideal one for your setup.

An advanced learning remote control is a remote capable of learning and producing multiple and sequential commands from the touch of one button. Suppose that you have hooked up your video from a DVD player via the direct connect method straight into a direct view television set. You also have the audio from the DVD player hooked up to the receiver or processor. With an advanced remote control, you can program one button to turn on your video monitor, turn on your A/V receiver or processor, select the audio input on the receiver/processor to play your DVD player, and select the DVD player's video on the video monitor. This flexibility of control can completely eliminate the complicated remote control actions that you would have to perform to switch video and audio. We will discuss this setup further on Sunday, when all your components are connected and you have all your remotes available.

Use Both Direct Connect and Receiver/Processor Switching

For some of your source devices, however, it is extremely critical to direct-connect to your video monitor. For others, it is less important for resolution (often because their resolution is not very good anyway—your VCR is an example).

Therefore, it is often an excellent idea to connect some source devices directly, especially if they will benefit from such a connection. One such device is your DVD player, which has the highest resolution of almost all your source devices and has a type of connection that will maximize the already amazing picture.

So, to video switch and access a particular device, such as the DVD player, without the extra button press of your video monitor's remote control, the integration of video switching into an advanced learning remote will be worth it. Also, this combination system will simplify your connections and assure you that your video monitor will have enough inputs for all your source devices. For most of your other sources, video switching through your receiver will be convenient and will not cause a tremendous loss of performance. We will discuss the best connections and when to direct-connect for each piece of source equipment in the individual sections on the source devices.

Video Cables You Will Use

You will use four types of video cables to connect the video to the device that you choose to perform the video switching. We will take a look at each one so that when you make your individual source component connections, you'll know which type of cable to grab out of that daunting pile of wire that you have in the theater room.

Composite Video Cables

You are probably already familiar with composite video cables, but you probably don't know them by that name. Chances are that you have opened your VCR or cable box and have seen the thin cable with two yellow ends called RCA connections (see Figure 4.1).

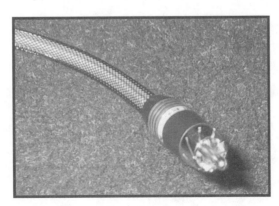

Figure 4.1

A composite video cable with an RCA connection.

The word *composite* refers to the signal that is being sent over the wire. To create a picture, two types of information must be passed by a cable. The first is luminance, which is the brightness of each of the individual points on the screen. The second is the color of that point, called chrominance. Using a grid of these small points, each at different light levels and different colors, you can compose an image and get video.

However, the problem with composite cables is that the separate luminance and chrominance information types that are passed along the cable exist in very close proximity to each other. Therefore, the two types of information tend to interact with each other to swap the chrominance for luminance and vice versa. This produces a series of stripes across certain places in an image that have tightly packed lines in the video presentation.

Almost all devices in your home theater will have a composite output, so for many pieces of source gear and your video monitor, the composite video cable is a must.

S-Video Cables

The next best wire for optimal video performance compared to composite video is S-video (see Figure 4.2). This particular cable is being used with increasing frequency in many home theater source devices. If your source device has an S-video connection and your video monitor does too, chances are that you will use it for connection.

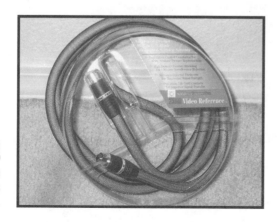

Figure 4.2

An S-video cable identified by its unique connection.

The critical element that sets the S-video cable above composite cable in performance is the separation of luminance and chrominance signals. The S-video signal path has one wire for luminance and one wire for chrominance. This is a much purer signal than composite cables offer and is generally a more desirable connection for a source device to the monitor or to the receiver/processor.

The first important problem with S-video is that not all devices use S-video signals and have S-video connections. Therefore, you must connect both an S-video connection to your monitor *and* regular composite video to get all your source device's video to the monitor.

Second, long runs of 12 feet or more of inexpensive S-video cable can often degrade the video picture enough that a run of composite video at the longer distance is still preferable. This is especially critical when the video monitor is a good distance away from the source devices and the receiver.

Finally, the benefits of carrying the luminance and chrominance information separately are eliminated when the original source material was recorded or coded through composite video cables. If the interaction between the two signals has already occurred through composite signals, using an S-video cable connection will have no perceivable benefits. We will discuss this problem when you connect your video from each of your source devices.

Component Video Cables

The newest video cable to arrive for the home consumer is also the best. This cable is called Component Video Cable and it is reserved for use on higher resolution source devices, such as DVD players and HDTV tuners.

The component cable carries video information on a much different level. Rather than transmitting the brightness and color information for each point, the component cable carries the amount of red, green, and blue necessary to define that point. The resulting picture is vastly superior to both S-video and composite video cables because it is in an even more pure state than the chrominance and luminance combination.

However, to achieve this excellent level of performance, there are three independent wires (confusingly, with RCA connections on them) that compose a component connection. Figure 4.3 shows a component cable and its three RCA connections.

The connections are colored red, green, and blue, and are often labeled Y (green), Cr (red), and Cb (blue) along the sides of the RCA ends of the cable. Each of these connections must be made in order to produce the picture.

As this type of advanced video becomes more prevalent in home theater (especially with the rise of digital source devices and signals, such as DVD and HDTV), we will see more and more video monitors, receivers, and processors with this type of connection. However, currently only a few sources and monitors have component inputs and outputs. Additionally, because three separate cables are necessary to transmit a signal, component video can be more expensive and more difficult to run than the traditional single cable system.

Coaxial Cable

You are already familiar with coaxial cable. After all, it's because of this wire that cable TV is called *cable*. This is a different type of wire than composite, S-video, and component cables because it carries both audio *and* video information in one cable (see Figure 4.4). Coaxial cable is also called Coaxial RF Cable and RG-6 cable.

Figure 4.3

A component cable with the three RCA connections.

Figure 4.4

Coaxial video cable.

The cable wire itself is the thin wire at the center of the connector that sticks out and locks into place when you screw on the connector to the source gear or the video monitor. The video is composite-based, with luminance and chrominance data passed along separately to compose the image.

Although this type of wire has been available in the same form for almost as long as television has been in existence, several devices still use it as their primary method for the delivery of audio and video. These devices are your cable company's signal wire and cable descrambler box, your DSS dish and receiver, and your VCR, all of which feed into almost every type of video monitor. You cannot purchase a direct view or rear projection television today without at least one coaxial input on the back.

Most people are accustomed to connecting their "cable" (which is really coaxial RF cable) that comes out of the wall into their VCR, and then using a second coaxial cable to get the audio and video to the video monitor.

Instead, most receivers and processors do not have connections for accepting a coaxial cable signal, because the devices that use coaxial generally provide the poorest picture and sound available in consumer home theater. With all that information packed onto one cable, there is an abundance of video noise and audio noise that degrades the cable's performance. Mostly you will be using cable just to provide your regular television signals from the cable company and from the satellite dish. Only in very rare circumstances will you use the coaxial cable to get signals into the television. Therefore, you are going to take the standard coaxial cable out of this loop of the central home theater circuitry as much as possible, to give you the greater performance benefits of regular television on your home theater system.

Now that you have a good idea as to the types of video cables available, let's start connecting that source gear.

Component Placement— Cables, Racks, and Components

To be completely set up for tomorrow's connection period, you need to determine where you will place your rack or entertainment center, the piece that will hold and store all your components, from your DVD player to your amplifiers.

Determining Proximity and Selecting Cable Lengths

Now that your room is completely empty of everything, except for a couch, your video monitor, and your speakers, it should be no problem for you to determine where you will place your rack.

We generally like to place the components up front where you can see them. However, others like to hide the components to the right and left sides of the room, or sometimes even in the rear of the room. These alternatives are fine, but you must consider a few things if you take such a route.

First, do you have enough power outlets for your home theater where you want to set up the components? Each circuit is designed to handle and draw roughly 20 amps. Some high-end amplifiers, such as the MPA-501, are designed to pull 30 amps out of the wall. If that is the case, you might need to have another circuit wired into that room, or just make sure that you are not pulling too much power; otherwise, you will trip the circuit breaker.

Now that you have a close proximity determined for your true power source, determine the maximum speaker cable lengths that you will need to run from that location to your speakers. Each length should be exactly the same if you want to be a perfectionist, but if not, just make sure that you have enough lengths of cables to handle the task.

If you decide that your rack and components will reside in a position other than in front of you, remember where you usually aim your remote control when you are watching a movie—right in front of you. If the components are to the left or right of you, that will be annoying. You will need to invest in an electronic eye and place it so that it sits in front by your video monitor, and then transmits over to wherever your components are (see Figure 4.5).

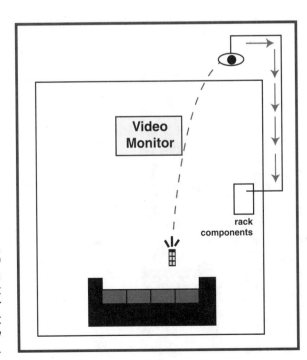

Figure 4.5

Diagram of an electronic eye set up to control your components that do not sit directly in front of you.

Electronic eye systems are quite affordable, so adding one is not a problem. However, it is something that you want to take into account now rather than later.

Also keep in mind that most amplifiers and receivers get rather warm, so make sure that the rack or enclosure does have some way to circulate cool regular air through it.

Setting Up Your Rack

Now that you have put a big black *X* where you want your components to lay, it is time to unpack the rack that will house them. You might have already done this if you are using an entertainment center, but if you are using racking systems, read on.

We use the Lovan Sovereign series racks. They are practical because they are modular, meaning you can add to or subtract from the rack as your needs change over time. You can choose from two different types of racks: the rack for the video-centric type, or the rack that holds only components. Figures 4.6 and 4.7 show examples of both.

Figure 4.6

Lovan component rack.

Figure 4.7

Lovan audio/video combination rack.

The video-centric rack (Figure 4.7) has a limitation in that it can hold only whatever it can store below the television. You might think that you can stack more and more under the TV, but remember that you don't want to be staring up at the TV as it nearly touches the ceiling! However, the video-centric rack keeps everything neat and tidy, especially for a compact home theater system that consists of only a DVD player, a receiver, and possibly a VCR. For such systems, the video-centric rack is perfect.

However, if you need all the components, the component rack (Figure 4.6) is the answer. Notice that it comes with dual-size modular racks that enable you to stack variable-size components up and down the rack.

One nice feature of both these racks is that their back and sides are accessible, even when the components are stacked. If you use an enclosed rack, make sure that you position it away from the wall initially so that you can get behind it and wire the setup correctly tomorrow. Nothing is more frustrating than trying to squeeze into an enclosed space and perform intricate tasks.

Unboxing Your Components

When we set up a home theater, we like to designate a room as the "staging area." Nothing leaves the staging area until it is ready to be fully connected to the system. And nothing stays in the home theater room unless it is fully connected. In other words, do not bring in all your boxes and try to connect all of them at once. All you will end up doing is completely disorganizing your instruction manuals, remotes, and supplied cables and finally tripping over boxes, all packing materials, and components.

So, after you find a place where you can stack all your components, you can begin unpacking them and getting them ready for tomorrow. Your goal here is to make sure that you have everything that is supposed to come with them before you start. I once bought a printer from a well-known computer company, and then drove 30 minutes back home only to find that the package did not include a printer cable or a power cord. You will try to avoid similar frustration now by doing a little preparation.

First, buy yourself a binder, along with some plastic liner inserts that can clip into the binder. As you unpack the components, you will add the instructions to the binder. This might seem quite detail-oriented (Freud might have another term for this). However, when the time comes when you really need to understand a feature of your home theater, all the documentation will be at your fingertips in the binder. So, as the box opens and you remove the documentation, put the instructions in the binder and that will be your home theater comprehensive manual. Trust us, you will thank us later if you run into any issues with your theater.

As you take out each component, put it aside. Connect any power cords. Open the plastic bags that come with each component, making sure all the necessary cables are there (if you are using good cable such as Monster Cable, this should not be an issue). Remove the remotes, and put batteries in them so that they are ready to go. But most of all, keep all the information in one central location per component.

The next step is optional, but we suggest "playing" with your rack configuration. With your rack assembled, put all your components up and down the rack and figure out what order looks the best. We recommend placing the amplifier as low as possible to lower the center of gravity of your rack.

Let's take a look at a few configurations. Figure 4.8 shows the amplifier sitting at the bottom of the rack. Sometimes these amps require more clearance, so a higher stacked rack space is necessary for this setup.

NOTE If you are using a receiver instead of an amplifier, place the heaviest component on the base of the rack.

If you add on to this, the receiver or processor usually should sit at the top of the rack (see Figure 4.9). This is the component that you will be dealing with the most, playing with it, connecting new components, and adding on to it as your home theater grows. It should be in a place that is easily accessible to you and your fingers.

Figure 4.8

The configuration of your components should start with the amplifier at the base of the rack.

Figure 4.9

Place the processor
on top so that you
have access to its
back panel.

Now it is just a matter of aesthetics. How would you like to see your components stacked? Or would you consider hiding them in an entertainment center or cabinet?

This stacking is important because you can now determine which cable lengths go with which component. You need the correct optical, coaxial, and component interconnects to make it from your component to the processor. Also, you need to be able to run the speaker wire from the position of the amplifier or the receiver to the speakers themselves.

Conclusion

It is time to call it a night. Yes, we know that you are very excited, but the next steps will require quite a bit of concentration. If you are not fully rested and ready to go, you can easily make some very frustrating mistakes, requiring hours if not days to debug and figure out.

Tomorrow morning you will get up early and connect the source components—the processor or receiver, the amps, and the speakers. This means that you will be crawling behind components, running cable along your room (or inside the walls), and generally doing a lot of detailed work. After that is complete, tomorrow afternoon you will connect all your components to the processor or the receiver. After that is done, you will be able to enjoy the benefit of your incredible new home theater. So, in summary, all your components and cables are laid out, everything is ready to go, so now we just need to connect everything. See you in the morning, and sleep well.

Bringing It All Together

- ✪ Connecting the processor to the amplifiers
- ✪ Running the speaker cable from speakers to equipment
- ✪ Connecting the subwoofer

O kay, we're going to dive right in and handle a critical two-part task. The first part of this task is to connect the processor and amplifier(s)—if you have purchased such a system instead of a receiver or integrated amplifier.

NOTE If you have a receiver, there are no connections of this nature necessary to make. A receiver already has the amplifiers connected, so there is no need to wire the signal from the processor to the amplifiers, because this is done internally. You can move right ahead to the next step.

After you complete any connections from the processor to the amplifier, you will then run the speaker wire necessary to connect all your speakers. Let's get to it, because running the wire in Step 2 will take a good amount of time.

Connecting the Processor to the Amplifiers

When a speaker plays, it is receiving a signal from the processor (or receiver) that contains the particular sounds that it is supposed to play, which are then amplified, or given power, from the amplifier. This amplified signal then runs to the speaker itself and actually pushes the drivers in and out to make the vibrations that re-create sounds.

In a receiver or integrated amplifier, this process is performed internally with the signal passing from the decoding chip (which takes a source device's signal and splits it into signals for each speaker to play) and then on to the five internal amplifiers in the receiver/integrated amplifier (see Figure 5.1).

However, when you split the processing section from the amplifier section, you must make a connection between these two units to continue the signal path. That is your next task.

NOTE The subwoofer connection in both a receiver/integrated amplifier and processor/amplifier combination is different from the connection for your other speakers. You will hook up this connection after you connect the other speakers.

Materials You Need: You will need five audio cables of suitable length to get from the pre-amplifier/processor to the amplifier (which you should have set up close to the processor/pre-amplifier). These cables must have RCA connecting terminals on the ends because this is the only system used for such connections.

Most RCA cables are sold in pairs, so you will need three pairs of cables. If the cables are sold attached to each other by pairs, you will need to pull them apart to make your connections. This means pulling gently until the central rubber between the cables tears, forming two cables that are no longer attached.

Figure 5.1

The different signal paths of processor/ pre-amplifier and amplifier combo, and an integrated receiver.

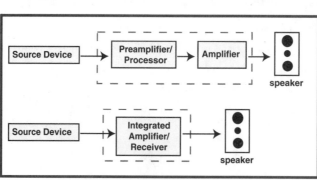

It is also very important that you have some method for labeling each of these cables at both ends. This will keep you from misconnecting all those wires. Several products will allow you to label the cables cleanly, including shrink-wrapped labels to surround the cables, small stick-on tags, and color-coded dots. However, all you really need are 10 address labels (such as you would use on a letter) and a marking pen. You can write on these labels and then wrap them around the cables.

NOTE As you perform this step in your setup, make sure that the amplifiers and the processor are turned off. Leaving your equipment on during any setup activities can cause serious damage to the components and speakers.

Connecting Channel Cables Step 1

The first step in this procedure is to label each one of the five cables. You will use whatever means you have chosen and label one cable at a time on both ends: Left, Right, Center, Left Surround, and Right Surround. (It is a good practice to use the key letters in a speaker's location—L, R, C, LS, and RS—for labeling. Most home theater users and professionals universally understand this designation.)

Connecting Channel Cables Step 2

Next, you will need to connect the first cable. Let's start with the left channel. Start by locating the area on the back of the processor called the "Speaker Outputs," "Channel Outputs," or "Analog Outputs." You will see a cluster of six RCA connections, labeled in the familiar channel designations of Left and Right (usually the RCA connections are on top of each other), Left Rear/Surround and Right Rear/Surround (also usually on top of each other), and Center and Subwoofer (usually on top of each other at the farthest right point of the connections). (See Figure 5.2.)

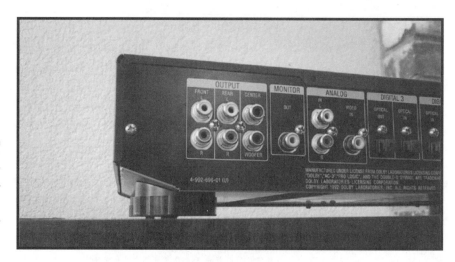

Figure 5.2

The back panel of a processor/ pre-amplifier with the six-channel RCA female outputs visible.

Because you are starting with the left channel, take one end of the wire labeled "LEFT" and insert the RCA male connection into the RCA female connection on the back of the receiver.

◄ ◄

Male and Female Connectors: Remember that the MALE connector or end will always have the protruding part and is generally only found on the end of the cable. The FEMALE connector will always be the receiver to the male cable's protruding section. Female connectors are always on the equipment. (Oh. This does sound vaguely unwholesome, but these are really the correct terms.)

◄ ◄

Connecting Channel Cables Step 3

You must now find the RCA input on the back of the amplifier that is designated as the left channel (see Figure 5.3). Some amplifiers will have only numbers to label their connections.

If your amplifier has only numbers for channel labels, you need to follow some basic guidelines for the matching of channels to amplifiers. Let's look at the potential amplifier combinations you might have.

Figure 5.3

The back panel of
a five-channel
amplifier.

1. **Five-Channel Amplifier:** If you have a five-channel amplifier, it is best to connect the channels in the following configuration, starting from left to right: 1 = Left Surround, 2 = Left, 3 = Center, 4 = Right, 5 = Right Surround. This configuration accomplishes two things. First, it places the speakers in a layout similar to the manner in which they are laid out in the room. Second, if you purchase an amplifier with level meters (the small bank of lights that light up and down as the amplifier plays at higher or lower volume), the meters will move symmetrically with the center channel in the middle and the other speakers around it. Let's face it—this just looks really cool.

2. **A Six-Channel Amplifier:** Many companies are now providing six-channel amplifiers to allow all five channels and a subwoofer to be connected to a single amplifier. If you have this amp in your home theater, choose a channel setup like a five-channel system, but with the subwoofer left over as a sixth channel. Therefore, your channels would be 1 = Left Surround, 2 = Left, 3 = Center, 4 = Right, 5 = Right Surround, and 6 = Subwoofer.

3. **A Three-Channel Amplifier and a Two-Channel Amplifier with the Three-Channel Amp Having More Watts per Channel Than the Two-Channel Amplifier:** It is best then to connect the left, center, and right speakers to the three-channel amplifier as channels 1 = Left, 2 = Center, and 3 = Right, especially because this amplifier is more powerful than the two-channel amp. Then you would connect the two rear speakers, which require less power (because they receive less overall information in movie soundtracks), to the two-channel amp as 1 = Left Surround and 2 = Right Surround.

4. **A Three-Channel Amplifier and a Two-Channel Amplifier with the Two-Channel Amp Having More Watts per Channel Than the Three-Channel Amplifier:** This configuration is a toss-up. It is more desirable to have the front three speakers play off the same amplifier because they will have the same general sonic characteristics from the amplifier's "sound." However, if you have a more powerful amplifier, it is best to put it to good use and not waste its power on the rear speakers, which do not receive a large portion of information in movie soundtracks. Therefore, it is advisable that you use the more powerful two-channel amplifier for the left and right speakers so that they can play louder and are better in two-channel stereo, when they are the only speakers playing. The configuration would be 1 = Left and 2 = Right, and the three-channel amplifier would run with 1 = Left Surround, 2 = Center, and 3 = Right Surround.

5. **Five Single-Channel Amplifiers (Monoblocks):** This configuration is pretty self-explanatory. Each individual amplifier is paired to a single speaker. Just make sure that all your cables correspond to the right channels. This configuration also tends to yield better sound because each amplifier only has to work on one speaker, and does not have to juggle the demands of multiple speakers all asking for power at the same time.

Now slide the male RCA connector over the female RCA connector for the numbered channel that you have picked as the left channel, making sure that the connection is snug and will not budge when you lightly tug on it.

Connecting Channel Cables Step 4

Now that you have the left channel cable in its proper place and hooked up, you can move on to the remaining four wires and complete the same steps for the left surround, the center, the right surround, and the right speaker. Remember to take extra precautions to get the correct output on the processor/pre-amplifier to the correct input on the amplifier. This will ensure that you do not have dialog coming out of the right-rear of your home theater when it belongs directly in front of you. Imagine Mel Gibson delivering his stirring monologue to rally the troops from center stage in the movie *Braveheart* and have him speaking from behind you!

After you have completed the four remaining connections, you will be all set if you have a processor/pre-amplifier and amplifier combo. Now let's get the same five speakers hooked up with their speaker wire.

Running the Speaker Cable from Speakers to Equipment

We'd like to welcome back those of you with receivers and integrated amplifiers. The group with a separate processor and amplifier(s) already has five more wires installed than you, but you're lucky because your receiver transfers this signal internally and you don't have to spend the time and money on these extra connections.

Regardless of what type of main components you have, the next step is for everyone with a home theater—connecting your speaker wire....

Materials You Need: The most critical element of this task is the speaker wire that you will use. It is best to have a roll of speaker wire at your disposal for this entire process, but if you have measured lengths, they will work as well—just as long as you have lengths that will run comfortably from the amplifier to the speaker, especially as far as the rear speakers.

You will also need the proper connectors from the speaker wire to the speaker and from the speaker wire to the back panel of the receiver/

processor. Such connectors can include banana plugs, spade lugs, or simply wire that you have stripped to leave a twisted end.

You will also need a pair of wire cutters and wire strippers, plus your tape measure. In addition, you must have another set of labels to mark each speaker wire at both ends.

NOTE Remember to turn off everything in your system (the components should all be unplugged at this point in the setup because we have not yet addressed power cords) so that you do not risk damage to your components and yourself from the electrical signals traveling through your equipment.

Connection of the Left Speaker

Now it is on to the speakers themselves—you will start with the front speakers, specifically the left-front speaker.

Step 1: Determining Wire Distance and Cutting

The first thing to do when connecting the left speaker is to measure how much wire you will need to reach the speaker from the amplifier or receiver. Before you begin measuring distances on the ground, remember that a wire run must also account for the drop from the speaker connector to the ground, and then run up the side of the equipment stack to the receiver/amplifier connection.

Plus, you will need to map out the exact route that your cable will take for aesthetics. You obviously do not want a whole series of cables running all around the room. You will want to run the wire close to walls so that you don't look like you are also preparing to launch the Space Shuttle at NASA. Instead, you want to create a wonderful sounding *and* looking home theater environment, and the wire route is a critical step in such a presentation.

Now that you can identify the wire's run location, get out the handy tape measure and make a rough set of measurements that take into account this entire run.

Now add on 4 feet. This is your overrun distance. Undoubtedly, you will want to make some adjustments to the speaker, angling or shifting it a couple of inches when you fine-tune the room so that you have some extra distance to provide a comfort zone.

Step 2: Cutting the Wire to Distance and Labeling

Now go ahead and cut your first cable from the roll with your wire cutters. If you have measured lengths, check to make sure that your earlier wire estimates were correct and that your wire length for the left speaker will make the distance comfortably.

Remember that 12-gauge wire is optimal for the front speakers. Only if the connections on the back of the amplifier do not allow such a large gauge wire to be inserted should you use 14-gauge, or in the absolute worst case scenario, 16-gauge.

Next, after you have the speaker cable run in front of you for the left speaker, it's time to label the cable. With your marker and sticker, or labeling kit, mark this cable at both ends roughly 6 inches from the end as "Left Speaker" or simply "Left."

Step 3: Stripping the Wire

The reason that you must label the cable roughly 6 inches down from the cut is that you will now have to strip the cable to attach the connecting end terminals (or just connect the stripped ends).

Your next step depends on which type of cable you decided to use. Some cable comes with an outer jacket that wraps around both of the wires (one wire is positive and the other is negative), which have their own individual jackets, whereas other cable just comes with two wires wrapped in their own individual jackets (see Figure 5.4).

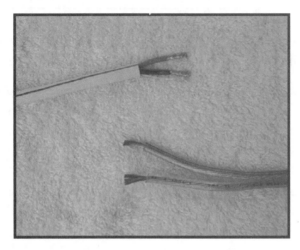

Figure 5.4

Both types of speaker wire—individually jacketed and dual jacketed.

If your wire has an external jacket, take your wire cutters and carefully cut the outside jacket for 2–3 inches down the length of the cable and peel away the two parts that you have created. Then trim those two parts with the wire cutters to reveal two exposed wires, one red and one black, of the gauge that you selected.

If your wire does not have a jacket, the wires are probably connected together with a thin strip made up of their individual jackets. You must now separate them by lightly tugging the two wires apart and ripping their mutual connection so that you have some distance between them to work and so that they will not get close to touching each other when connected. You can probably rip about 3 inches down the cable.

Jacketed or unjacketed, your wire should have two exposed wires in a *Y* formation. Now, with your wire strippers and in the proper gauge cutter (the gauge will be labeled on the side of the cutter—this is where the wire rests for stripping), clamp down lightly on one end of the wire roughly 1/2 inch down from the tip. Now give the strippers a slight angle down from the cable and pull on the strippers and on the wire in your other hand. This motion should remove the wire's jacket and expose the actual copper strands inside (see Figure 5.5).

Figure 5.5

The exposed copper strands of your wire.

If, while you strip your first wire, you accidentally cut some of the small copper strand inside the wire too, it is important to redo the wire strip. Having too many of these strands missing defeats the purpose of using thicker wire because you do not have as much copper for the signal transfer. Therefore, it is advisable that you redo the strip so that fewer or none of the strands are removed from the bulk of the wire's core.

 NOTE Don't worry if you have a hard time with wire stripping to start. With the number of wires that you have to strip (roughly 24–28), you will soon get a feel for the process and be able to do it quickly and without losing many strands.

Now you will need to repeat this process until all four individual wires (two at both ends) are stripped with little copper strand loss and roughly 1/2 inch of exposed copper remaining.

Step 4: Twisting the Copper Strands

Being careful not to rip out any of the copper strands, twist them around in your fingers until they form a tight spiral (see Figure 5.6).

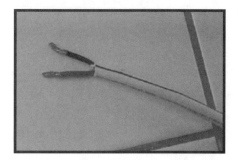

Figure 5.6

A pair of bare wires twisted and ready for connectors.

Almost every connection that you make will require that these wires be relatively thin and dense, so twisting the strands to a tight connection is a must.

Step 5: Attaching the Connectors

The next step varies widely from home theater builder to home theater builder. Depending on the connections that you require and the speaker/component wire inputs, you will need a particular type of connector. We'll examine the most popular and how to get them onto your wire.

NOTE   Examine your connections at both ends of the wire's destination. It is possible to mix and match the types of connectors that we will now discuss on either end of the wire, if necessary. This is in case a particular wire connector will work with your speaker and another type will work with your amplifier.

No Connector—Bare Wire

This is the simplest option for connection because it requires no work and no additional expense. The bare wire (after you twist the strands) is inserted into the speaker wire receptacle on the speaker, and on the connector on the back panel of the amplifier or receiver. There is no prep work to be done here, so move on to the actual connections.

Banana Connectors

This is probably the most popular connector type in the home theater industry. It allows for easy on/off connections and is relatively secure after it has been inserted into a banana terminal or binding post. You can choose from four types of connectors: twist-on single-wire banana connectors, crimped single-wire banana connectors, screw-in single-wire banana connectors, and screw-in dual-wire banana connectors.

Twist-on Single-Wire Connectors

These connectors first require a small rubber sheath that fits over the bare wire (see Figure 5.7). The sheath is color-coded red or black. Therefore, you need to find which wire has the stripe on it. This wire will be the red one (or positive wire) and requires the red sheath. The other wire receives the black sheath. The sheath then slides down past the bare wire and rests there momentarily. Next, you place the single connector onto the exposed copper strands and twist counterclockwise. The connector bunches the wires up inside and creates a fairly strong attachment. Then, take the sheath and slide it back up to cover the tail end of the banana connector and provide a color-coded identification of which wire is being used.

Repeat this for the black wire and then again if you need bananas at the other end of the speaker wire.

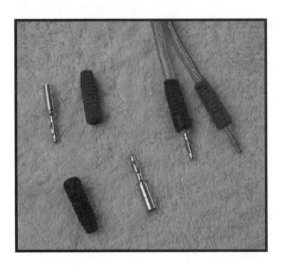

Figure 5.7

A pair of twist-on banana plug connectors.

Crimped Single-Wire Connectors

To attach these connectors, you need a crimping tool. You start by sliding the color-coded red or black sheaths over the bare wire ends. The red wire is the one with the stripe printed on the side. The other wire receives the black sheath. The sheath then slides down past the bare wire and rests there momentarily. Now place the banana connector on the end with the exposed wire, so that all the bare wire sits inside the connector. Then, with your crimping tool, place the back section of the connector in the tool and squeeze down. This dents the base of the connector and crushes the wire strands into the connector. Now slide the sheath up onto the base of the banana connector, and you're done. These connectors should look the same as the twist-on connections due to the sheath, which covers the crimped connector. Repeat this for the black wire, and the two wires on the other end of the speaker wire, if required.

Screw-in Single-Wire Banana Connectors

These connectors are much easier to attach to the copper strands (see Figure 5.8). First, identify the striped wire, which will get the connector with the red stripe around it. At the base of each connector is a twisting screw that will loosen the screw in the little hole at the middle of the connector. Unscrew this back section until you can see through the hole. Now insert the striped wire into the hole and hold it so that just a small amount of wire sticks out the other side. Then re-twist the screw unit at the base of the connector to tighten the screw into the hole and crunch the wire. Keep screwing until you can screw no more. Now the connector is set.

Repeat this for the black wire, and then move on to the other side of the cable.

Screw-in Dual-Wire Banana Connectors

These are two single-screw type connectors that have been joined by a plastic holding unit (see Figure 5.9). This holding unit separates the two banana screw units from each other, but is the exact distance to connect

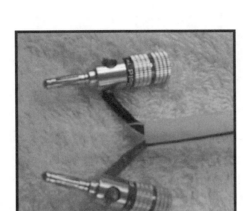

Figure 5.8

A pair of screw-in single-wire banana plug connectors.

to side-by-side banana terminals on your receiver or speakers. Repeat the same process as for screw-in single-wire connectors, making sure to attach the red to the striped cable and the black to the nonstriped cable.

Spade Lug Connectors

Usually reserved for higher-end systems, spade lugs are *U*-shaped connectors that fit around the central section of a binding post. They come in two varieties: crimped spade lug connectors and twist-on spade lug connectors.

Figure 5.9

A screw-in dual-wire banana plug connector.

Crimped Spade Lug Connectors

Start by sliding the rubber color-coded red or black sheaths over the bare wire ends. Make sure that the red rubber sheath goes over the wire with the stripe printed on the side. Use the black sheath on the unmarked black wire. Slide the sheath down past the bare wire and leave it there for now. Next, place the spade lug connector so that the hole covers the exposed wire. All the bare wire will be inside the connector. Then, with your crimping tool, put the back of the connector (with the wire still inside) in the tool and squeeze down. This compresses the connector's base and jams the wire strands into the connector. Now slide the sheath back up onto the base of the spade lug connector and you're done (see Figure 5.10).

Repeat this for the black wire, and then for the two wires on the other end of the speaker wire.

Twist-on Spade Lug Connectors

You will find these same *U*-shaped connectors in the less popular twist-on form. As with the twist-on banana connectors, you must identify the striped wire and place the red rubber sheath down past the bare wire end. The other wire receives the black sheath. Next, place the twist-on spade

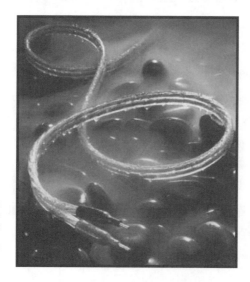

Figure 5.10

A pair of crimped spade lug connectors.

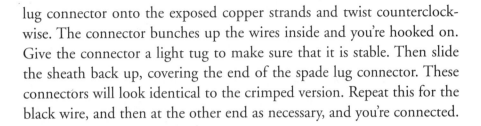

lug connector onto the exposed copper strands and twist counterclockwise. The connector bunches up the wires inside and you're hooked on. Give the connector a light tug to make sure that it is stable. Then slide the sheath back up, covering the end of the spade lug connector. These connectors will look identical to the crimped version. Repeat this for the black wire, and then at the other end as necessary, and you're connected.

Step 6: Attaching the Wire to the Left Speaker

The next step is much easier than attaching all those connectors. It's time to connect the speaker wire to the speakers.

Look first on the back of the left speaker. You will see either a set of spring clip connectors (see Figure 5.11) or, most likely, a pair of binding posts. The connection differs for either connector.

For spring clips, the only option that you have is bare wire connections of thin enough gauge to fit inside the small hole. To connect, press and hold the small tab at the bottom of the small square to open the hole in the center of the connector. After the hole is fully open, put the twisted strands of cable into the hole and release the tab. Give the wire a small tug to make sure that it is connected tightly.

Figure 5.11

A pair of spring clip connectors on the back of a speaker.

When your speaker has two binding posts (one red, the other black) in the back, you have a variety of options based on the connector method that you used to attach the left speaker wire a few minutes ago.

If you are using bare wire with no connectors, unscrew the top portion of the connector to open it. You must open the connector wide enough to allow you to wrap the bare wire around the central post in the middle (see Figure 5.12). Then, while holding the wire in place, rescrew the terminal back in to grab onto the wire. Give it a small tug to make sure that it is tight and will not come loose.

CAUTION

Be very careful that too much wire isn't sticking out of the connector toward the other binding post. If you allow this wire to touch both the red binding post and the black binding post at the same time, or the red and black wires touch while connected in their binding post when the speaker is playing, you will probably regret the large popping noise made by the speaker—which just might be the last noise the speaker will ever make. (You've shorted the speaker and blown the drivers.) This is a very dangerous situation, so be very careful when working with bare wire connections.

Figure 5.12

A pair of binding post connectors with bare wire attached.

If you have any of the variety of banana terminals available, you need only stick the banana plug into the hole on the top of the binding post connector. Make sure that red is connected to red, and black to black. The banana plug should plug into the post with a good tightness that results in a solid fit. As always, give the two wires a gentle tug to ensure a solid connection. Now put the other wire's banana cable in as well (see Figure 5.13).

Finally, if you are using spade lugs, unscrew the top part of each binding post (the one marked red and the one marked black) to reveal the post that sits in the middle of the connector. After you have it open wide enough, you can slide the spade lug flat around the center post until it goes into the post as far as possible. Then screw the binding post top section down so that it grabs onto the spade lug and holds it in place (see Figure 5.14). Tug gently on the wires to make sure that you have a tight fit. Repeat this process with the other wire connection.

CAUTION With large spade lugs, you could reach so far across the gap area between the binding posts that you could touch the other side's large spade lug. If this is the case, or the space between the binding posts is small, you should probably change your speaker wire connection type to avoid these two wires touching and frying the amplifier or speakers with a short.

Figure 5.13

A pair of binding post connectors with dual banana plugs attached.

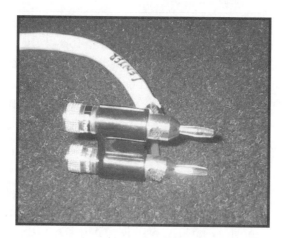

Figure 5.14

A pair of binding post connectors with spade lugs attached.

Step 7: Running the Wire to the Receiver/Amplifier

Now that you have a cable connection, it is important to run your wire to keep a relatively low profile. This usually means running it to the back wall, and then parallel to the back wall in the corner where the floor hits the wall. After you reach the stack of equipment, turn perpendicular to the wall and run toward the amplifier/receiver. That way, a minimum amount of the wire will be seen. Many speaker wires are available in wall-matched colors, or you can even paint them. If you purchased such a speaker wire, now is the time to paint it.

Step 8: Connecting the Wire to the Receiver/Amplifier

You should now be behind your receiver or amplifier with the left speaker wire in hand, ready to connect. As before, the connection type on your receiver will dictate the connection method (see Figure 5.15).

If the back panel of the receiver/amplifier has only spring clips, you will need bare speaker wire connections of thin enough gauge to fit inside the small hole. Press and hold the small tab at the bottom of the small square (it is black or red) to open the hole in the center of the connector. After the hole is fully open, put the twisted strands of cable into the hole and release the tab. Gently pull on the wire to confirm that it is connected tightly.

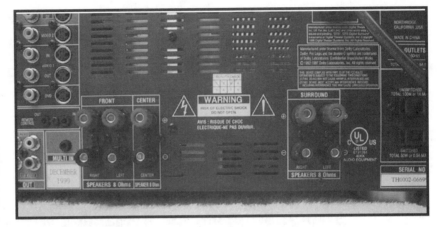

Figure 5.15

A good example of a binding post cluster on the back of a receiver.

With binding posts (one red and one black) in the back, you have a variety of options based on the connector method that you used to attach the left speaker wire a few minutes ago.

If you have bare wire without a connector for the red and black cable, unscrew the top portion of the connector on the amplifier to open it wide enough to enable you to wrap the bare wire around the central post. Then, screw the terminal back in to grab onto the wire that is held in place inside. A quick tug will confirm that the wire is tight and will not loosen.

◆ ◆

CAUTION   Remember, as before, to be very careful that you don't have too much wire sticking out of the connector toward the other binding post. Such excess wire might cause a short and severe damage to your equipment.

◆ ◆

With the various types of banana terminals, you must stick the banana plug into the receptacle at the top of the binding post on the receiver/amplifier. Red must be connected to red, and black connected to black. The banana plug should plug into the post with a solid grabbing fit. The customary light tug will ensure that there is a solid connection. Insert the other banana plug for the other wire as well.

If you have spade lugs, unscrew the binding post to slide the spade lug flat around the center post. Then screw down the binding post so that it holds the spade lug in place. Then make sure that you have a strong connection. Repeat these steps with the other wire connection.

◆ ◆

Remember that large spade lugs can touch in two binding posts next to each other if you do not pay close attention to the lugs' proximity.

◆ ◆

Step 9: Stripping the Remaining Wires and Connecting Them

Now that you have one speaker properly connected, you may continue with the remaining five speakers. However, before you repeat this process for the remaining speakers, let's go through a few brief notes on connecting each.

The Right Speaker

The connection of the right speaker will be very similar to that of the left speaker and should only require, at most, a different length of cable depending on where you place your equipment stack. Make sure not to confuse the red and black connections, though.

The Center Speaker

This speaker will probably have the shortest speaker wire run of any of the speakers you connect, because it is probably on top of the video monitor and in close proximity to the receiver/amplifier. This speaker should get the exact same speaker wire as the left and right channels so that everything about them is identical to get a seamless sound in the front of the room.

The Rear-Left and Rear-Right Speakers

The first issue for the left and right surround speakers is that you will need a much longer wire run than for any of the other speakers in your system. You will want to hug the wall with your cable to keep it somewhat hidden. Because of this, it is best to use the 12-gauge wire that you are using for the front three channels to retain the signal sent to the rear speakers over the long distance.

However, for many brands of receivers and integrated amplifiers, the connection on the back panel to the internal amplifiers is often spring clips. In addition, the spring clips will not accept a cable run that is 12-gauge or thicker. Instead, you need to use 14-gauge wire for the rear speakers. Although this is not optimal, it should affect rear speaker performance at an almost imperceptible level. (However, on exceptionally long runs, the cable tends to lose some of the information at the extremes of the frequency spectrum and makes the sound rather unexciting and less dynamic.)

The other issue is that in addition to the long run around the room to get to the back locations, you may also need to negotiate certain obstacles—doorways and thruways. You have basically two options. The first is to run the cable up and over the doorway with tacking nails to keep it in place. You can also lead the cable around the room in the opposite direction (which will be the longer way), past the other rear speaker and on its identical route to the equipment stack. This solution looks more elegant, but if you find that too much extra cable is necessary, this may be too expensive and may cause detail loss in the rear speakers.

A good solution to this dilemma is flat cable (see Figure 5.16). Using ordinary 12- or 14-gauge cable, the cable company will shape the copper strands inside into a very flat structure rather than a cylinder. This wire can very unobtrusively hug the walls with special minibrackets or, with a little more work, you can tuck it underneath the carpet.

Such a cable is perfect for the rear speakers, especially in the 12-gauge form, but thin enough to tuck underneath the carpet or between the seams in a doorway to the rear speakers.

Figure 5.16

Specialty flat cable for hiding your wire, especially to the rear channels.

That wraps it up for the speaker and amplifier connections. Wait! There is one speaker left. Your subwoofer!

NOTE

If you have front channel speakers with woofers built into them (this means that there is a driver in the left or right speaker enclosure that is 10 inches or more in diameter), you can skip this step. Usually such speakers already will have the necessary connection to the subwoofer through the left or right channel input on the back of the speaker terminal. If you see only one input, all the drivers run off the one speaker wire attached and the system is not designed to run with a subwoofer.

However, if you see an RCA connection or an additional set of terminals for speaker wire on the back, this speaker has a separate input for the woofers even though it is in the same enclosure as the left or right channel speaker. If this is the case, you will treat these connections as if they were subwoofers and you will continue to the section "Connecting the Subwoofer." The only difference is that your subwoofers are already placed because they *must* go where your left and right speakers would be located.

If you do not have a subwoofer, you can skip ahead and start connecting individual components.

Connecting the Subwoofer

The subwoofer is a very special speaker setup, as we discussed earlier. The biggest problem with a subwoofer or group of subwoofers is that its place-

ment in the room is an undefined variable at this stage. Only when you have gone through the entire setup procedure on Sunday night will you actually be able to test for subwoofer locations.

The connection method is from the receiver/processor's subwoofer output RCA jack on the back panel directly into the subwoofer's input RCA jack on its back panel. This is a direct signal connection to the subwoofer that will tell the subwoofer specifically what to play to generate low frequency effects.

The reason for this connection type is that as soundtracks from movies began to be coded into 5.1 multichannel audio, and the bass got its own channel, there no longer was a need for an internal crossover in the subwoofer. That was because the processor had already decoded the signal being sent to the subwoofer, so the signal coming out was already designed to be the only thing for the subwoofer to play. Therefore, you didn't have to worry about sounds higher than 80 Hz getting into the subwoofer, or sounds lower than 80 Hz getting into your left and right speakers.

Materials You Need: You will need one audio cable of suitable length to get from the receiver/processor to the subwoofer, which should be near a corner in the front of the room. This cable must have RCA connections on the ends because this is the only type of cable used for this connection.

NOTE As you perform this step in your setup, make sure that the amplifier(s), receiver/processor, and subwoofer are turned off. Leaving your equipment on during any setup activities can cause serious damage to the components and speakers.

Connecting Channel Cables Step 1

The first step in this procedure is to label each cable as "Subwoofer."

Connecting Channel Cables Step 2

Locate the area on the back of the subwoofer called the "Mono Input," or just "Sub Input." Usually there will be a left and right RCA input with one of them labeled "Mono." See Figure 5.17.

Go ahead and insert the RCA male connection into the RCA female connection on the back of the subwoofer with the "Mono Input" or "Sub Input" label.

Connecting Channel Cables Step 3

Finally, you must find the RCA input on the back of the amplifier that is designated as the subwoofer channel, and then slide the male RCA connector over the female RCA connector. Make sure that the connection is snug and will not budge when you lightly tug on it.

Figure 5.17

The back panel of a standard powered subwoofer.

NOTE

If you prefer a system with dual subwoofers (and we strongly encourage this to achieve better bass balance in your room), you will need to purchase a splitter cable (see Figure 5.18). This connector has a male RCA at one end and two female RCA connectors at the other.

This allows you to connect two RCA audio cables to the single subwoofer RCA jack on the back of your receiver/processor. Each cable will run to one of your subwoofers.

That completes the basic connection for the subwoofer with a 5.1 channel setup.

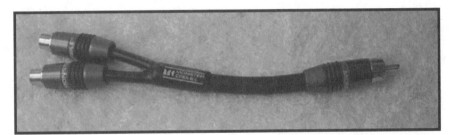

Figure 5.18

An RCA splitter cable.

Conclusion

Now that you have completed connecting the main components and the speakers, take a break and grab some lunch, and then we'll dive in to connecting all your source devices.

Connecting Your Source Devices

- ✿ Connecting your DVD player
- ✿ Connecting your home theater to broadcast television
- ✿ Connecting your CD player
- ✿ Connecting your CD recorder/minidisc player
- ✿ Connecting your tuner

Connecting Your DVD Player

You'll start with one of the most important components in your system: the DVD player. This source device provides the bulk of your home theater movie viewing and can also double as your single-disc CD player. This section examines the connections in two parts: first the video, and then the audio.

Video Connections

To connect your DVD player to deliver video, remember from the discussion on Saturday evening that there are two routing methods for the video signal when it comes to video switching: Either you switch video on the video monitor, or you have your receiver/processor do it for you.

 NOTE Remember that the proper universal remote control will eliminate many of your video switching issues. Such a remote will allow you to send two signals to your equipment: one to switch the sound on the receiver, and one to the video monitor to switch the video input.

You first must identify which connection types you have and then pick the best setup for the optimal video performance. Remember that a DVD player has the highest resolution of any of your source devices, so you are shooting for the best possible video connection for the best possible picture.

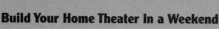

> **TIP**
>
> Because your DVD player has the highest resolution of any of your source devices, it's a good idea to use the best possible connection for the DVD player in order to achieve the best possible picture.

Let's take a look at each possible connection.

A DVD Player with Component Outputs and a Video Monitor with Component Inputs

This output/input combination provides the top video performance from a DVD player—so good that it can look like film in a movie theater. This is a direct connection between the DVD player and the video monitor, yielding no interrupts in the signal and preserving the quality of the DVD's video output.

However, when you turn on your DVD player for movie watching, this connection forces you to switch your receiver/processor to the DVD player input by pressing the DVD Input button, and then pressing the Input or TV/Video button on your video monitor. This locks the video monitor into the proper mode to receive the DVD's video signals. You'll perform this procedure at the end of your setup, on Sunday evening when you spin your first couple of movies.

How Do I Know I've Got It? You have this combination if your DVD player has component output listed as one of its features, or if the back panel has three RCA inputs color-coded green, red, and blue, and labeled Y, Cr, and Cb (see Figure 6.1).

You must also have the same set of corresponding inputs on the back of your video monitor.

Materials You Need: You need one component video cable long enough to reach comfortably from the DVD player to the video monitor.

1. Take one male end of your component video cable with the three color-coded RCA connectors, and attach each one to the connectors of corresponding colors on the DVD player. After you have each

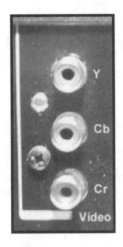

Figure 6.1

The back panel of a
DVD player with
component inputs.

connection in place, you will see that the Y, Cr, and Cb labels
around the connectors match the inputs on the back of the DVD
player marked Y, Cr, and Cb.

2. Take the other male end of the component cable with the matching
three RCA ends and go to the back of the video monitor. You
should have a wire length that is not taut, but that rests easily
between the video monitor and the DVD player. Repeat the same
type of connection that you made between the component cable
and the DVD player, with the corresponding color cables each connected to the like-colored RCA inputs on the back of the video
monitor. If you do this correctly, the connectors labeled Y, Cr, and
Cb will be attached to their identically labeled connections on the
video monitor. That's it. Your video is connected!

A DVD Player with Component Outputs, a Receiver/Processor with Component Outputs and Inputs, and a Video Monitor with Component Inputs

This setup combination is difficult to find on current home theater systems,
because most receivers and processors cannot yet perform video switching
on component video. This capability currently is available only with the
most expensive of components, especially pre-amplifiers and processors.

You should use this connection setup *only* if you have two separate devices in your system with component output going into one component input on your video monitor. That way, because you have only one input, you don't have to crawl behind your video monitor to switch the two cables back and forth.

Suppose that you have a DVD player with a component output, an HDTV decoder with a component output, and a new rear projection television with only one component input. You could only plug in either the DVD player or the HDTV decoder, but never both at the same time. But, if you can plug both the HDTV decoder and the DVD player into your processor and let it send out a single component video wire to the RPTV, you can accommodate both source devices. When you wanted to watch HDTV, you would select the HDTV input on your processor and it would route the HDTV video signal to the one component cable to the RPTV.

Having the processor handle the video switching makes the system easy to operate. However, suppose that you are watching a source device through any other type of video cable, such as a VCR, that uses a composite video cable. You would still need to change the rear projection television's input to component video to accept the new type of signal in the video monitor even though a processor is sending the signal.

How Do I Know I've Got It? You have this combination if your DVD player has component output as one of its features, or the back panel has three RCA inputs, color-coded red, green, and blue, and labeled Y, Cr, and Cb. Your receiver/processor will have two sets of three RCA connection component inputs and one set of three RCA connection component output (see Figure 6.2).

Finally, your video monitor's back panel will have one set of three RCA connections for component video input color-coded and labeled Y, Cr, and Cb.

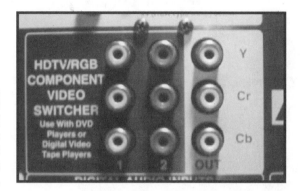

Figure 6.2

The back panel of a processor with two component inputs and one component output.

Materials You Need: You need two component video cables long enough to reach comfortably from the DVD player to the receiver/processor, and to get from the receiver/processor to the inputs on the video monitor.

1. Take your component video cable with one set of the three color-coded RCA male connectors, and attach each one to the female connectors with corresponding colors on the DVD player. After you have each connection in place, you will see that the Y, Cr, and Cb cables connect to the RCA inputs with the same letters (Y, Cr, and Cb) printed on the back of the DVD player.

2. Take the other end of the component cable with the matching three male ends and go to the back of the receiver/processor. You should have a wire length that is not taut, but that rests easily between the receiver/processor and the DVD player. Repeat the same type of connection that you made between the component cable and the DVD player, with the corresponding color cables—each connected to the RCA inputs with corresponding colors on the back of the receiver/processor—into the input labeled Component Video 1 or DVD Component Video.

3. Connect the second component video cable to the component video output on the receiver/processor using the same connection method as before, matching green, red, and blue, plus Y, Cr, and Cb (see Figure 6.3).

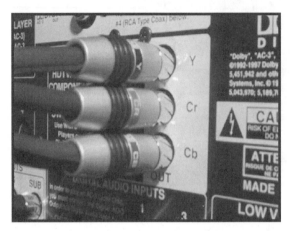

Figure 6.3

The back panel of the pre-amplifier/ processor with component video output connected.

4. Finish the hookup of the second component video connection (the output) by attaching the three color-coded RCA cables to the back panel of the video monitor so that red matches red, green matches green, and blue matches blue. The labels for the cable— Y, Cr, and Cb—should all match on the cable and on the back panel of the video monitor.

Your DVD player's video is now connected with the receiver or processor doing the video switching.

A DVD Player with S-Video Output and a Video Monitor with S-Video Input

After component video connections, S-video is the next best possible connection for video performance. Once again, because your DVD player is capable of the highest resolution of your audio/video source devices, the optimal connection is to hook an S-video cable directly between the DVD player and the video monitor.

This configuration also requires you to do your video switching through the video monitor. However, having to press an extra button on your video monitor remote or universal remote will be outweighed by the performance benefits.

How Do I Know I've Got It? An S-video connection is the small recessed hookup on the back panel of your source devices and your video monitor (see Figure 6.4). The wire part of the connection has four small pins and a rectangular guide. The input side of the connection has four small pin-holes and a rectangular hole for the plastic guide.

All DVD players currently on the market have an S-video output, so you should see this on the back panel. Plus, your video monitor most likely has at least one S-video input. (See Figure 6.5.)

However, if you have an older video monitor (a television set or rear projection television), make sure to check the back panel inputs for an S-video input, usually labeled Video-1 or S-Video.

Figure 6.4

The back panel of a DVD player with an S-video output.

Figure 6.5

The back panel of a video monitor with an S-video input.

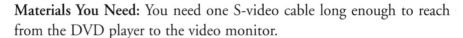

Materials You Need: You need one S-video cable long enough to reach from the DVD player to the video monitor.

1. Take your S-video cable and, being careful to align the pins properly with their holes, insert the S-video connector into the jack labeled S-Video on the DVD player.

2. Take the other male end of the S-video cable and head to the back of the video monitor. The wire length should be loose, not so tight that unnecessary pressure is placed on the wire or the connections. Place the wire's S-video connector in the back connection labeled S-Video on your video monitor. When the cable snugly fits into place, your connection is made.

A DVD Player with S-Video Output, a Receiver/ Processor with S-Video Outputs and Inputs, and a Video Monitor with S-Video Input

Again, you must pay close attention to your video switching for the DVD player. This particular setup will allow video switching through the receiver/processor so that you need only press a single button to jump from a DVD to a DSS.

Remember, however, that some receivers and processors do video switching without much loss of the S-video signal, whereas others introduce picture errors and noise that will decrease the DVD's picture performance. You should always connect via direct monitor connection and via the receiver/processor hookup that you are working on here, unless you have multiple S-video devices that need to go into a single S-video input on your video monitor.

Most receivers and processors on the market today include video switching on S-video sources, so it's a good bet that your receiver or processor has several S-video inputs on the back panel corresponding to some or all of the source devices. (Often, there are both S-video *and* composite video connections for each source device.)

NOTE

Remember that even though you may be able to switch between S-video sources using your receiver or processor without touching your video monitor's inputs, you may still need to switch the video monitor's input manually with the remote when you are jumping from an S-video source to a composite video source. You will have to trigger a whole new input on the video monitor that is accepting your composite video sources. The video monitor must therefore have an available input dedicated to each video cable type, such as Video 1 = Component input, Video 2 = S-video input, Video 3 = Composite input.

The only way to do video switching entirely through your receiver or processor is with outputs that are *all* S-video, *all* composite video, or *all* component video.

This connection is required when you have several other S-video source devices but only one S-video input on your video monitor. By connecting all the S-video sources to the receiver or processor, and then connecting a single S-video cable to the receiver that outputs to the video monitor whatever signal you choose on the receiver, you can attach all your S-video source devices.

How Do I Know I've Got It? Your DVD player has S-video output listed as one of its features; if you look on the back panel, you will see the input. Your receiver/processor probably also has a set of inputs labeled either Video 1, 2, 3, and so on, with S-video jacks, or has an input specifically labeled DVD Player that includes an S-video connection.

The receiver/processor must also have an S-video output in the form of a monitor output jack. This one connection is the output connection to the video monitor that enables the receiver to send the selected video source to the video monitor. Check to see that you have at least one such connection on the back panel (see Figure 6.6). If your receiver/processor has S-video inputs, though, you have at least one S-video output.

Figure 6.6

The back panel
of a processor
with multiple
S-video inputs and
S-video outputs.

Finally, your video monitor will have at least one S-video input connection on its back panel, as either Video 1, or a specially labeled input S-Video.

Materials You Need: You need two S-video cables long enough to reach comfortably from the DVD player to the receiver/processor, and to get from the receiver/processor to the inputs on the video monitor. However, it is important to minimize these cable lengths because long S-video runs of cable (more than 12 feet) tend to decrease the performance of the signal unless you purchase a premium S-video cable designed for long runs.

1. Attach one male end of your S-video cable to the DVD player's S-video female input. Make sure that you insert the cable correctly. You can easily damage the S-video connector pins by trying to force in the connection upside down.

2. Take the other male end of the S-video cable and get to the back of the receiver/processor. You should have a wire length that is not taut, but that rests easily between the receiver/processor and the DVD player. Carefully insert the S-video cable into the receiver/processor's S-video input labeled Video 1 or DVD Player. (You should give the DVD player the Video 1 designation because it will be the most heavily used source device in your system—trust us.)

3. Connect the other S-video cable's male end to the S-video output connection on the receiver/processor. This connection is often labeled S-Video Output or Monitor on the receiver/processor.

4. Hook up the remaining S-video connection to the video monitor's back panel. This connection is often labeled Video-1 or S-Video Input. You should always make this connection with the first S-video input if the panel has more than one.

Your DVD's S-video output is now connected with the video switching handled by the receiver/processor.

A DVD Player with Composite Output and a Video Monitor with Composite Input

This connection is really a mixed blessing. Yes, it does get you into the amazing digital video of DVD, but the performance from composite outputs is not nearly as crisp and clear as that of a component or S-video connection. However, many older video monitors have no component input connections or S-video inputs. If you have such a monitor, you have to settle for the composite video. Think of it as the lowest common denominator—every video monitor offers composite video.

To minimize signal loss and achieve the highest picture quality possible, the best composite connection is direct from the DVD player to one composite video input on the video monitor. Once again, this configuration also requires you to do your video switching using the video monitor's remote control, but having to press the extra button is outweighed by better performance.

How Do I Know I've Got It? The back panel of your DVD player is certain to include a composite connection. This connection is a single RCA output jack with a yellow center, usually near the S-video jack (see Figure 6.7). Sometimes a DVD player will have two composite connections labeled #1 and #2.

Your video monitor will also have at least one composite video input (and often many more) labeled Video 1, 2, 3, and so on (see Figure 6.8).

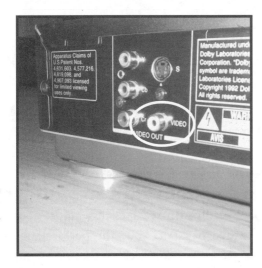

Figure 6.7

The back panel
of a DVD player
with a composite
output jack.

Figure 6.8

The back panel
of a video monitor
with several
composite inputs.

Materials You Need: You need one composite video cable long enough to reach from the DVD player to the video monitor.

1. Take your composite cable and insert the male RCA connector into the female RCA jack colored yellow and labeled Video on the DVD player.

2. Take the other male end of the composite video cable and head to the back of the video monitor. The wire length should be loose,

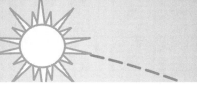

not tight, so that no unnecessary pressure is placed on the wire or the connection. Attach the composite video cable's RCA connector to the video monitor's input jack labeled Video-1. When the cable fits snugly into place, your connection is made.

A DVD Player with Composite Output, a Receiver/ Processor with Composite Outputs and Inputs, and a Video Monitor with Composite Input

This is the last resort setup for your DVD player; this connection method yields poor performance compared to the others already discussed. If you have a component input on the video monitor, use it. If you have an S-video input on the video monitor, use it. But if your video monitor has *only* composite video, only then should you continue with this connection. If so, you are unfortunately using an interrupted signal path and the lowest performance video cable available.

However, even if this is the only method available to hook up your video monitor, that doesn't mean that you shouldn't buy a home theater or a DVD player—quite to the contrary. This setup method is the least desirable of an already huge step up in quality from what most consumers have ever seen. Plus, the price, performance, features, and convenience of DVDs make purchasing a DVD player a no-brainer.

The principal benefit of this system is that you can do almost all your video switching through the receiver/processor. For convenience, this cannot be beaten. Also, this system is required if you have only a single composite video input on your video monitor. By connecting all your source devices into the receiver/pre-amplifier and then hooking up only the one wire to send video to the video monitor, you can have multiple inputs where there was only one.

Every receiver and processor on the market today includes video switching for composite video sources, so you can check the back panel of your unit to find the yellow RCA input jacks for video input.

How Do I Know I've Got It? Your DVD player will have one or two composite video output jacks on the back panel. Your receiver/processor will probably also have a set or row of yellow composite inputs labeled either Video 1, 2, 3, and so on, or have an input specifically labeled DVD Player that has a composite connection.

The receiver/processor will also have a composite output connection in the form of a monitor output jack (see Figure 6.9). This hooks up to the video monitor so that the receiver sends the picture from the video source that you want to watch.

Finally, your video monitor should have at least one composite input connection on its back panel—another yellow RCA jack labeled Video 1. Often the panel will have more than one composite connection. However, because your receiver/processor is doing the video switching, you need only one connection, so use the prime Video 1 position.

Materials You Need: You need two composite cables long enough to reach comfortably from the DVD player to the receiver/processor, and to get from the receiver/processor to the inputs on the video monitor.

1. Attach one male end of your composite cable to the DVD player's composite female input. Make sure that the connection is slightly tight and that there is no excessive weight or pull on the wire.

Figure 6.9

The back panel of a processor with multiple composite inputs and outputs.

2. Take the other male end of composite cable and go to the back of the receiver/processor. You should have a wire length that is not taut, but that rests easily between the receiver/processor and the DVD player. Slide the single-pin composite connector onto the female jack labeled Video 1 on the back panel of the receiver/processor.

NOTE Although you may have a variety of source devices using the composite connections, you should give the DVD player the Video 1 designation because it will be the most heavily used source device in your system—trust us.

3. Slide the other composite cable's male end into the composite video output RCA jack on the receiver/processor. This connection is often labeled Video Output or Monitor on the receiver/processor.

4. Hook up the last unattached cable end to the video monitor's back panel. This connection is often labeled Video-1 or Video Input. You should always make this connection with the first composite video input because this input is responsible for all the video for all the source devices connected to the receiver/processor.

Now that you have completed connecting the video portion of your DVD player, let's move on to establishing the incredible sounds that you're going to hear in your home theater.

Audio Connections

There are a few methods of connecting the audio on your DVD player to your receiver/processor. You *must* connect your DVD player to your receiver/processor to steer the sound to each of your speaker locations and give you the true benefits of a home theater presentation.

Again, we'll rank the connection methods from the highest performance and convenience to the lowest so that you can get the optimal hookup for your home theater's equipment.

A DVD Player with Coaxial Digital Output and a Receiver/Processor with Coaxial Digital Inputs

Remember that the audio information sent out of your DVD player is in the digital realm and is a series of 1s and 0s that make up what you hear from your home theater. Therefore, a special digital cable is used to transfer this information to the receiver/processor so that decoding of those 1s and 0s can occur. This cable provides the information used by the Dolby Digital and DTS surround sound decoder system in your receiver or processor, which is the same processing used in movie theaters.

The cable that you'll use to transfer this information and send it for decoding is digital coaxial cable.

NOTE Remember that the digital coaxial cable looks like a regular audio interconnect cable because it has male RCA connectors at both ends. However, you should purchase a cable that is specifically tailored to pass digital information, which is the purpose of digital coaxial connections.

How Do I Know I've Got It? Check the back of your DVD player. If there is a single RCA connector that has a ring of orange in the center of the connector and is labeled either Digital Audio Output, PCM/ Bitstream Out, or Coaxial Digital Out, then your DVD player is all set (see Figure 6.10).

Figure 6.10

The back panel of a processor with a coaxial digital input.

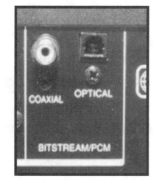

On your receiver/processor, you will find an input section devoted to one or more of the following:

○ Digital inputs and outputs all clustered together

○ DVD player inputs with all the inputs needed to connect a DVD player clustered together

○ Video-1 inputs with all kinds of inputs for a variety of video sources, including a DVD player

Among these input sections, you should also find an orange coaxial digital cable input if your receiver or processor has one.

Materials You Need: All you need for this connection is a single coaxial digital cable long enough to connect to the back of the receiver or processor. Keep this wire as short as possible but, as always, never so tight that it pulls on the inputs when you connect it.

1. Push one male end of the coaxial digital cable onto the RCA connector with the orange interior ring and labeled Audio Output, PCM/Bitstream Output, or even Digital Output. The RCA connection should be tight and not budge even when the cable is pulled very lightly.

2. Take the other male end of the coaxial digital cable and find the digital coaxial input on the back of the receiver or processor. If the inputs are labeled numerically, use the number one input, but if there is an input specifically labeled DVD Player or a section of inputs for DVD players, make sure to use one of those; otherwise, you won't hear anything! Slide the cable's male RCA connector onto the receiver/processor's input.

That's all it takes.

A DVD Player with Toslink/Optical Digital Output and a Receiver/Processor with Toslink/Optical Digital Inputs

The other type of digital cable that you can use is the Toslink/optical cable (see Figure 6.11). (Remember that Toslink cable and optical cable are the same thing.) This fiber-optic cable provides the exact same information as the coaxial digital cable, but due to the nature of the signal method that it uses (light pulsation), it is inadvisable (and expensive) to use long lengths of this cable (you shouldn't use more than about 6 feet).

Otherwise, the Toslink/optical cable is just an alternative to the coaxial digital cable, although it is not as robust and durable.

How Do I Know I've Got It? Take a look at your DVD player's back panel (see Figure 6.12). In the area marked Digital Outputs, you should see either a small, square Toslink/optical connection (often next to the coaxial digital connector) or the protective insert that has a small handle that you can remove to allow access to the Toslink/optical connection. Every DVD player has one of these features.

Figure 6.11

A Toslink/
optical cable.

Figure 6.12

The back panel of a
DVD player with
the Toslink/optical
protector on and
with the Toslink/
optical protector
off; notice the
angled bottom
sides, which allow
connection at only
one angle.

On your receiver/processor, you will find an input section devoted to one or more of the following:

- Digital inputs and outputs all clustered together
- DVD player inputs with all the inputs needed to connect a DVD player clustered together
- Video-1 inputs with all kinds of inputs for a variety of video sources, including a DVD player

Among these input sections, you should also find an exact match of the square Toslink/optical connector, or the protective insert in place that you can remove to allow access to the Toslink/optical connection.

Materials You Need: All you need for this connection is a single Toslink/optical digital cable long enough to reach the back of the receiver or processor and connect. Be very careful when purchasing this wire; make sure that the length you choose is not too long or too short, but just long enough for a tight connection. The Toslink/optical connection is somewhat flimsy and can lead to wire or equipment damage if it is pulled accidentally or rests too tightly against other equipment, corners, and so on.

1. Remove the protective covering over the actual Toslink/optical wire connectors. This is a small sheath of plastic that covers the tip of the optical connection that goes into the DVD player and the receiver/processor. Make sure to remove this protector from both ends. Otherwise the protector could get stuck in the Toslink/optical connector and then screw up the input.

2. Take one male end of the Toslink/optical cable and find the corresponding output on the back of the DVD player. Connect the cable connector into the DVD player until it locks into the output with a small click. The cable will fit only one way because there are two angled sides to the connector that must fit into the output in the right configuration.

3. Take the other male end of the Toslink/optical cable and find the input on the receiver/processor. This input is usually labeled as

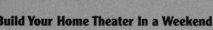

DVD Player Digital Audio Input, Optical 1, Video 1, Toslink/ Optical Input, or something similar. Connect the Toslink/optical connector into the receiver/processor so that it locks into the output with a small click. Be careful, however, not to strain the input or the cable too much. This is the only really delicate cable that you must work with, so watch out!

That's it for the two digital connections you can make. By now, no matter what your DVD player and receiver/processor combination is, your video and audio are connected, so it is time to move on to your next source device.

Connecting Your Home Theater to Broadcast Television

The next task in connecting the system is to hook up your home theater to receive broadcast channels. There are various connection methods to accomplish this task.

Four source components are involved in this connection: a DSS satellite system, a cable converter box, a personal television recorder (PTVR) system, and your VCR. Your setup from this point on will be determined by the components you have and the method you use for receiving television broadcasts. This section describes the following configurations:

- A DSS satellite receiver or cable converter box with a personal television recorder and a VCR
- A DSS satellite receiver or cable converter box with only a VCR
- A personal television recorder with only a VCR
- A VCR only

Your system should fall into one of these categories. Let's get to it.

A DSS Satellite Receiver or Cable Converter Box with a Personal Television Recorder and a VCR

This connection is the most complicated to set up, but it allows you to use a PTVR with a DSS or cable box to get local channels and record programs, plus make hard-copy recordings onto VCR tapes.

You'll start by connecting the DSS system or a cable converter box, which is always the first to receive the broadcast signals. Luckily, the general inputs and outputs are exactly the same for either device. We will call these two devices *set-top boxes*.

Connection Step 1: A Coaxial (RG-6) Cable Connection from a DSS Antenna or Cable Provider Signal

DSS Dish Systems

One project that used to be a part of home theater setup was the installation of the DSS dish on your roof or deck. However, with the costs of these dishes dropping dramatically, paying the initial fee for installation is an excellent investment that can save you the time and hassle of installing the dish yourself. A setup professional will come to your house and mount the dish where it is best hidden and then align it with the satellite, finally running the RG-6 coaxial cable wire to the location that you need in the home theater. Generally, this service may be free or may be around $99 for the complete package. If you purchase this service, your money will be well spent.

After installation, you will have an RG-6 cable somewhere in your home theater room (see Figure 6.13).

This cable provides the video and audio content of your television channels. In addition, you will have a DSS receiver box that has this RG-6 cable connected to it so that it may unscramble the signals brought in from the satellite. This DSS receiver box is the gateway to your television content and is the item that you must integrate into your home theater components.

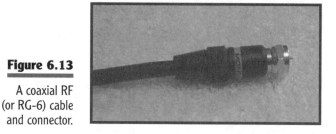

Figure 6.13

A coaxial RF
(or RG-6) cable
and connector.

NOTE

Don't confuse this type of coaxial RF (RG-6) cable with the digital RCA interconnect
cable used for digital signal transfer on DVD players, CD players, and other digital
sources.

Cable Converter Boxes

If you do not have a DSS system, you may have a cable converter box
provided by the cable company to bring your broadcast channels into
your home theater. If this is the case, you already have an RG-6 connection to the back panel of the cable box in the Cable-In connection.

If the RG-6 cable connected to the DSS receiver box or the cable converter box does not reach the component stack location, you need to purchase a female-to-female coaxial cable connector and an additional length
of coaxial cable. This will extend the range of the set-top box. As always,
try to minimize the cable lengths to avoid excessive signal loss and tangling with other cables in the equipment stack.

Connection Step 2: Video and Audio Connection from a DSS Receiver/Cable Box to a Personal Television Recorder

This connection now allows the DSS or cable system to provide its
content to the personal television recorder to create its unique television
viewing experience.

AN OPTIONAL ADVANCED CONNECTION: DIRECT CONNECTION OF A DSS/CABLE SET-TOP BOX TO A RECEIVER/PROCESSOR FOR DIGITAL AUDIO CONNECTION

This is a special connection to make if your DSS receiver box or cable converter box happens to have a digital output connector for digital sound. Currently, some pay-per-view programming and special events are being broadcast in full Dolby Digital sound. *Only if you plan to use these services should you do this task.*

To make this connection, bypass the normal route to the PTVR and connect directly to the receiver/processor. However, make this connection only if you have enough video and digital inputs on the receiver/processor to accommodate an additional device.

1. Connect the video from the DSS/cable box to the receiver/processor.

    Check the back of your DSS/cable box and also of your receiver/processor. If both components have open S-video connectors, connect an S-video cable between them. On the DSS/cable box, connect to the S-video output labeled S-Video Out, and on the receiver/processor, hook up the S-video cable to the lowest numbered S-video connector in the S-video input group (usually labeled S-Video 1, 2, 3, and so on) or the section labeled DSS or Cable.

    If no S-video connection is possible, you must connect with a composite cable. The back panel of the DSS/cable box will have a yellow RCA composite connection. You must check for an open composite cable input on the receiver/processor. If one exists, connect a single composite video cable from the Video Out connector on the DSS/cable box to the Video 1, 2, 3... In, DSS In, or Cable In connector on the receiver/processor.

2. Connect the digital audio connection from the DSS/cable box to the receiver/processor.

    Check the back of your DSS/cable box and also of your receiver/processor. If there is a connector labeled Digital Out on the back of your DSS/cable box, you're in business for this connection.

Now make sure that the same type of connector (digital RCA interconnect or Toslink/optical) is available and open on the receiver/processor. You will then connect a cable of that type from the Digital Out input on the DSS/cable box to the input labeled Coaxial 1 In, Optical-1, 2, 3... In, DSS Digital Audio In, or Cable Digital Audio In on the receiver with the open connector. (You will already have one digital cable connected for the DVD player.)

3. **Connect the DSS/cable box to the personal television recorder.**

    You must still connect the DSS/cable box to the PTVR so that the recorder can do its magic with broadcast television. To do this, the DSS/cable box should have an unused RF coaxial cable output. Attach an RF coaxial cable to this connector, which is usually labeled RF Out, and then connect the cable to the RF coaxial input labeled Antenna In on the PTVR (see Figure 6.14).

    This connection will allow you to use every function of the PTVR. Thus you can watch and record regular broadcast television and even watch it over the home theater system.

Figure 6.14

The back panel of a PTVR with the RF coaxial cable attached to the Antenna In RF connector.

Video Connection

A set-top box offers two types of video connections to provide video information to the PTVR: S-video and composite connections.

A DSS/Cable Set-Top Box with S-Video Output

The optimal video resolution for your DSS system comes through direct connection from the DSS receiver box to the PTVR through an S-video cable.

How Do I Know I've Got It? An S-video connection is the small, recessed hookup on the back panel of the DSS receiver box and on your PTVR (see Figure 6.15).

The wire part of the connection has four small pins and a plastic rectangular guide. The input side of the connection has four small pinholes and a rectangular hole for the plastic guide.

Figure 6.15

The S-video connection on the back panel of a PTVR.

Materials You Need: You need one S-video cable long enough to reach from the DSS receiver box to the PTVR.

1. Take your S-video cable and align the pins properly in their holes with the plastic guide. Then slide the S-video connector into the output jack labeled S-Video on the DSS receiver.

2. Get behind your PTVR. Your wire length run should be loose—not so tight that there is pressure on the wire, but not so loose that there is a bunch of wire left on the floor. Connect the wire to the S-Video connector labeled S-Video Input or S-Video In on the back panel of the PTVR.

A DSS/Cable Set-Top Box with Composite Output and a Personal Television Recorder with Composite Input

Every DSS receiver box and cable converter box comes with at least one composite video output. However, the performance of this connection is less than optimal, especially if you get accustomed to the crystal clear images of DVD.

How Do I Know I've Got It? Without fail, the back of your DSS receiver box or cable converter box will have a composite output terminal. It is a single RCA output jack with a yellow center and is usually labeled Video Out or just Video in the Output section of connectors.

Your PTVR will also have at least one composite video input, usually labeled Video In or just Video, that is placed in the Input section of connectors (see Figure 6.16).

Materials You Need: You need one composite video cable long enough to reach from the DSS receiver box to the PTVR.

1. Take your composite cable and insert the male RCA connector into the female RCA jack colored yellow and labeled Video on the DSS receiver/cable converter box. Tug on the cable slightly to ensure that the connection is solid.

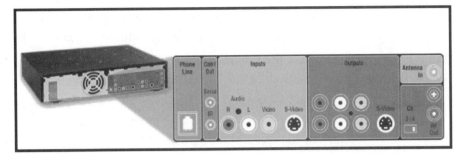

Figure 6.16

The composite input connector on the PTVR.

2. Attach this same composite video cable's RCA connector to the yellow RCA connector labeled Video In on the PTVR. As always, make sure that the connection is firm and will not come undone with a light tug.

Audio Connection

The audio connection for your DSS/cable box to the PTVR is a standard dual stereo RCA interconnect pair.

A DSS/Cable Box with Stereo Analog RCA Outputs and a PTVR with Stereo Analog RCA Inputs

How Do I Know I've Got It? You'll have it, guaranteed. Your DSS/cable box will have a pair of stereo RCA outputs, and your PTVR will also have a pair of RCA stereo (left and right) inputs (refer to Figure 6.16).

Materials You Need: To connect the audio from the DSS/cable box, you need dual RCA stereo interconnect cables (left and right) that reach from the DSS/cable box to the PTVR.

1. Take the white or black audio cable (there is a stripe on the wire or the RCA connector is colored white/black to designate the left channel) and go to the back panel of the DSS receiver box or cable converter box. You will find the pair of stereo outputs labeled Audio Out or Stereo Output. After locating the outputs, plug the white and black wire with the RCA connectors into the corresponding input that has a white or black center ring and is labeled "Left."

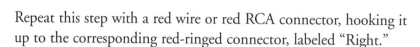

Repeat this step with a red wire or red RCA connector, hooking it up to the corresponding red-ringed connector, labeled "Right."

2. Take the unconnected left and right RCA cable ends and move to the back of the PTVR. Find the input labeled Audio In. This input has two colored RCA jacks of the same kind as those on the back of the VCR. Connect the remaining two stereo left and right cables to the corresponding inputs. Make sure that the left and right cables are connected properly; otherwise, you will have left sound coming out of the right side speaker, and right sound coming out of the left speaker, creating a very weird home theater presentation.

Connection Step 3: Controlling Your DSS Receiver/Cable Box Through the PTVR

First, your PTVR must communicate with your cable converter box or your DSS receiver box. Two methods exist for such a connection, and the PTVR system usually includes both required cables. By attaching one of these cables, your PTVR can tell the cable converter box or the DSS receiver box to change the channel.

You may control the cable converter box or the DSS receiver box with a special cable called a serial cable. This connector has a single small ⅛-inch plug connector on one side that connects to the input labeled Serial on the PTVR. On the other end, your cable box or DSS receiver will have a serial connection (similar to a serial cable on a computer) with nine pins in a five–over-four configuration. This connector attaches to a corresponding female connector on the set-top box.

You may also use an IR (infrared) controller cable, which sends a remote control signal from the PTVR to the cable box or DSS receiver to change the channel. This cable also has a ⅛-inch plug that connects directly to the IR-labeled connector on the PTVR. The other end is shaped like an *L* and has a small bulb on it. This bulb must be pointed at the IR receiver section of the cable box or DSS receiver.

You can find the location of the IR input by checking the front panel for a small piece of transparent plastic, or a section on the front display's plastic that has a small circle behind it. This is the IR receiver. Then, with a piece of sticky tape, place the controller cable's end at the IR location on the cable box or DSS receiver.

Connection Step 4: A Video and Audio Connection from the PTVR to the Receiver/Processor

Now you must make a connection between the PTVR and the receiver/processor to allow you to watch your favorite programs and hear them on your home theater in surround sound.

Video Connection

Now you must connect the video for the PTVR into the home theater system to obtain an image on the video monitor. As before, we will have to pay special attention to the video switching issue so that you can get the best possible video available, but with ease of use.

A PTVR with S-Video Output, a Receiver/Processor with S-Video Input, and a Video Monitor with S-Video Input

How Do I Know I've Got It? Your PTVR will most likely have an S-video output on the back panel. Your receiver/processor will also have a set of inputs labeled either Video 1, 2, 3, and so on, with S-video jacks, or have an input specifically labeled PTVR Input that includes an S-video connection.

The receiver/processor also needs an S-video output in the form of a monitor output jack.

This connection attaches to the video monitor so that the receiver can send the selected video source to the video monitor. If your receiver/processor has S-video inputs, you will have at least one S-video output.

NOTE Remember that your video monitor needs one open S-video connection to provide the S-video images routed through your receiver/processor. If you have earlier chosen to connect your DVD player directly to the S-video monitor, it is important to check for another free S-video connector on the video monitor to accept video signals from the receiver/processor.

Materials You Need: You need an S-video cable for this connection (unless you have already attached an S-video cable to the back panel in the connection of your DVD player). The cable must be long enough to get from the PTVR to the receiver/processor. You may also need a second S-video cable for connection from the receiver/processor to the video monitor.

1. Attach the male end of your S-video cable to the PTVR's S-video female output, which should be labeled S-Video Output or Video Output. Make sure that you insert the cable correctly so that the pins in the connector line up exactly right. Do not force the connector, but slide it in only when you feel it fitting in comfortably.

2. Hold the male end of the S-video cable that you just attached to the PTVR S-video output and go to the back of the receiver/processor. You should have a wire length that is not taut, but that rests easily between the PTVR and the receiver/processor. Insert the S-video cable into the receiver/processor's S-video input labeled Video 2 (the DVD player is Video 1) or perhaps labeled PTVR. Lightly tug the cable to make sure that you have a firm connection.

3. If you have not connected an S-video cable from the receiver/processor for another source device, connect the other S-video cable's male end to the S-video output connection on the receiver/processor. This connection is often labeled S-Video Output or Monitor.

4. Hook up the remaining S-video connection to the video monitor's back panel (see Figure 6.17).

Figure 6.17

The back panel of a direct view monitor with an S-video input jack.

 NOTE If you already have connected an S-video DVD player on a video monitor with two S-video inputs, use S-Video Input 2. If you have only one S-video input on the video monitor, you will already have a connection there from the DVD player, so you'll have to scratch this setup configuration and move to the next.

A PTVR with Composite Output, a Receiver/Processor with Composite Input and Output, and a Video Monitor with Composite Input

You should use this setup only if your video monitor has only one S-video input that your DVD player is currently using, or if your video monitor does not have any S-video inputs. By connecting all your source devices into the receiver/processor first and then hooking up only the one composite cable to send video to the video monitor, you will have multiple inputs where there formerly was only one.

How Do I Know I've Got It? Your PTVR will always have one or two composite video output jacks on the back panel in their customary yellow RCA connectors. Your receiver/processor will also have a set or row of yellow composite inputs labeled either Video 1, 2, 3, and so on, or have

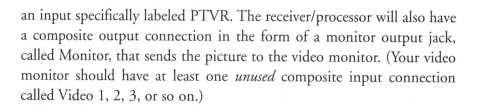

an input specifically labeled PTVR. The receiver/processor will also have a composite output connection in the form of a monitor output jack, called Monitor, that sends the picture to the video monitor. (Your video monitor should have at least one *unused* composite input connection called Video 1, 2, 3, or so on.)

NOTE

Remember that you cannot use multiple connection types on the video monitor's inputs even though there may be both S-video and composite video connections on the input group (like Video 1). If an S-video cable is connected to Video 2, you cannot run on Video 2 and must move to Video 3. If you use up too many of these inputs, it is best to consolidate your composite video devices and do your video switching through the receiver/processor.

Materials You Need: You need a composite cable long enough to reach comfortably from the PTVR to the receiver/processor. You may also need a second S-video cable for connection from the receiver/processor to the video monitor.

1. Attach one of the male ends of your composite cable to the PTVR's composite female output. Make sure that the connection is slightly tight and that there is no excessive weight or pull on the wire.

2. Take the other male end of the composite video cable and move to the rear of the receiver/processor. You should have a wire length that rests easily between the receiver/processor and the PTVR. Slide the single-pin composite connector onto the female jack on the back panel of the receiver/processor. This input is labeled Video 2 (if the DVD player is using Video 1).

3. If you have not already done so for the DVD player, slide the other composite cable's male end into the composite video output RCA jack on the receiver/processor. This connection is often labeled Video Output or Monitor on the receiver/processor.

4. Hook up the last unattached cable end to the video monitor's back panel. Generally, you should make this connection with the first

available composite video input because this input is responsible for all the video for all the source devices connected to the receiver/processor. Just remember not to hook up this cable end to an input bank (such as Video 1) that already has an S-video cable connected for the DVD player.

Audio Connection

The audio connection for your PTVR is only a stereo signal like the kind produced by your CD player. This connection will still provide the ability to use Dolby Pro Logic sound. Your receiver and processor will take the two stereo signals from the two outputs on the PTVR and create a Dolby Pro Logic soundtrack.

Materials You Need: To connect the audio from the PTVR, you need only two RCA audio cables that can reach from the PTVR to the receiver/processor.

1. Take the white or black audio cable (there is either a white or black stripe on the cable, or the RCA connector will be colored to designate the left channel) and go to the back panel of the PTVR. You will find a pair of stereo outputs labeled Audio Out or Stereo Output. Plug the white or black wire into the corresponding input with a white or black center ring on the connector. Repeat with the red wire and red connector.

2. Take the left and right unconnected RCA cable ends and move to the back of the receiver/processor. Find the input on the back that corresponds to the video cable that you connected earlier from the PTVR. If you connected that video cable as Video 2, use Video 2, and so on. Now connect the remaining two left and right stereo cables to the corresponding inputs.

Make sure that the left and right cables are connected to their inputs; otherwise, you will have left sound coming out of the right speaker, and right sound coming out of the left speaker.

Connection Step 5: Video and Audio Connection from the PTVR to the VCR

Now you must make a video and audio connection between the PTVR and a VCR to allow you to produce hard copies of the programs that you have recorded on your personal television recorder system.

Video Connection

The video connection can be broken down into two possibilities: S-video and composite.

A PTVR with Available S-Video Output and a VCR with Available S-Video Input
How Do I Know I've Got It? Check the back panel of your PTVR. If you identify an *available* S-video connector (you may have only one that is already being used by the connection to the receiver/processor), then check the back of the VCR. If this is an S-video VCR, you will have an available S-video input on the back panel.

Materials You Need: You will need an S-video cable long enough to reach from the PTVR to the VCR. The cable should not be too tight to pull on the connectors, but not so long as to leave excess cable on the floor.

1. Connect one of the S-video male connector ends of the cable to the S-video output on the PTVR. This output will be labeled S-Video Output or be in the section labeled Output.

2. Connect the remaining S-video male connector to the S-video input on the VCR. This input will be labeled S-Video Input or be in the section labeled Input on the back panel.

A PTVR with Available Composite Output and a VCR with Available Composite Input
You will need to use this system to make your connection if you have only one S-video output on the PTVR that you are using.

How Do I Know I've Got It? Check the back panel of your PTVR. It will have a composite video connector. It will also have an available composite input on the back panel of the VCR (see Figure 6.18).

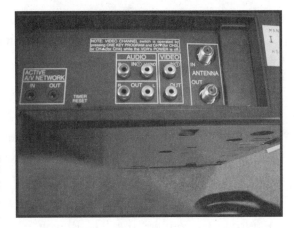

Figure 6.18

A composite input on the back panel of a VCR.

Materials You Need: You need an S-video cable long enough to reach from the PTVR to the VCR. The cable should be not too tight to pull on the connectors, but not so long as to leave excess cable on the floor.

1. Connect the composite video RCA connector end of the cable to the composite video RCA output on the PTVR. This output will be labeled Video Output or be in the section labeled Output.

2. Connect the remaining composite RCA connector to the composite input on the VCR. This input will be labeled Video Input or be in the section labeled Inputs on the back panel.

Audio Connection

The audio connection to the VCR is always a stereo signal. The PTVR will send the two stereo signals from its two outputs. When you play back audio through the receiver/processor, it will create a Dolby Pro Logic soundtrack.

Materials You Need: For connecting the audio from the PTVR, you need only two RCA audio cables that can reach from the PTVR to the VCR.

1. Find a pair of stereo outputs labeled Audio Out or Stereo Output on the PTVR. The PTVR's back panel should have two sets in the Output section of connectors. Plug the white and black audio cable into the white connector and the red wire into the red connector.

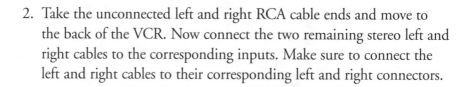
2. Take the unconnected left and right RCA cable ends and move to the back of the VCR. Now connect the two remaining stereo left and right cables to the corresponding inputs. Make sure to connect the left and right cables to their corresponding left and right connectors.

Connection Step 6: The RF Coaxial (RG-6) Cable from the PTVR to the Video Monitor

This connection provides your video monitor with a basic television signal so that you may run the PTVR system without the rest of the full home theater experience. This is best for just news or sitcom-type programs.

Material You Need: To connect the PTVR, you need an RF coaxial RG-6 cable long enough to reach from the PTVR to the video monitor.

1. First locate on the PTVR the RG-6 coaxial cable connector labeled RF Out or Antenna Out (see Figure 6.19).

2. Now screw the coaxial connector onto the connector until it snugly fits around the connector and is screwed in all the way.

3. On the video monitor's back panel, find a corresponding RF coaxial RG-6 cable connector. Screw the other end of the RF coaxial RG-6 cable from the PTVR into the video monitor's input.

Figure 6.19

The RF coaxial RG-6 cable output on a PTVR.

Connection Step 7: The VCR to the Receiver/Processor

If you still want to be able to play your videotape collection or watch anything that you have recorded from the PTVR down to a VCR tape, you will also require a direct connection to the receiver/processor. This connection will allow you to play tapes in Dolby surround mode through your home theater.

Video Connections

Only two types of video connections are available on a VCR to provide video information to the receiver/processor: S-video and composite connections. This section discusses each in turn. Keep in mind our earlier discussion on video switching and its critical role in the setup process.

A VCR with S-Video Output and a Receiver/Processor with S-Video Input

This particular setup will allow you to get an S-video connection into the receiver/processor for the optimal VCR video connection. If you have only one S-video connection on the video monitor, or are using the first S-video input for a DVD player and the second S-video connection for all your S-video sources routed through the receiver/processor, this is the best connection for your VCR.

NOTE Even though you may be able to switch between S-video sources using your receiver or processor, you still have to switch the video monitor's input manually (using the video monitor's remote control, via the "TV/Video" button or the "Input" button) when moving from an S-video source to a composite video source. You need to reach a new input on the video monitor for any composite video sources in your home theater. The only way to do video switching entirely through your receiver or processor is with outputs that are *all* S-video, *all* composite video, or *all* component video.

How Do I Know I've Got It? Your VCR will have an S-video output only if it is equipped as an S-VHS VCR.

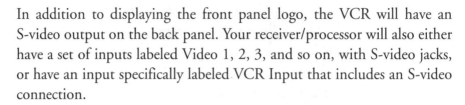

In addition to displaying the front panel logo, the VCR will have an S-video output on the back panel. Your receiver/processor will also either have a set of inputs labeled Video 1, 2, 3, and so on, with S-video jacks, or have an input specifically labeled VCR Input that includes an S-video connection.

The receiver/processor needs an S-video output in the form of a monitor output jack. From your installation of the PTVR, you should already have a connection from the receiver/processor to the video monitor. This connection is S-video and is attached to the S-Video 2 connection, if you have the DVD player in S-Video 1.

Materials You Need: For this connection, you need one S-video cable long enough to reach from the VCR to the receiver/processor. It is wise to purchase premium cables for this connection, especially if you have a long run of cable (longer than 12 feet) to get from the receiver/processor to the video monitor, which can be located away from the equipment stack.

1. Attach the male end of your S-video cable to the VCR's S-video female output, which should be labeled S-Video Output or Video Output. Make sure to insert the cable correctly so that the pins in the connector line up exactly right. Do not force the connector, but slide it in only when you feel it fitting comfortably.

2. Take the male end of the S-video cable that you just attached to the VCR S-video output and go to the back of the receiver/processor. You should have a wire length that is not taut, but that rests easily between the receiver/processor and the VCR. Insert the S-video cable into the receiver/processor's S-video input labeled Video 2 (the DVD player should be Video 1) or VCR. Tug the cable lightly to make sure that you have a firm connection.

A VCR with Composite Output and a Receiver/Processor with Composite Input
If your VCR has only composite video, you must make a composite video connection to the receiver/processor. If you connected the PTVR with an

S-video connection, you also need to connect a single composite cable to the video monitor from the receiver/processor to transmit video because the composite signal will not transfer over the S-video wire.

How Do I Know I've Got It? All VCRs have one or two composite video output jacks on the back panel in their customary yellow RCA connectors. Your receiver/processor probably also has a set or row of yellow composite inputs labeled either Video 1, 2, 3, and so on, or has an input specifically labeled VCR.

The receiver/processor will also have a composite output connection in the form of a monitor output jack, called Monitor, that sends the picture to the video monitor. Finally, you need to make sure that the video monitor has an open composite connection that does not have a composite cable already plugged in. There cannot be any other video connection on a video monitor's Video Input if it has both S-Video and Composite Video connectors. For example, if an S-Video cable is connected to Video 2, you cannot run on Video 2 and must move to Video 3.

Materials You Need: You need two composite cables long enough to reach comfortably from the VCR to the receiver/processor, and to reach from the receiver/processor to the input on the video monitor.

1. Attach the male end of one of your composite cables to the VCR's composite female output. Make sure that the connection is slightly tight and that there is no excessive weight or pull on the wire.

2. Take the other male end of composite cable and move to the rear of the receiver/processor. You should have a wire length that rests easily between the receiver/processor and the VCR. Slide the single-pin composite connector onto the female jack on the back panel of the receiver/processor. This input is labeled Video 2 (which may be used by the PTVR), Video 3, or VCR.

3. Slide the other composite cable's male end into the composite video output RCA jack on the receiver/processor. This connection is often labeled Video Output or Monitor.

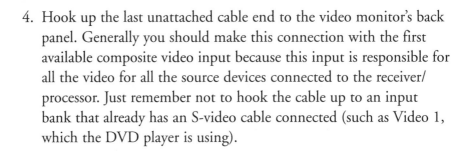

4. Hook up the last unattached cable end to the video monitor's back panel. Generally you should make this connection with the first available composite video input because this input is responsible for all the video for all the source devices connected to the receiver/ processor. Just remember not to hook the cable up to an input bank that already has an S-video cable connected (such as Video 1, which the DVD player is using).

Audio Connections

The audio connection for your VCR is relatively simple because only one type of sound information is available from the source device. Videotapes can deliver a maximum of only two channels of sound into your home theater: the left and right channels. This is a standard stereo signal like the kind produced by your CD player.

NOTE Keep in mind that you are setting up the system with a stereo VCR. Stereo is standard for home theater VCRs. However, VCRs can also be purchased in a mono configuration that has only one channel of audio output. Such a VCR with a single channel of output is basically useless in a home theater because only a single speaker will be playing out of your whole system. Because a stereo VCR is roughly $50 more than a mono one, this is one component for which you should invest a few more dollars, and one that may be ripe for upgrading if you already have a mono VCR.

Although a stereo signal is generally played in the stereo mode on your receiver/processor, your system will play back your VCR tapes in the Dolby Pro Logic mode to enhance the presentation with surround sound and a center channel. Your receiver/processor will take the two stereo signals from the two outputs on the VCR and create a Dolby Pro Logic soundtrack. In particular, movie tapes that you have purchased for your collection will benefit from this setup.

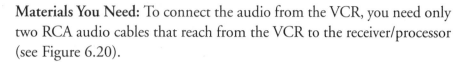

Materials You Need: To connect the audio from the VCR, you need only two RCA audio cables that reach from the VCR to the receiver/processor (see Figure 6.20).

1. Take the white or black audio cable (it will have a white/black stripe or the RCA connector will be colored white or black to designate the left channel) and go to the back panel of the VCR. You will find a pair of stereo outputs labeled Audio Out or Stereo Output (see Figure 6.21).

2. After locating the outputs, plug the white and black wire with the RCA connectors into the corresponding white/black ringed input connector. Repeat this step with the red RCA wire and connector, hooking it up to the corresponding red connector input.

3. Take the unconnected left and right RCA cable ends and move to the back of the receiver/processor. Find the input on the back

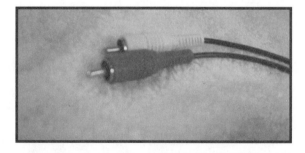

Figure 6.20

A pair of RCA audio cables for stereo hookup.

Figure 6.21

Stereo outputs on the VCR.

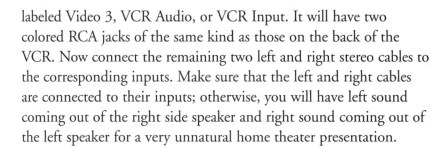

labeled Video 3, VCR Audio, or VCR Input. It will have two colored RCA jacks of the same kind as those on the back of the VCR. Now connect the remaining two left and right stereo cables to the corresponding inputs. Make sure that the left and right cables are connected to their inputs; otherwise, you will have left sound coming out of the right side speaker and right sound coming out of the left speaker for a very unnatural home theater presentation.

That's it. You have made all the necessary connections for this system, so you can skip to the CD player connection task and continue.

A DSS Receiver Box or Cable Converter Box with a VCR Only

To bring channels into the video monitor without a PTVR, the most important device in your system is your set-top box. This component (either a DSS receiver or a cable converter box) makes sense of the cable information coming in and allows you to manage it by changing the channel, volume, and basic information.

Therefore, you will proceed to connect your set-top box to the home theater so that you can watch broadcast television with the full benefits of your home theater.

This section examines the setup connections for the set-top box, VCR, and receiver/processor in three parts: the coaxial RF connections, the video connections, and the audio connections.

Connection Step 1: The Coaxial (RG-6) Cable Connection from the Antenna to the DSS, Then to the VCR, Then to the Video Monitor

One project that used to be a part of your home theater setup was the installation of the DSS dish on your roof or deck. However, the cost of these dishes has dropped severely, and simply paying the initial fee for installation is an excellent investment that can save you the time and

hassle of installing the dish yourself. Generally this service may be free or may be around $99 for the complete package. It is money well spent.

Regardless of whether you have a DSS receiver or a cable converter box, you will have an RG-6 cable protruding from the wall in your home theater room (see Figure 6.22).

This cable provides the video and audio content of your television channels and connects to the DSS/cable box.

NOTE Don't confuse this type of coaxial cable (RG-6) with the digital RCA interconnect cable used for digital signal transfer on DVD players, CD players, and other digital sources.

If the RG-6 cable does not reach the DSS/cable box location, you need to purchase a female-to-female coaxial cable connector and an additional length of coaxial cable to reach the location.

Keep the cable lengths to a minimum to avoid excessive signal loss and tangling with other cables in the equipment stack. Also, try to run the cable along the side wall to minimize the aesthetic intrusion into the room.

Materials You Need: You need two coaxial RF cables to get from the DSS receiver to the VCR and then to the video monitor. This will allow you to watch television without the home theater active, which is good for most programming situations.

Figure 6.22

The standard RF coaxial RG-6 cable coming out of the wall.

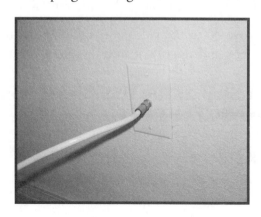

1. Go to the back of the DSS/cable box. On the RF output labeled Antenna Out or Coaxial Out on the DSS/cable box, screw one coaxial cable into the input (be careful not to bend the wire at the center of the connector). You should be able to pull on the cable lightly without disconnecting it.

2. Screw the coaxial cable end into the input on the VCR labeled Antenna In or Coaxial In. As before, the connection should be tight enough that the cable cannot come loose. Give it a light tug to make sure that it is tight.

3. Screw the other coaxial cable into the input on the VCR labeled Antenna Out, Coaxial Out, or To TV. Make sure that you slide the center wire in without bending it and then screw in the jacket connector. Tug the connection to make sure that it is tight.

4. Connect the last end of the coaxial RF cable to the input labeled Antenna In or Cable In on the back of the video monitor.

The single connector should slide easily into the center hole connector and then the jacket should screw around the input connector. Give the cable a short tug to ensure a good connection.

Now you do not have to turn on the entire home theater system to watch television through your video monitor, and with sound only coming from the video monitor. You will select programs through the DSS/cable box, and the VCR will be left in its video input channel to pass the broadcasts directly through the VCR and on to the video monitor.

Next, we will move on to the video and audio connections to integrate your DSS/cable box and your VCR into the home theater.

Connection Step 2: The DSS/Cable Box to the Receiver/Processor

This connection enables you to play broadcast programs over your home theater system directly from the DSS/cable box.

Video Connections

A DSS receiver box or cable converter box provides two types of video connections to send video information to the home theater: S-video and composite connections. You'll now connect one type, based on your analysis of your video switching and its critical role in the setup process.

A DSS/Cable Box with S-Video Output, a Receiver/Processor with S-Video Input, and a Video Monitor with an Open S-Video Input

The optimal video resolution for your DSS/cable box comes through direct connection from the DSS receiver box to the video monitor through an S-video cable.

How Do I Know I've Got It? An S-video connection is the small, recessed hookup on the back panel of the DSS receiver/cable converter box and on your video monitor. The wire part of the connection has four small pins and a plastic rectangular guide. The input side of the connection has four small pinholes and a rectangular hole for the plastic guide.

Check the DSS/cable box's back panel. If the panel has an S-video connection, your DSS receiver or cable box is ready for this connection.

In addition, you must have an open S-video input on your receiver/processor.

Also, unless you have attached an S-video cable from the DVD player to the receiver/processor and then to the video monitor, you need to make this connection in this task.

Materials You Need: You need one S-video cable long enough to reach from the DSS receiver box to the receiver/processor, and, if necessary, one additional S-video cable to go from the receiver/processor to the video monitor.

1. Take your S-video cable and align the pins properly in their holes with the plastic guide. Slide the S-video connector into the output jack labeled S-Video on the DSS receiver box.

2. Go to the back of the receiver/processor. Your wire length run should be loose—not so tight that there is pressure on the wire, but not so loose that a bunch of wire is left on the floor. Connect the wire to the S-video connector labeled S-Video 2 or Video-2 on the back panel of the receiver/processor or in a special input group labeled DSS/Cable. Usually, for this task, the DVD player will take up the Video-1 input on the receiver/processor. When the cable snugly fits into place, your connection is made.

3. If you did not run an S-video cable between the receiver/processor for the DVD player to use for video, you now must connect one. On the back of the receiver/processor, find the S-video output jack labeled Monitor Out or S-Video Out. Connect another S-video cable to this output.

4. Connect the S-video cable from the Monitor Out jack on the receiver/processor to the S-video input terminal on the video monitor labeled S-Video 2 or Video 2. Your DVD player is probably using the Video 1 position.

A VCR with Composite Output, a Receiver/Processor with Composite Output and Input, and a Video Monitor with Composite Input

If your DSS receiver box has only composite video or your video monitor does not have enough S-video inputs to accommodate both your DVD player *and* DSS/cable box, this is the only remaining connection option that you have. Unfortunately, the connection provides mediocre performance, with an interrupted signal path and the lowest performance video cable.

How Do I Know I've Got It? Your DSS receiver/cable converter box will have a composite video output jack on the back panel in a standard yellow RCA connector. Your receiver/processor will also have yellow composite inputs labeled either Video 1, 2, 3, and so on, or have an input specifically labeled DSS/Cable. The receiver/processor will also have a composite output connection in the form of a monitor output jack, called Monitor Out. Finally, your video monitor should have at least one unused composite input connection called Video 1, 2, 3, and so on.

NOTE

Remember that there cannot be any other video connection on the Video input group that you use. For example, if an S-Video cable is connected to Video 1 for the DVD player, you cannot use the composite input also on Video 1 and must move to Video 2.

Materials You Need: You need two composite cables long enough to reach from the DSS receiver box to the receiver/processor, and to reach from the receiver/processor to the input on the video monitor.

1. Attach one of your composite cables to the DSS receiver box's composite female output, labeled Video Out, checking for a solid connection with a light pull.

2. Take the other male end of the composite cable and slide the single-pin composite connector onto the female jack on the back panel of the receiver/processor. Use the lowest number composite input that is available (see Figure 6.23). It will be labeled Video 1, 2, 3, and so on, or DSS/Cable.

   Chances are that the DVD player is currently using your Video 1 input group, so stay away from Video 1.

3. If there is not a composite connection already between the receiver/ processor and the video monitor for the DVD player, you must make one. Slide the unused composite cable's male end into the

Figure 6.23

Composite inputs on a receiver.

composite video output RCA jack on the receiver/processor. This connection is often labeled Video Output or Monitor on the receiver/processor.

4. Hook up the remaining unattached composite cable end to the video monitor's back panel. You usually should make this connection with the lowest numbered composite video input without any other connections. Remember not to hook up the cable to an input bank (such as Video 1) that already has an S-video cable connected.

You may already have a DVD player in Video 1 (via an S-video connection), and the DSS through the receiver/processor in Video 2 (via an S-video connection); now you will add the VCR in Video 3 via a composite connection. However, if you have already attached the DSS via a composite connection through the receiver/processor, you will not need this connection because you already have a connection through the receiver/processor, which can switch between the DSS and the VCR's composite output to the video monitor.

Audio Connections

The audio connection for your DSS receiver box or cable converter box can consist of two types of connections. The first is a digital connection of either digital coaxial interconnect cable or a Toslink/optical interconnect cable. Some broadcasts over the DSS system are now appearing with a Dolby Digital signal, and you will want to take advantage of this sound system. Cable programming sound is also increasingly being broadcast in this manner. The other connection type is a standard dual stereo RCA interconnect pair.

A DSS Receiver Box or Cable Converter Box with Coaxial Digital Output and a Receiver/Processor with an Available Coaxial Digital Input

Digital RCA coaxial interconnect cable looks like a single regular audio interconnect cable because it has male RCA connectors at both ends. However, this cable is specifically tailored to pass digital information through digital coaxial connections. You should use this type of cable for this connection.

How Do I Know I've Got It? Check the back of your DSS receiver. If there is a single RCA connector with an orange interior and that is labeled Digital Audio Output, Bitstream Out, or Coaxial Digital Out, your DSS receiver can make the connection.

On your receiver/processor, you will find an input section in one of the following configurations:

- A series of digital inputs and outputs all clustered together—some coaxial digital, some Toslink/optical
- A DSS input section with a stereo analog RCA connection pair, a composite or S-video input, and perhaps a digital input (with either coaxial or optical connectors, or both)
- Inputs labeled Video 1, 2, 3, and so on, each with a stereo analog RCA connection pair and perhaps a digital input (with either coaxial or optical connectors, or both)

Among these input sections, you must find an open orange coaxial digital cable input. If one is not present, move on to the next type of connection method.

Materials You Need: This connection requires one coaxial digital cable long enough to connect from the DSS receiver box or cable converter box to the back of the receiver/processor.

1. Push one male end of the coaxial digital cable onto the orange RCA connector labeled Audio Output or Digital Output on the back of the DSS receiver box or cable converter box. Make sure that the connector attaches snugly and will not slip off.

2. Connect the other male end of the coaxial digital RCA interconnect cable to the RCA connector on the back of the receiver or processor. If the inputs are labeled numerically, use the lowest number available; but if there is one input specifically labeled DSS Receiver Box/Cable Converter Box or there is a section of inputs for DSS receiver boxes or cable converter boxes, use that input.

3. Slide the cable's male RCA connector onto the receiver/processor's digital coaxial interconnect input.

A DSS Receiver Box with Toslink/Optical Digital Outputs and a Receiver/Processor with Toslink/Optical Digital Inputs

The other digital cable that you can use is Toslink/optical cable, which is much more prevalent on DSS receiver boxes and cable converter boxes. Remember to keep your runs of optical cable to a minimum because the signal method that it uses (light pulsation) tends to cause digital jitter over long runs. Try to use premium cable for longer runs and keep them to a maximum of 12 feet.

How Do I Know I've Got It? Take a look at your DSS receiver/cable converter box's back panel. If you see a small, square Toslink/optical connection or a protective insert that has a small handle that you can remove to allow access to the Toslink/optical connection, you can make a Toslink/optical connection to the receiver/processor.

On your receiver/processor, you should find an input group corresponding to one of the following sets:

- Digital inputs and outputs of both digital coaxial interconnect cable and Toslink/optical cable all clustered together
- A DSS receiver box input section with a stereo analog RCA connection pair and perhaps a digital input (either coaxial or optical, or both)
- Inputs labeled Video 1, 2, 3, and so on, each with a stereo analog RCA connection pair, a composite or S-video input, and perhaps a digital audio input (either coaxial or optical, or both)

Among one of these input sections, you should find an open Toslink/optical cable female connector.

Materials You Need: You need one Toslink/optical digital cable long enough to reach from the DSS receiver/cable converter box to the back

of the receiver/processor and connect them. When you purchase this wire, make sure that it is just the right length to reach, but not so tight that it pulls on the delicate Toslink/optical connection.

1. Remove the protective covering over the Toslink/optical wire connectors. This small plastic sheath covers the tip of the optical connection. Remove this protector from both ends of the cable because failing to do so could damage this input by causing the protector to get stuck in the connector.

2. Take a male end of the Toslink/optical cable and find the corresponding output on the back of the DSS receiver box.

   Slide the connector into the DSS receiver box until it locks into the output with a small click. The cable will fit only one way because the connector has two angled sides that must fit into the output in the right configuration.

3. Take the other male end of the Toslink/optical cable and find the input on the receiver/processor. This input is usually labeled as DSS Digital Audio Input, Cable Optical Input, Optical-1, 2, 3, and so on, Toslink/Optical Input, or something similar. Connect the Toslink/optical connector into the lowest numbered input available on the receiver/processor or an input labeled DSS or Cable. The connector will slide in enough that it locks into the output with a small click, just as your first connection did. You're all set.

A DSS Receiver Box with Stereo Analog RCA Outputs and a Receiver/Processor with Stereo Analog RCA Inputs

This is the default connection method for your DSS receiver box or cable converter box to the home theater system.

How Do I Know I've Got It? You are guaranteed to have it. Your DSS receiver box or cable converter box will have a pair of stereo RCA outputs, and your receiver/processor will also have multiple pairs of RCA stereo (left and right) inputs.

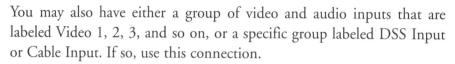

You may also have either a group of video and audio inputs that are labeled Video 1, 2, 3, and so on, or a specific group labeled DSS Input or Cable Input. If so, use this connection.

Materials You Need: To connect the audio from the DSS/cable box, you need only two RCA stereo interconnect cables that reach from the DSS receiver box or cable converter box to the receiver/processor.

1. Take the white or black audio cable (there will be a white or black stripe on the cable or the RCA connector will be colored white to designate the left channel) and go to the back panel of the DSS receiver/cable converter box. You will find a pair of stereo outputs labeled Audio Out or Stereo Output.

   After locating the outputs, plug the white or black wire or the white or black RCA connectors into the corresponding Left input. Repeat this step with a red RCA connector, hooking it up to the corresponding Right connector, which is colored red.

2. Now, take the unconnected left and right RCA cable ends and move to the back of the receiver/processor. On the back of the receiver/processor, find the input labeled Video 1, 2, 3, and so on, DSS Audio, or Cable Input. The input will have two colored RCA jacks of the same kind as those on the back of the DSS/cable box. Remember to use the same input number as the video connection that you have made for the DSS/cable box.

3. Now connect the remaining two stereo left and right cables to the corresponding inputs. Make sure that the left and right cables are connected properly; otherwise, you will have left sound coming out of the right side speaker and right sound coming out of the left speaker, creating an unnatural home theater presentation.

Connection Step 3: The VCR to the Receiver/Processor

Finally, you still need to connect your VCR to the receiver/processor to get a home theater connection from your VCR. If you are like millions of

VCR owners who have a library of movies on tape, you will want to watch them in surround sound. This connection enables you to view your video library on your home theater.

Video Connections

Only two types of video connections are available on a VCR to provide video information into the receiver/processor: S-video and composite connections. This section discusses each in turn. Keep in mind the earlier discussion on video switching and its critical role in the setup process.

A VCR with S-Video Output and a Receiver/Processor with S-Video Input

This particular setup will allow you to get an S-video connection into the receiver/processor for the optimal VCR video connection. If you only have one S-video connection on the video monitor, or are using the first S-video input for a DVD player and the second S-video connection for all your S-video sources routed through the receiver/processor, this is the best connection for your VCR.

How Do I Know I've Got It? Your VCR will have an S-video output only if it is an S-VHS VCR. The front panel will state that the model is an S-VHS VCR, and the back panel will have an S-video output. Your receiver/processor will also have a set of inputs labeled either Video 1, 2, 3, and so on, with S-video jacks, or have an input specifically labeled VCR Input that will include an S-video connection.

Materials You Need: For this connection, you need one S-video cable long enough to reach from the VCR to the receiver/processor. It is wise to purchase premium cables for this connection, especially if you have a long run of cable (longer than 12 feet) to get from the receiver/processor to the video monitor, which can be located away from the equipment stack.

1. Attach the male end of your S-video cable to the VCR's S-video female output, which should be labeled S-Video Output or Video Output. Make sure to insert the cable correctly so that the pins in the connector line up exactly right.

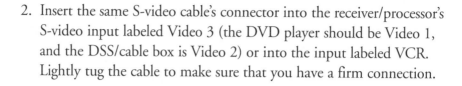

2. Insert the same S-video cable's connector into the receiver/processor's S-video input labeled Video 3 (the DVD player should be Video 1, and the DSS/cable box is Video 2) or into the input labeled VCR. Lightly tug the cable to make sure that you have a firm connection.

A VCR with Composite Output and a Receiver/Processor with Composite Input If your VCR has only composite video, you must make a composite video connection to the receiver/processor. If you also connected the DSS/cable box with an S-video connection, you also need to connect a single composite cable to the video monitor from the receiver/processor to transmit video because it cannot send S-video information over the video wire.

How Do I Know I've Got It? Your VCR will always have one or two composite video output jacks on the back panel in their traditional yellow RCA connectors. Your receiver/processor will probably also have a set or row of yellow composite inputs labeled either Video 1, 2, 3, and so on, or have an input specifically labeled VCR.

The receiver/processor will also have a composite output connection in the form of a monitor output jack, labeled Monitor, that sends the picture to the video monitor. Finally, you need to make sure that the video monitor has an open composite connection that does not already have a composite cable plugged in. There cannot be any other video connection to the set of video inputs you use for the video monitor. If an S-video cable is connected to Video 2 from the DSS/cable box, you cannot run on Video 2 and must move to Video 3 for source devices that use a composite type video cable.

Materials You Need: You need two composite cables long enough to reach comfortably from the VCR to the receiver/processor, and if necessary, to reach from the receiver/processor to the input on the video monitor.

1. Attach the male end of one of your composite cables to the VCR's composite female output. Make sure that the connection is slightly tight and that there is no excessive weight or pull on the wire.

2. Take the other male end of composite cable and move to the rear of the receiver/processor. You should have a wire length that rests easily between the receiver/processor and the VCR. Slide the single-pin composite connector onto the female jack labeled Video 2 (this input may be used by the PTVR), Video 3, or VCR on the back panel of the receiver/processor.

3. If there is no composite cable going to the video monitor yet, slide the other composite cable's male end into the composite video output RCA jack on the receiver/processor. This connection is often labeled Video Output or Monitor.

4. Hook up the last unattached cable end to the video monitor's back panel. Usually you should make this connection with the first available composite video input because this input is responsible for all the video for all the source devices connected to the receiver/processor. Just remember not to hook up the cable to an input bank that already has an S-video cable connected (such as the Video 1 input used by the DVD player).

Audio Connections

The audio connection for your VCR provides a maximum of two channels of sound into your home theater: the left and right channels. This is a standard stereo signal like the kind produced by your CD player.

NOTE Keep in mind that you are setting up the system with a stereo VCR. Stereo is standard for home theater VCRs. However, you can also purchase mono VCRs, which have only one channel of audio output. Such a VCR with a single channel of output is basically useless in a home theater because only a single speaker will be playing out of your whole system. Because a stereo VCR is roughly $50 more than a mono one, this is one component for which you should invest a few more dollars, and one that may be ripe for upgrading if you already have a mono VCR.

Although a stereo signal is generally played in the stereo mode on your receiver/processor, your VCR tapes will be played back in the Dolby Pro Logic mode to enhance the presentation with surround sound and a center channel. Your receiver and processor will take the two stereo signals from the two outputs on the VCR and create a Dolby Pro Logic soundtrack. In particular, movie tapes that you have purchased for your collection will benefit from this setup.

Materials You Need: To connect the audio from the VCR, you need only two RCA audio cables that reach from the VCR to the receiver/processor.

1. Take the white or black audio cable (it will be white or black striped or have a white or black colored RCA connector to designate the left channel) and go to the back panel of the VCR. You will find a pair of stereo outputs labeled Audio Out or Stereo Output.

2. After locating the outputs, plug the white or black labeled wire into the corresponding white or black center ringed left channel input. Repeat this step with a red RCA connector, hooking it up to the corresponding right channel red connector.

3. Take the unconnected left and right RCA cable ends and move to the back of the receiver/processor. On the back panel, find the input labeled Video 3, VCR Audio, or VCR Input. The input will have two colored RCA jacks of the same kind as those on the back of the VCR. Now connect the remaining two left and right stereo cables to the corresponding left and right inputs.

Now that you have connected your DSS receiver box or cable converter box, you can move on to the next source device that you have.

A Personal Television Recorder with a VCR Only

First, let's think of the PTVR as a substitute for the VCR in your home theater setup. You will now watch television through your PTVR, with the home theater providing the audio during programs. Suppose that you are a big fan of *Who Wants to Be a Millionaire?* With your PTVR, you can

watch the show in surround sound through your home theater speakers. Plus, when you record the program on the PTVR, you can watch it in surround sound through the home theater as well.

Start with the connection of the RF coaxial cable that comes from the wall. Connect this cable to the back panel of the PTVR in the input labeled Antenna In.

Connection Step 1: Video and Audio Connection from the PTVR to the Receiver/Processor

Now you must make a connection between the PTVR and the receiver/processor to allow you to watch your favorite programs through your home theater in surround sound.

Video Connection

You will first need to make the connection between the PTVR and the video monitor to watch the image. As always, it is critical that you pay special attention to the video switching principles we have discussed throughout installation.

A PTVR with S-Video Output, a Receiver/Processor with S-Video Input, and a Video Monitor with S-Video Input

How Do I Know I've Got It? Your PTVR will most likely have an S-video output on the back panel (see Figure 6.24). Your receiver/processor will also have a set of inputs labeled either Video 1, 2, 3, and so on, with S-video jacks, or have an input specifically labeled PTVR Input that will include an S-video connection.

Figure 6.24

The S-video connection on the back of the PTVR.

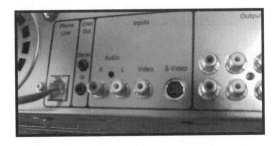

The receiver/processor also needs an S-video output in the form of a monitor output jack. This connection attaches to the video monitor so that the receiver can send the selected video source to the video monitor. If your receiver/processor has S-video inputs, you need at least one S-video output.

NOTE

Remember that your video monitor needs one open S-video connection to provide the S-video images routed through your receiver/processor. If you have chosen to connect your DVD player in this manner, it is important to check for another free S-video connector to receive the other S-video signal from the receiver/processor.

Materials You Need: You need an S-video cable for this connection (unless you have already attached an S-video cable to the back panel in the connection of your DVD player). The cable must be long enough to reach from the PTVR to the receiver/processor. You may also need a second S-video cable for connection from the receiver/processor to the video monitor.

1. Attach the male end of your S-video cable to the PTVR's S-video female output, which should be labeled S-Video Output or Video Output. Make sure to insert the cable correctly so that the pins in the connector line up exactly right. Do not force the connector, but slide it in only when you feel it fitting comfortably.

2. Take the male end of the S-video cable that you just attached to the PTVR S-video output and go to the back of the receiver/processor. You should have a wire length that is not taut, but that rests easily between the PTVR and the receiver/processor. Insert the S-video cable into the receiver/processor's S-video input labeled Video 2 (the DVD player, if connected, is Video 1; otherwise, if the Video 1 input is open, use it) or labeled PTVR. Lightly tug the cable to make sure that you have a firm connection.

3. If you have not connected an S-video cable from the receiver/processor for another source device, connect the other S-video cable's male end to the S-video output connection on the receiver/processor. This connection is often labeled S-Video Output or Monitor.

4. Hook up the remaining S-video connection to the video monitor's back panel. If you already have connected an S-video DVD player on a 2 S-video system, use S-video input number 2. If your video monitor has only one S-video input, you already have a connection from the DVD player. That's it.

A PTVR with Composite Output, a Receiver/Processor with Composite Input and Output, and a Video Monitor with Composite Input

You should use this setup only if your video monitor has only one S-video input that the DVD player is currently using, or if your video monitor does not have any S-video inputs. By connecting all your source devices into the receiver/processor first and then hooking up only the one composite cable to send video to the video monitor, you will have multiple inputs where there was only one.

How Do I Know I've Got It? Your PTVR will always have one or two composite video output jacks on the back panel in their customary yellow RCA connectors (see Figure 6.25). Your receiver/processor will also have a set or row of yellow composite inputs labeled either Video 1, 2, 3, and so on, or have an input specifically labeled PTVR.

Figure 6.25

The PTVR composite video output jacks.

The receiver/processor will also have a composite output connection in the form of a monitor output jack, called Monitor, that sends the picture to the video monitor. (Your video monitor should have at least one unused composite input connection labeled Video 1, 2, 3, and so on.)

NOTE

Remember that on the video monitor, you cannot be using any other video connection on the Video input group (like all of the inputs labeled Video 1) if it has both S-video and composite inputs. If an S-video cable is connected to Video 2, you cannot run a composite cable into Video 2 and must instead move to Video 3. If too many inputs are used up, it is best to consolidate your composite video devices and do your video switching through the receiver/processor.

Materials You Need: You need a composite cable long enough to reach comfortably from the PTVR to the receiver/processor. You may also need a second S-video cable for connection from the receiver/processor to the video monitor.

1. Attach the male end of one of your composite cables to the PTVR's composite female output. Make sure that the connection is slightly tight and that there is no excessive weight or pull on the wire.

2. Take the other male end of the composite video cable and move to the rear of the receiver/processor. You should have a wire length that rests easily between the receiver/processor and the PTVR. Slide the single-pin composite connector onto the female jack labeled Video 2 (if the DVD player is using Video 1) on the back panel of the receiver/processor.

3. If you have not done so for the DVD player, slide the other composite cable's male end into the composite video output RCA jack on the receiver/processor. This connection is often labeled Video Output or Monitor on the receiver/processor.

4. Hook up the last unattached cable end to the video monitor's back panel. Usually you should make this connection with the first available composite video input because this input is responsible for all the video for all the source devices connected to the receiver/processor. Just remember not to hook up this cable to an input bank (such as Video 1) that already has an S-video cable connected for the DVD player.

Audio Connection

The audio connection for your PTVR is a stereo signal like the kind produced by your CD player. This connection still enables your system to produce Dolby Pro Logic sound. Your receiver and processor take the two stereo signals from the two outputs on the PTVR and create a Dolby Pro Logic soundtrack.

Materials You Need: To connect the audio from the PTVR, you need only two RCA audio cables that can reach from the PTVR to the receiver/processor.

1. Take the white or black audio cable (the connector will be colored white or black, or the cable will have a white/black stripe to designate it as used for the left channel) and go to the back panel of the PTVR. You will find a pair of stereo outputs labeled Audio Out or Stereo Output. Plug the white or black wire into the corresponding input with a white or black center ring on the input. Repeat with the red connector.

2. Take the unconnected left and right RCA cable ends and move to the back of the receiver/processor. Find the input on the back that corresponds to the video cable that you connected earlier from the PTVR. If you connected the PTVR's video on the receiver/processor to the Video 2 input group, then remain consistent and use the white/black and red stereo input cables for Video 2, and so on. Now connect the remaining two left and right stereo cables to the

corresponding inputs. Make sure that the left and right cables are connected to their inputs; otherwise, you will have left sound coming out of the right side speaker, and right sound coming out of the left speaker.

Connection Step 2: Video and Audio Connection from the PTVR to the VCR

Now you must make a video and audio connection between the PTVR and a VCR to allow you to produce hard copies of the programs that you have recorded on your personal television recorder system.

Video Connection

The video connection can be broken down into two possibilities: S-video and composite.

A PTVR with Available S-Video Output and a VCR with Available S-Video Input
How Do I Know I've Got It? Check the back panel of your PTVR. If you identify an available S-video connector (you may have only one that is already being used by the connection to the receiver/processor), then check the back of the VCR. If this is an S-video VCR, you will have an available S-video input on the back panel.

Materials You Need: You need an S-video cable long enough to reach from the PTVR to the VCR. The cable should be not too tight to pull on the connectors, but not so long as to leave excess cable on the floor.

1. Connect one of the S-video male connector ends of the cable to the S-video output on the PTVR. This output will be labeled S-Video Output or be in the section labeled Output.

2. Connect the remaining S-video male connector to the S-video input on the VCR. This input will be labeled S-Video Input or be in the section on the back panel labeled Input.

Audio Connection

The audio connection to the VCR is a stereo signal. The PTVR sends the two stereo signals from its two outputs. When you play back through the receiver/processor, it will create a Dolby Pro Logic soundtrack.

Materials You Need: To connect the audio from the PTVR, you need only two RCA audio cables that can reach from the PTVR to the VCR.

1. Take the white or black audio cable and find a pair of stereo outputs labeled Audio Out or Stereo Output on the PTVR. It should have two sets in the Output section of connectors. Plug the white or black wire into the white connector and the red wire into the red connector.

2. Take the unconnected left and right RCA cable ends and move to the back of the VCR. Now connect the remaining two left and right stereo cables to the corresponding inputs. Make sure that the left and right cables are connected to their corresponding inputs.

Connection Step 3: Coaxial (RG-6) Cable from the PTVR to the Video Monitor

This connection provides your video monitor with a basic television signal so that you may run the PTVR system without the full home theater experience. This is best for just news or sitcom-type programs.

Materials You Need: To connect the PTVR, you need an RG-6 coaxial cable long enough to reach from the PTVR to the video monitor.

1. Locate the RG-6 coaxial cable connector on the PTVR labeled RF Out or Antenna Out. Now screw the coaxial connector onto the connector until it snugly fits around the connector and is screwed in all the way.

2. Go to the back of the video monitor and find a corresponding coaxial RG-6 cable connector. Screw the other end of the coaxial RG-6 cable from the PTVR into the video monitor's input.

Connection Step 4: Connection from the VCR to the Receiver/Processor

If you still want to play your videotape collection, or to watch anything that you have recorded from the PTVR to a VCR tape, you will also require a direct connection to the receiver/processor. This connection will allow you to play tapes in Dolby surround mode through your home theater.

Video Connections

Only two types of video connections are available on a VCR to provide video information into the receiver/processor: S-video and composite connections. This section discusses each in turn. Keep in mind our earlier discussion on video switching and its critical role in the setup process.

A VCR with S-Video Output and a Receiver/Processor with S-Video Input

With this particular setup, you can get an S-video connection into the receiver/processor for the optimal VCR video connection. If you have only one S-video connection on the video monitor, or are using the first S-video input for a DVD player and the second S-video connection for all your S-video sources routed through the receiver/processor, this is the best connection for your VCR.

NOTE   Even though you may be able to switch between S-video sources using your receiver or processor, you still need to switch the video monitor's input manually with the remote control (by pressing "TV/Video" or "Input") when you are jumping from an S-video source to a composite video source. This will activate the composite input on the video monitor instead of the S-video input. The only way to do video switching entirely through your receiver or processor is with outputs that are *all* S-video, *all* composite video, or *all* component video.

How Do I Know I've Got It? Your VCR will have an S-video output only if it is equipped as an S-VHS VCR. This output will be plainly identified on the front panel. In addition, the VCR will have an S-video output on the back panel. Your receiver/processor will also have a set of inputs labeled Video 1, 2, 3, and so on, with S-video jacks, or have an input specifically labeled VCR Input that will include an S-video connection.

The receiver/processor needs an S-video output in the form of a monitor output jack. You should already have a connection from the receiver/processor to the video monitor from your installation of the PTVR. This connection should be S-video and be attached to the S-Video 2 connection, if you have the DVD player attached to S-Video 1.

Materials You Need: For this connection, you need one S-video cable long enough to reach from the VCR to the receiver/processor. It is wise to purchase premium cables for this connection, especially if you have a long run of cable (longer than 12 feet) to get from the receiver/processor to the video monitor, which can be located away from the equipment stack.

1. Attach the male end of your S-video cable to the VCR's S-video female output, which should be labeled S-Video Output or Video Output. Make sure to insert the cable correctly so that the pins in the connector line up exactly right. Do not force the connector, but slide it in only when you feel it fitting comfortably.

2. Take the male end of the S-video cable that you just attached to the VCR S-video output and go to the back of the receiver/processor. You should have a wire length that is not taut, but that rests easily between the receiver/processor and the VCR. Insert the S-video cable into the receiver/processor's S-video input labeled Video 2 (the DVD player should be Video 1) or VCR. Tug the cable lightly to make sure that you have a firm connection.

A VCR with Composite Output and a Receiver/Processor with Composite Input
If your VCR has only composite video, you must make a composite video connection to the receiver/processor. If you also connected the PTVR

with an S-video connection, you also need to connect a single composite cable to the video monitor from the receiver/processor to transmit video.

How Do I Know I've Got It? All VCRs have one or two composite video output jacks on the back panel in their customary yellow RCA connectors. Your receiver/processor will probably also have a set or row of yellow composite inputs labeled Video 1, 2, 3, and so on, or have an input specifically labeled VCR.

The receiver/processor will also have a composite output connection in the form of a monitor output jack, labeled Monitor, that sends the picture to the video monitor. Finally, you need to make sure that the video monitor has an open composite connection that does not already have a composite cable plugged in. The video input group (on the back of the video monitor, labeled Video 1, Video 2, and so on) that you use cannot have any other video connection. If an S-video cable is connected to Video 2, you cannot run on Video 2 and must move to Video 3.

Materials You Need: You need two composite cables long enough to reach comfortably from the VCR to the receiver/processor, and to reach from the receiver/processor to the input on the video monitor.

1. Attach the male end of one of your composite cables to the VCR's composite female output. Make sure that the connection is slightly tight and that there is no excessive weight or pull on the wire.

2. Take the other male end of composite cable and move to the rear of the receiver/processor. You should have a wire length that rests easily between the receiver/processor and the VCR. Slide the single-pin composite connector onto the female jack labeled Video 2 (which may be used by the PTVR), Video 3, or VCR on the back panel of the receiver/processor.

3. Slide the other composite cable's male end into the composite video output RCA jack on the receiver/processor. This connection is often labeled Video Output or Monitor.

4. Hook up the last unattached cable end to the video monitor's back panel. Usually you should make this connection with the first available composite video input because this input is responsible for all the video for all the source devices connected to the receiver/processor. Just remember not to hook up the cable to an input bank that already has an S-video cable connected (such as Video 1, which the DVD player is using).

Audio Connections

The audio connection for your VCR is relatively simple because only one type of sound information is available from the source device. Videotapes can deliver a maximum of only two channels of sound into your home theater: the left and right channels. This is a standard stereo signal like the kind produced by your CD player.

NOTE Keep in mind that you are setting up the system with a stereo VCR. Stereo is a standard feature for home theater VCRs. However, you can also purchase mono VCRs that have only one channel of video output. Such a VCR with a single channel of output is basically useless in a home theater because only a single speaker will be playing out of your whole system. A stereo VCR is roughly $50 more than a mono one, so this is one component for which you should invest a few more dollars, and one that may be ripe for upgrading if you already have a mono VCR.

Although your receiver/processor generally plays a stereo signal in the stereo mode, your VCR tapes will be played back in the Dolby Pro Logic mode to enhance the presentation with surround sound and a center channel. Your receiver and processor will take the two stereo signals from the two outputs on the VCR and create a Dolby Pro Logic soundtrack. In particular, movie tapes that you have purchased for your collection will benefit from this setup.

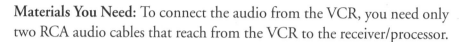

Materials You Need: To connect the audio from the VCR, you need only two RCA audio cables that reach from the VCR to the receiver/processor.

1. Take the white or black audio cable (it will be striped white or black or the RCA connector will be colored white or black to designate the left channel) and go to the back panel of the VCR. You will find a pair of stereo outputs labeled Audio Out or Stereo Output.

   After locating the outputs, plug the white or black wire/RCA connectors into the corresponding white/black center ringed input. Repeat this step with a red RCA connector, hooking it up to the corresponding red connector on the back panel.

2. Take the unconnected left and right RCA cable ends and move to the back of the receiver/processor. Find the input on the back labeled Video 3, VCR Audio, or VCR Input. The input will have two colored RCA jacks of the same kind as those on the back of the VCR.

   Now connect the remaining two left and right stereo cables to the corresponding inputs. Make sure that the left and right cables are connected to their inputs; otherwise, you will have left sound coming out of the right side speaker and right sound coming out of the left speaker, producing a very unnatural home theater presentation.

A VCR Only

If you do not have a DSS system, a cable box, or a PTVR, you must still connect your VCR to provide audio and video into your home theater system. This section examines the setup connections in three parts: the cable television connection, the video connection, and the audio connection.

Coaxial Television Connection

You most likely are quite familiar with this aspect of a VCR's connection because you probably have this feature connected in your home right now. The coaxial RG-6 cable brings in television signals from your cable

provider so that you can get broadcast television. It allows you to select channels, and to accept the input from a cable decoder box for pay-TV channels and pay-per-view.

NOTE Don't confuse this type of coaxial cable with the digital cable with RCA connectors used for digital signal transfer on DVD players, CD players, and other digital sources.

It is important that you put the VCR and cable television into perspective in regard to the home theater system. The VCR is now going to provide all your television signals and send their video and audio to the home theater system.

However, you will also leave a cable connection directly to the video monitor so that you can continue to watch television without the entire system active. You will find that programs such as the news and sitcoms do not require the full home theater experience and, in fact, would be audio overkill.

Materials You Need: To connect your television to your cable provider's signals, you need an existing coaxial cable line coming out of the wall in the home theater room. If this cable does not stretch to the VCR location, you need to purchase a female-to-female coaxial cable connector and an additional length of coaxial cable to reach the VCR. As always, try to keep the cable lengths to a minimum to avoid excessive signal loss and tangling with other cables in the equipment stack.

Also, you need a second coaxial cable long enough to reach directly to the video monitor from the VCR for watching television without the home theater active.

1. Take the coaxial cable's male end, which is sticking out of the outlet or hole in the wall in the home theater room. If you had to add cable at the end coming out of the wall to reach the VCR, take the male end of the extended cable. On the input labeled Antenna In or Coaxial In on the VCR, screw the coaxial cable (be careful

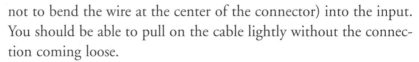

not to bend the wire at the center of the connector) into the input. You should be able to pull on the cable lightly without the connection coming loose.

2. Screw the other coaxial cable into the VCR input labeled Antenna Out or Coaxial Out. As before, the connection should be tight enough that the cable cannot come loose. Give it a light tug to make sure.

3. Take the male end of the coaxial cable connected to the VCR and go to the back panel of the video monitor. Then connect the male coaxial end to the input labeled Coaxial In or Antenna In. This connection will allow you to watch television with the audio coming only from the internal video monitor's speakers. *Friends* in surround sound is a little excessive.

Now that you have connected the cable television, you can move on to the video and audio connections.

Video Connections

Only two types of video connections are available on a VCR to provide video information into the home theater: S-video and composite connections. This section discusses each in turn. Keep in mind the earlier discussion on video switching and its critical role in the setup process.

A VCR with S-Video Output and a Video Monitor with S-Video Input

Currently, S-VHS VCRs represent the optimal video resolution for this source device because it can output through an S-video cable. Therefore, as you have generally attempted to retain the highest level of video quality in your installation, the best connection for your system with an S-VHS VCR is direct connection to the video monitor through an S-video cable.

However, you must also have an open S-video connection that the DVD player is not currently using. If your video monitor only has one S-video input that the DVD player is using, you must skip this section and proceed to connect using a composite video connection.

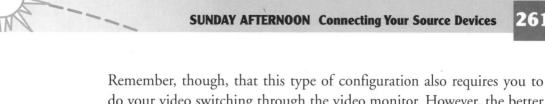

Remember, though, that this type of configuration also requires you to do your video switching through the video monitor. However, the better performance from the S-video connection is more significant than the required extra button to press on your video monitor's remote. And even then, with a little extra investment in your home theater, you can purchase a universal remote that will instantly handle this switch.

How Do I Know I've Got It? An S-video connection is the small recessed hookup on the back panel of the VCR and on your video monitor. The wire part of the connection has four small pins and a plastic rectangular guide. The input side of the connection has four small pinholes and a rectangular hole for the plastic guide.

Your video monitor will most likely have an S-video input on its back panel, especially if you have purchased your video monitor in the past three to four years. S-video connections have become almost a standard for video monitors. Usually these inputs are part of the connection terminals labeled Video 1 or S-Video. (Your video monitor probably will also have a composite video connection and a set of left and right audio connections.)

Materials You Need: You need one S-video cable long enough to reach from the VCR to the video monitor.

1. Take your S-video cable and carefully align the pins properly in their holes. Slide the S-video connector into the jack labeled S-Video Out on the VCR.

2. Move to the back of the video monitor. Your wire length run should be loose, not so tight that there is pressure on the wire. Most monitors have only one or two S-video inputs. As a result, if you already have a DVD player connected to a single S-video input (which should get a higher priority for video performance), you may be out of inputs. If this is the case, you must skip to the next type of installation option for the VCR, below.

A VCR with S-Video Output, a Receiver/Processor with S-Video Inputs and Outputs, and a Video Monitor with S-Video Input

If you have only one S-video connection and one S-video DVD connection, and prefer the convenience of video switching through the receiver/processor, this is the best connection for your VCR.

How Do I Know I've Got It? Your VCR will have an S-video output only if it is equipped as an S-VHS VCR. This will be plainly identified on the front panel. In addition, the VCR will have an S-video output on the back panel. Your receiver/processor will also have a set of inputs labeled either Video 1, 2, 3, and so on, with S-video jacks, or have an input specifically labeled VCR Input that will include an S-video connection.

The receiver/processor also needs an S-video output in the form of a monitor output jack. This connection attaches to the video monitor so that the receiver can send the selected video source to the video monitor. If your receiver/processor has S-video inputs, you need at least one S-video output.

Finally, your video monitor needs at least one S-video input connection on the back panel.

Materials You Need: You need two S-video cables for this connection (unless you have already attached an S-video cable to the back panel for the DVD player because you are video switching through the receiver/ processor). The cables need to be long enough to reach from the VCR to the receiver/processor, and then to the S-video input on the video monitor. It is wise to purchase premium cables for this connection, especially if you have a long run of cable (longer than 12 feet) to get from the receiver/processor to the video monitor, which can be located away from the equipment stack.

1. Attach the male end of your S-video cable to the VCR's S-video female output, which should be labeled S-Video Output or Video Output. Make sure to insert the cable correctly so that the pins in the connector line up exactly right. Do not force the connector, but slide it in only when you feel it fitting comfortably.

2. Take the male end of the S-video cable that you just attached to the VCR S-video output and go to the back of the receiver/processor. You should have a wire length that is not taut, but that rests easily between the receiver/processor and the VCR. Insert the S-video cable into the receiver/processor's S-video input labeled Video 2 or Video 3 (the DVD player is Video 1, then you can assign your components to inputs by your viewing priority) or labeled VCR. Lightly tug on the cable to make sure that you have a firm connection.

3. If you have not connected an S-video cable from the receiver/processor for another source device, connect the other S-video cable's male end to the S-video output connection on the receiver/processor. This connection is often labeled S-Video Output or Monitor on the receiver/processor.

4. Hook up the remaining S-video connection to the video monitor's back panel. If you already have connected an S-video DVD player on a 2 S-video system, use S-Video Input #2. If you only have one S-video input on the video monitor, you already have a connection there from the DVD player. That's it.

A VCR with Composite Output and a Video Monitor with Composite Input

For VCR outputs, this connection is without a doubt the standard. Every VCR comes with at least one composite video output. However, the picture quality is far from excellent, especially if you get accustomed to the razor-sharp images of DVD.

We'll do our best to maximize the video output of your VCR, and the first step is to identify that the best composite connection is direct from the VCR to one composite video input on the video monitor. As discussed earlier, this setup method forces you to perform video switching with the video monitor's remote control.

NOTE

● ●
If there is only one composite connector on the back of your video monitor, and it is connected to the DVD player through either S-video or composite video, you are in trouble. You must now disconnect the DVD player and reconnect it using composite video switched through the receiver/processor. Otherwise, you will not be able to run an input for your VCR through the home theater.
● ●

How Do I Know I've Got It? Without fail, your VCR's back panel will have a composite terminal. It is a single RCA output jack with a yellow center. Sometimes a VCR player will have two composite terminals, labeled #1 and #2.

Your video monitor will also have at least one composite video input (and often many more) labeled Video 1, 2, 3, and so on.

Materials You Need: You need one composite video cable long enough to reach from the VCR to the video monitor.

1. Take your composite cable and insert the male RCA connector into the female RCA jack colored yellow and labeled Video on the VCR.

2. Attach the composite video cable's RCA connector to the video monitor's input jack labeled Video 2. You cannot plug this cable into a group of inputs if an S-video cable is already present. In other words, you want to plug the VCR's composite cable into the Video 1 input, but you cannot if there is already an S-video cable from the DVD plugged into the S-video input Video 1. Move to Video 2.

   As is our common practice, make sure that the connection is firm and will not come undone with a light tug.

A VCR with Composite Output, a Receiver/Processor with Composite Outputs and Inputs, and a Video Monitor with Composite Input

If your VCR has only composite video and you must share the composite video inputs on the video monitor with other devices, you use this connection. By connecting all your source devices to the receiver/

pre-amplifier and then hooking up only the one wire to send video to the video monitor, you now have multiple inputs where there was only one. Unfortunately, this connection represents an interrupted signal path and the lowest performance video cable available.

How Do I Know I've Got It? All VCRs have one or two composite video output jacks on the back panel in their customary yellow RCA connectors. Your receiver/processor will probably also have a set or row of yellow composite inputs labeled either Video 1, 2, 3, and so on, or have an input specifically labeled VCR.

The receiver/processor will also have a composite output connection in the form of a monitor output jack, called Monitor, that sends the picture to the video monitor.

Finally, your video monitor should have at least one unused composite input connection called Video 1, 2, 3, and so on.

Remember that there cannot be any other video connection on the Video input group that you use on the back of the video monitor. If the DVD player's video cable is already connected to Video 1 through S-video, you cannot run the VCR's composite signal on Video 1 and must move to Video 2.

Materials You Need: You need two composite cables long enough to reach comfortably from the VCR to the receiver/processor, and to reach from the receiver/processor to the input on the video monitor.

1. Attach the male end of one of your composite cables to the VCR's composite female output, colored yellow and labeled Video Out. Make sure that the connection is slightly tight and that there is no excessive weight or pull on the wire.

2. Take the other male end of composite cable and move to the rear of the receiver/processor. You should have a wire length that rests easily between the receiver/processor and the VCR. Slide the single-pin composite connector onto the female jack labeled Video 2 or simply VCR on the back panel of the receiver/processor.

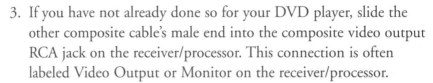

3. If you have not already done so for your DVD player, slide the other composite cable's male end into the composite video output RCA jack on the receiver/processor. This connection is often labeled Video Output or Monitor on the receiver/processor.

4. Hook up the last unattached cable end to the video monitor's back panel. Usually you should make this connection with the first available composite video input because this input is responsible for all the video for all the source devices connected to the receiver/processor. Just remember not to hook up the cable to an input bank that already has a cable connected (such as Video 1 if it is being used by the DVD player's S-video or composite connection).

Audio Connections

The audio connection for your VCR is relatively simple because only one type of sound information is available from the source device. Videotapes can deliver a maximum of only two channels of sound into your home theater: the left and right channels. This is a standard stereo signal like the kind produced by your CD player.

NOTE Keep in mind that you are setting up the system with a stereo VCR. Stereo is a standard feature for home theater VCRs. However, you can also purchase mono VCRs that have only one channel of video output. Such a VCR with a single channel of output is basically useless in a home theater because only a single speaker will be playing out of your whole system. Because a stereo VCR is roughly $50 more than a mono one, this is one component for which you should invest a few more dollars, and one that may be ripe for upgrading if you already have a mono VCR.

Although a stereo signal is generally played in the stereo mode on your receiver/processor, your system will play back your VCR tapes in the Dolby Pro Logic mode to enhance the presentation with surround sound and a center channel. Your receiver and processor will take the two stereo signals from the two outputs on the VCR and create a Dolby Pro Logic soundtrack. In particular, movie tapes you have purchased for your collection will benefit from this setup.

Materials You Need: To connect the audio from the VCR, you need only two RCA audio cables that reach from the VCR to the receiver/processor.

1. Take the white or black audio cable (it has a white or black stripe on the cable or a white or black RCA connector that designates it as the left channel cable) and go to the back panel of the VCR. You will find a pair of stereo outputs labeled Audio Out or Stereo Output.

   After locating the outputs, plug the white or black wire with the white/black cable label or white/black RCA connectors into the corresponding white or black input on the VCR. Repeat this step with a red RCA connector, hooking it up to the corresponding red output connector on the VCR.

2. Take the unconnected left and right RCA cable ends and move to the back of the receiver/processor. Find the input on the back of the receiver/processor labeled Video 3, VCR Audio, or VCR Input. It will have two colored RCA jacks of the same kind as those on the back of the VCR.

3. Now connect the remaining two left and right stereo cables to the corresponding inputs. Make sure that the left and right cables are connected to their inputs; otherwise, you will have left sound coming out of the right side speaker and right sound coming out of the left speaker for a very unnatural home theater presentation.

Now that you have connected your VCR, you can move on to your audio source devices.

Connecting Your CD Player

Over the past several years, our attitude toward the compact disc has radically changed. No longer are CDs the mysterious digital technology that was so radically different from tape or vinyl records. Instead, the compact disc has grown to become the media of choice to deliver audio content.

Compact discs may be one of the reasons that you are reading this book. You got hooked by those little shiny CDs (after buying your record collection *again*), which sparked an interest in the world of audio reproduction and sound so good that you'd swear you were there, and holds you entranced by its majesty. It was an easy step from enjoying digital music to desiring the sights *and* sounds of home theater.

So, even though you are building a home theater, you will definitely want to install a CD player for when you just want to listen to music.

Luckily, for your CD player setup task, just about every type of CD player on the market today has the same connections, whether the component is a single-disc unit, a five- or six-disc changer, or a 100- to 300-disc megachanger. In addition, unlike most of your other components, your CD player does not require a video connection. Let's dive in and hook up this component.

Audio Connections

Like all digital devices, your CD player has two methods for providing its audio information to your receiver/processor. The first is the method to which you have been accustomed for a long time: analog. This method uses a stereo pair of RCA interconnect cables to transfer an analog signal. The only disadvantage of this system is that you are relying on the internal digital-to-analog (D/A) converter inside the CD player to change the data in the digital 1s and 0s into analog signals. Some higher-priced CD players can do this exceptionally well, but most compact disc units have cheap D/A converters in them that just don't cut it sonically.

Therefore, on an inexpensive to medium-priced CD player ($100–$600), you can get around the D/A converter inside the player by outputting the digital information directly into the receiver/processor. You will obtain better performance using the D/A converter inside the receiver/processor rather than the one in the CD player. Of course, this is provided you have such an input on your receiver/processor.

We discussed this option in your research on Friday night, and we hope that you have chosen a receiver/processor that includes several digital inputs to accept all your digital sources, including your CD player for a direct digital connection.

NOTE Remember that the order of these setup sections has been designed by priority of components. If, for example, you have only two digital inputs and both are being used by your DVD player and a TiVo system, you will not have an open digital connection. Therefore, you will proceed to make an analog connection because it is more critical to have the digital connections devoted to the components that you have already connected.

Digital Connections

The two types of digital audio cables are coaxial digital and optical digital cables. This section discusses both setup options so that you can determine which is best for your system.

A CD Player with Coaxial Digital Output and a Receiver/Processor with Available Coaxial Digital Input

Digital coaxial cable looks like a regular audio interconnect cable because it has male RCA connectors at both ends. However, you should purchase a cable that is specifically tailored to pass digital information for the purpose of digital coaxial connections.

How Do I Know I've Got It? Check the back of your CD player. If there is an RCA connector that has an orange color in the center of the RCA connector, and is labeled either Digital Audio Output, Bitstream Out, or Coaxial Digital Out, your CD player is capable of the direct connection to the receiver/processor (see Figure 6.26).

On your receiver/processor, you will find an input section devoted to one or more of the following:

✿ Digital inputs and outputs all clustered together

Figure 6.26

The back panel of a CD player with a coaxial digital input in its unique orange coloring.

○ A CD player input section with a stereo analog RCA connection pair and perhaps a digital input (with coaxial or optical connectors, or both)

○ Inputs labeled Audio 1, 2, 3, and so on, each with a stereo analog RCA connection pair and perhaps a digital input (with coaxial or optical connectors, or both)

Among one of these input sections, you should find an open orange coaxial digital cable input.

Materials You Need: This connection requires one coaxial digital cable long enough to connect to the back of the receiver/processor without being too tight.

1. Push one male end of the coaxial digital cable onto the orange RCA connector on the back panel labeled Audio Output or Digital Output on the CD player.

2. Connect the other male end of the coaxial digital cable to the RCA connector on the back of the receiver or processor. If inputs are labeled numerically, use the input with the lowest number available, but if there is one specifically labeled CD Player or there is a section of inputs for CD players, use one of those. Slide the cable's male RCA connector onto the receiver/processor's input.

That's all it takes.

A DVD Player with Toslink/Optical Digital Output and a Receiver/Processor with Toslink/Optical Digital Inputs

The other digital cable that you can use is the Toslink/optical cable (remember that Toslink and optical cable are the same, with different names). (Refer to Figure 6.26.) Remember to keep your runs of optical cable to a minimum because the signal method that it uses (light pulsation) tends to cause digital jitter over long runs. Therefore, it is inadvisable to use lengths over 6 feet.

How Do I Know I've Got It? The optical connection is actually more popular for CD players than digital coaxial cable connections. So, take a look at your CD player's back panel. If you see a small, square Toslink/optical connection or the protective insert that has a small handle that you can remove to allow access to the Toslink/optical connection, you can provide a digital signal from the CD player to the receiver/processor.

On your receiver/processor, you should find an input group corresponding to one of the following:

- Digital inputs and outputs all clustered together
- A CD player input section with a stereo analog RCA connection pair and perhaps a digital input (with coaxial or optical connections, or both)
- Inputs labeled Audio 1, 2, 3, and so on, each with a stereo analog RCA connection pair and perhaps a digital input (with coaxial or optical connections, or both)

Among one of these input sections, you should find an open Toslink/optical cable female connector.

Materials You Need: You need one Toslink/optical digital cable long enough to reach from the CD player to the back of the receiver or processor and connect them. When you measure this wire for purchase, make sure that it is just the right length to reach, but not too tight to pull on the Toslink/optical connection, which is somewhat flimsy. Accidentally pulling this connection or resting it too tightly in its connector can lead to wire or equipment damage.

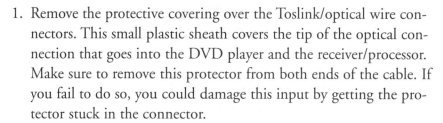

1. Remove the protective covering over the Toslink/optical wire connectors. This small plastic sheath covers the tip of the optical connection that goes into the DVD player and the receiver/processor. Make sure to remove this protector from both ends of the cable. If you fail to do so, you could damage this input by getting the protector stuck in the connector.

2. Take one male end of the Toslink/optical cable and find the corresponding output on the back of the CD player. Connect the Toslink/optical connector to the CD player until it locks into the output with a small click. The cable fits only one way because there are two angled sides to the connector that must fit into the output in the right configuration.

3. Take the other male end of the Toslink/optical cable and find the input on the receiver/processor. This input is usually labeled as CD Player Digital Audio Input, Optical 1, Toslink/Optical Input, or something similar. Connect the Toslink/optical connector to the receiver/processor so that it locks into the output with a small click, just as with your first connection.

Analog Connections

If you do not have the option of connecting the CD player digitally, you must use an analog connection.

A CD Player with Two RCA Stereo Analog Outputs and a Receiver/Processor with Two RCA Stereo Analog Inputs

This is the default connection method for most CD players. The connection outputs a stereo signal in the analog domain (using the CD player's D/A converter) through two cables carrying left speaker information and right speaker information.

How Do I Know I've Got It? All CD players have two outputs for stereo operation, labeled Left and Right and colored customarily white (left) and red (right). All receivers/processors have at least one RCA connector stereo pair of audio inputs, also labeled Left and Right and usually in a section labeled Audio 1, 2, 3, and so on.

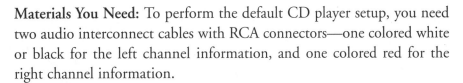

Materials You Need: To perform the default CD player setup, you need two audio interconnect cables with RCA connectors—one colored white or black for the left channel information, and one colored red for the right channel information.

1. Attach each of the two RCA connectors to the two connectors on the CD player labeled Mixed Out, Stereo Out, Analog Out, or 2-Channel Output. The white or black RCA connector on the cable should slide on the white or black output RCA connector on the CD player. Remember to check that the connectors are on snugly and that they are not too tight.

2. You now have two audio cables coming out of the CD player's back panel—one for left speaker information, the other for right speaker information. You must now hook up the two cables to the corresponding inputs on the receiver/processor. Connect the RCA audio connectors to the RCA inputs labeled Audio 1, 2, 3, and so on, selecting the lowest numbered input that isn't already being used. If there is a section on the receiver/processor labeled CD Player with two analog RCA inputs, attach the connectors there. Make sure that from the CD player to the receiver/processor, Left matches Left, and Right matches Right. Plus, make sure that the RCA connectors are snugly attached.

Now you've laid the groundwork for your music listening, so let's move on to the next source device.

Connecting Your CD Recorder/Minidisc Player

One of the most important aspects of home theater that is just now coming to the spotlight is the ability to make digital recordings of your digital source media. Many of you are familiar with the classic cassette tape deck, which could make analog copies of your CDs, LPs, and other tapes. However, over the past five years, digital reproduction technology has filtered down to the consumer market and now you have the ability to make exact copies of your CDs.

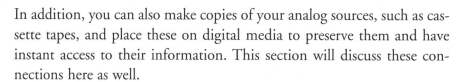

In addition, you can also make copies of your analog sources, such as cassette tapes, and place these on digital media to preserve them and have instant access to their information. This section will discuss these connections here as well.

The two devices that allow you to do this are the minidisc player/recorder and the CD recorder. You have already learned about both these units in your research on Friday night, so let's begin the setup, which is identical for both pieces of equipment.

NOTE   Some new CD and minidisc recorders have both a single (and in some components, three) compact disc player *plus* the CD or minidisc recorder in the same component. Treat this type of a unit as a standard CD recorder or minidisc recorder even though most recording occurs within the unit and only playback is routed to the receiver/processor.

Input Through a Digital or Analog Connection

To get the digital signal that you are going to record from the CD player or other digital source, you must make a digital connection directly from the source to the CD or minidisc recorder or route it through your receiver/processor.

The key to this digital connection is to analyze your source outputs. Most CD players have only one digital output on the back panel. Because it is vastly more important to have the CD player play through a digital connection, you should reserve this connection for hookup to your receiver/processor. Therefore, you will need to route the signal from the source device to the receiver/processor, and then to the digital recorder.

If you happen to have dual digital outputs on your CD player, you can use one output for the receiver/processor for playback, and the second can go directly to the CD or minidisc recorder.

It is also important to note that in addition to making a digital connection, you may also want to connect a set of analog RCA cables so that you can record from your analog sources, such as your tuner.

This section considers all these potential setup options.

A CD Player with Dual Digital Coaxial Outputs and a CD or Minidisc Recorder with Digital Coaxial Input

Start with a single coaxial digital cable going to the recorder from the CD player.

How Do I Know I've Got It? First, check the back of your CD player for digital outputs. If you have a single RCA connection (often colored orange) labeled Digital Audio Output, Bitstream Out, or Coaxial Digital Out, your CD player is properly equipped with this type of connection. Next, examine your CD or minidisc player for the same type of connection on the back panel. If you locate a single RCA connector labeled Digital Audio In, Bitstream In, or Coaxial Digital In, you are in business.

Materials You Need: You need one coaxial digital cable long enough to connect comfortably from the back of the CD player to the CD or minidisc recorder.

1. Slide the male end of the coaxial digital cable onto the back panel's RCA connector labeled Audio Output or Digital Output on the CD player.

2. Hook up the other male end of the coaxial digital cable to the RCA digital coaxial connector on the back of the CD or minidisc recorder. The connector will be labeled Digital Input or Coaxial Digital Input.

Now proceed to the next section to add analog connections to the CD or minidisc recorder to record other sources that have only analog connections.

A CD Player with Dual Toslink/Optical Digital Outputs and a CD or Minidisc Recorder with Toslink/Optical Digital Input

It is much more likely that your CD player will have two Toslink/optical connectors on the back panel than dual coaxial connectors. This is also the general rule for the CD or minidisc recorder, which will most likely have a single Toslink/optical input.

How Do I Know I've Got It? First, take a look at your CD player. If it has two small, square Toslink/optical connections or the protective optical connector insert (which has a small handle that you can remove to allow access to the Toslink/optical connection), your CD player is equipped properly. Second, check your CD or minidisc recorder's back panel. You will need a matching Toslink/optical connection (or the protector covering it) for reception of the digital signal that you are going to record.

Materials You Need: You need a single Toslink/optical digital cable to reach from the CD player to the back of the CD or minidisc recorder. Make sure that the cable is just the right length to reach, but not so tight that it places stress on the Toslink/optical connection or cable.

1. Remove the protective covering over the Toslink/optical wire connectors on both sides of the wire. This small plastic sheath covers the tip of the optical connection where it goes into the CD player and into the CD or minidisc recorder. If you fail to remove this covering, you could damage the inputs by getting the protector stuck in the connector.

2. Take one male end of the Toslink/optical cable and find the Toslink/optical output on the back of the CD player. Make sure that you have also removed the Toslink/optical protector from the back panel. Connect the Toslink/optical connector into the CD or minidisc recorder until it locks into the output with a small click. The Toslink/optical connector has two angled sides that must fit into the output in the right configuration.

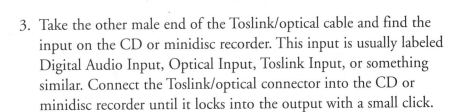

3. Take the other male end of the Toslink/optical cable and find the input on the CD or minidisc recorder. This input is usually labeled Digital Audio Input, Optical Input, Toslink Input, or something similar. Connect the Toslink/optical connector into the CD or minidisc recorder until it locks into the output with a small click.

Now proceed to the next section to add analog connections to the CD or minidisc recorder to record other sources that have only analog connections.

A CD Player with Single Digital Output, a Receiver/Processor with Digital Input and Output, and a CD or Minidisc Recorder with Digital Input

This connection method is used for a CD player with only one digital output (of either the digital interconnect type or Toslink/optical type). Because you need to send the single digital signal to both the receiver/processor for playback and the CD or minidisc recorder for recording, you must route the signal through the receiver/processor.

NOTE Your ability to connect in this manner and make digital recordings is entirely based on whether your receiver/processor has a digital output.

How Do I Know I've Got It? First, take a look at your CD player. If you see either a digital RCA Interconnect connector (often colored orange) or a square Toslink/optical input connector (remember that the protective Toslink/optical insert may still be on), probably labeled Digital Output, Coaxial Output, or Optical Output, then your CD player has the digital output necessary.

Next, look at the back panel of your receiver/processor. First, check for a digital output of either the digital RCA interconnect type or the Toslink/optical type. This connector will be labeled Digital Out, Digital Record Out, Optical Out, or Coaxial Out. If you have a single RCA connector (which is probably orange), your receiver/processor has a digital

RCA interconnect output. If you have the square input of a Toslink/optical connector, you are also ready to output a digital signal to the CD or minidisc recorder.

NOTE If your receiver/processor does not have a digital output of either type and your CD player has only one digital output of either type, you cannot properly connect with a digital cable to record. Your only solutions are to switch the output of the CD player directly into the CD or minidisc recorder every time you want to record, or make only analog recordings through the analog connections that you will make in a few minutes.

You must also have an open digital input for playback of whatever type of input the CD player has. If the CD player has a digital RCA interconnect output, with a single open RCA output (possibly colored orange), you need an open digital RCA interconnect output on the receiver/processor. If you have a Toslink/optical output on your CD player, you need a corresponding Toslink/optical input on the receiver/processor. You must have either the square Toslink/optical input or the protective Toslink/optical input on the receiver/processor.

Finally, check your CD or minidisc recorder's back panel. You will need a digital RCA interconnect connector or Toslink/optical connector (or the protector covering it) for reception of the digital signal that you are going to record. This connector will be labeled Digital Input, Coaxial Input, Toslink Input, or Optical Input.

Materials You Need: You need two digital cables that correspond to the outputs of your CD player and CD or minidisc recorder. You may need one digital RCA interconnect and one Toslink/optical input if there are different connections between the CD player to the receiver/processor and the receiver/processor to the CD or minidisc recorder. Make sure that the cable you get is long enough that it is not too tight and pulling on the connectors.

Start with the connection between the CD player and the receiver/processor.

NOTE By now, if you have a CD player with a single digital output, you will have made the digital connection to the receiver/processor.

1. The necessary connector will be labeled Digital Out, Optical Out, or Digital Coaxial Out. If you have a digital RCA interconnect connection between the CD player and the receiver/processor, first hook up the male RCA connector to the back panel of the CD player. If you have a Toslink/optical connection, remove the plastic sheath from the wire connector and remove the input protector. Then connect one end of the Toslink/optical cable to the CD player.

2. Attach to the receiver/processor whichever cable you have connected to the CD player. You will see an input section devoted to one or more of the following:

   ❂ Digital inputs and outputs all clustered together

   ❂ CD player inputs, with all the inputs needed to connect a CD player, clustered together

   ❂ Inputs labeled Audio 1, 2, 3, and so on, with all kinds of inputs for a variety of audio sources, including CD players

   Connect the cable to whichever input group corresponds to the CD player; if there is no labeled CD input, connect the cable to the available digital connector with the lowest number. You are ready for playback.

3. Now you must connect the digital cable that will transfer the digital signal from the receiver/processor to the CD or minidisc recorder. On the back panel of the receiver/processor you will locate the output labeled Digital Out, Coaxial Out, Toslink Out, or Optical Out. If you have a digital RCA interconnect connector, slide the RCA connector over the RCA digital interconnect connector to make a tight fit that does not move with a slight tug. If you have a Toslink/optical connector on the back of the receiver/processor,

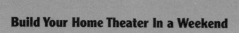
make sure to remove both the protective sheath and the plastic input protector. Now insert the cable's connector into the small, square input (with the square side facing up and the two notched corners facing down).

4. Now you must connect the digital cable that will transfer the digital signal from the receiver/processor to the digital recording device. Take the remaining end of the cable you just installed and attach it to the input on the CD or minidisc recorder. This input will be labeled Digital In, Coaxial In, Optical In, or Toslink In. If you have a male digital RCA interconnect connector, slide it over the CD or minidisc recorder's connector to make a solid, stable fit. If you have a Toslink/optical connector on the back of the CD or minidisc recorder, remove the protective sheath and the plastic input protector now. Insert the cable's connector into the small, square input (with the totally square side facing up and the two notched corners facing downward).

Now proceed to the next section to add analog connections to the CD or minidisc recorder to record other sources that have only analog connections.

A Receiver/Processor with RCA Stereo Analog Input and Output and a CD and Minidisc Recorder with RCA Stereo Analog Input

Every CD and minidisc player will include this connection set for analog connection to your receiver/processor. You should make this connection regardless of any digital connection that you have made; then you can make recordings from other sources besides digital ones. This method outputs a stereo signal through the two RCA interconnect cables.

How Do I Know I've Got It? All receivers/processors will have at least one RCA interconnect stereo pair of audio outputs, also labeled Left and Right and usually in a section called Audio 1, 2, 3, and so on, or in a cluster of inputs labeled for a specific piece of equipment. Sometimes there will be such a group called CD Recorder/Minidisc, or, more frequently, you will use the connection group labeled Tape 1.

Using the Tape 1 connection group is especially convenient because it includes a pair of input and output connectors for recording and playback. These connectors usually are labeled Tape 1 Play for the input set and Tape 1 Rec for the set that outputs from the receiver/processor.

The CD or minidisc recorder will also have a pair of stereo RCA inputs for recording from analog sources.

Materials You Need: To perform this setup, you need a stereo pair of audio interconnect cables with RCA connectors, one colored white or black for the left channel information and one colored red for the right channel information.

1. Attach each of the two RCA connectors to the two connectors on the receiver/processor labeled Tape 1 Out, Analog Out, or 2-Channel Output. The white or black RCA connector on the cable should slide on the white or black output RCA connector. Remember to check that the connectors are not too tight.

2. Using the two audio cables connected to the receiver/processor's back panel—one left speaker information, the other right speaker information—hook up the two cables to the corresponding inputs on the CD or minidisc recorder. These connectors will be labeled Analog In or Stereo Input. Make sure that from the CD or minidisc recorder to the receiver/processor, Left matches Left and Right matches Right. In addition, the connector must be on tightly so that it cannot slide off with light pressure.

Output Through a Digital or Analog Connection

Your CD recorder or minidisc player has the customary dual methods for outputting audio information to your receiver/processor—analog through dual RCA interconnect cables, and digitally through a single digital coaxial cable or a single digital optical cable.

The rule of thumb is always to connect a digital recording device for playback with the receiver/processor using a digital connector if possible. For the most part, these devices fall into the same category as CD players in the quality of their D/A converters. On an inexpensive to medium CD recorder or minidisc player ($100–600), you should circumvent the D/A converter inside the recorder by outputting digital information directly into the receiver/processor. But remember that you must have a digital connector input on the receiver/processor.

NOTE We discussed this option in your research on Friday night, and we hope that you have chosen a receiver/processor that includes several digital inputs to accept all your digital sources, including your CD recorder, in this manner. Remember that these setup sections are arranged by priority of components. If, for example, you have only two digital inputs and both are being used by your DVD player and a TiVo system, you will not have an open digital connection. Therefore, you will proceed to make an analog connection because it is more critical to have the digital connections devoted to the components that you have already connected.

A CD Recorder or Minidisc Player with Coaxial Digital Output and a Receiver/Processor with Available Coaxial Digital Input

Digital coaxial cable looks like regular analog RCA interconnect cable, but you must make sure that you purchase an interconnect that is labeled and created specifically for the purpose of digital coaxial connections to pass digital information.

How Do I Know I've Got It? Check the back of your CD recorder or minidisc player. If there is an RCA connector colored orange in the interior and labeled Digital Audio Output, Bitstream Out, or Coaxial Digital Out, your CD recorder or minidisc player is capable of the direct connection to the receiver/processor.

On your receiver/processor, you will find an input section with the following configurations:

- Digital inputs and outputs all clustered together
- A CD or minidisc recorder input section with a stereo analog RCA connection pair and digital inputs (with coaxial or optical connections, or both)
- Inputs labeled Audio 1, 2, 3, and so on, each with a stereo analog RCA connection pair and perhaps a digital input (with coaxial or optical connections, or both)

Among one of these input sections, you should find an orange coaxial digital cable input that is open.

Materials You Need: You need one coaxial digital cable long enough to connect comfortably to the back of the receiver/processor.

1. Push one of the male ends of the coaxial digital cable onto the RCA connector on the back panel labeled Audio Output or Digital Output on the CD or minidisc recorder.

2. Slide the other male end of the coaxial digital cable onto the RCA connector on the back of the receiver or processor. If the inputs are labeled numerically, use the one with the lowest number available, but if there is a single input or a section of inputs labeled CD Recorder or Minidisc, use one of those. There may also be a set of inputs labeled Tape 1 (originally for use with a cassette recorder) that may have a digital coaxial type input as well.

   Slide the cable's male RCA connector onto the receiver/processor's input so that it rests comfortably on the RCA connector and can comfortably reach between the digital recorder and the receiver/processor.

Now your CD or minidisc recorder is ready to play your digital and analog custom creations.

A CD or Minidisc Recorder with Toslink/Optical Digital Output and a Receiver/Processor with Toslink/Optical Digital Inputs

The Toslink/optical cable is definitely more prevalent than digital coaxial cable on CD and minidisc recorders, so chances are your component will require the steps described in this section. Remember to minimize the lengths of optical cable because the signal method it uses (light pulsation) tends to cause digital jitter over long runs.

How Do I Know I've Got It? First, take a look at your CD or minidisc recorder's back panel. If you see a small, square Toslink/optical connection or the protective optical connector insert (which has a small handle that you can remove to allow access to the Toslink/optical connection), your digital recorder is equipped properly.

On your receiver/processor, as before, you will see an input group corresponding to one of the following configurations:

- Multiple digital inputs and outputs all clustered together, usually labeled Optical 1, 2, 3, and so on, and Coaxial Digital 1, 2, 3, and so on

- A digital recorder input section with a stereo analog RCA connection pair and perhaps a digital input (with coaxial or optical connections, or both)

- Inputs labeled Audio 1, 2, 3, and so on, each with a stereo analog RCA connection pair and perhaps a digital input (with coaxial or optical connections, or both)

Among one of these input sections, you should find an open Toslink/optical cable connector or the Toslink/optical cable protector.

Materials You Need: This setup requires a Toslink/optical digital cable long enough to reach from the CD or minidisc recorder to the back of the receiver or processor. When you measure this wire for purchase, make sure that it is just the right length to reach, but not so tight to pull on the Toslink/optical connection, which is fragile. Too much tension can damage the equipment and cable.

1. Remove the protective covering over the Toslink/optical wire connectors on both sides. This small plastic sheath covers the tip of the optical connection where it goes into the CD or minidisc recorder and into the receiver/processor. Make sure to remove this protector from both ends of the cable. If you fail to do so, you could damage this input by getting the protector stuck in the connector.

2. Take one male end of the Toslink/optical cable and find the corresponding output on the back of the CD or minidisc recorder. Connect the Toslink/optical connector to the CD or minidisc recorder until the connector locks into the output with a small click. The cable fits only one way because the Toslink/optical connector has two angled sides to the connector that must fit into the output in the right configuration.

3. Take the other male end of the Toslink/optical cable and find the input on the receiver/processor. This input is usually labeled as CD Recorder/Minidisc Digital Audio Input, Optical 1, 2, 3, and so on, Toslink/Optical Input, or something similar. Connect the Toslink/ optical connector to the receiver/processor so that it locks into the output with a small click, just as with your first connection.

Analog Connections

If you do not have an available digital input on your receiver/processor, you will be unable to play through the digital connection on your recorder. However, this is not the end of the world because you almost certainly have the alternative analog connections available.

A CD Player with Two RCA Stereo Analog Outputs (Left/Right) and a Receiver/Processor with Two RCA Stereo Analog Inputs (Left/Right)

Every CD recorder and minidisc player includes this connection set for analog connection to your receiver/processor. This method outputs a stereo signal through the two RCA interconnect cables.

How Do I Know I've Got It? As mentioned before, all CD and minidisc recorders have two outputs for stereo operation, labeled Left (colored white) and Right (colored red). All receivers and processors have at least one RCA connector stereo pair of audio inputs, also labeled Left and Right and usually in a section called Audio 1, 2, 3, and so on, or in a cluster of inputs labeled for a specific piece of equipment. Sometimes such a group is called CD Recorder/Minidisc, but more frequently you will use the connection group labeled Tape 1. The Tape 1 connection group is especially convenient because, as we have already discussed, this group also has a pair of output connectors for recording.

NOTE

If you are already out of available inputs on your receiver or processor, you are in a real pickle. There are a few methods for expanding the number of available source hookups that you can get, but the bottom line is that these methods can only serve as a bandage solution to a larger problem—you may need a new receiver/processor. Remember this advice: Make sure you have enough inputs for now *and* later!

Materials You Need: To perform this setup, you need two audio interconnect cables with RCA connectors, one colored white or black for the left channel information and one colored red for the right channel information.

1. Attach each of the two RCA connectors to the two connectors labeled Stereo Out, Analog Out, or 2-Channel Output on the CD or minidisc recorder. The white or black RCA connector on the cable should slide on the white or black output RCA connector on the CD or minidisc recorder. Remember to check that the connectors are not too tight.

2. Using the two audio cables connected to the CD or minidisc recorder's back panel—one left speaker information, the other right speaker information—hook up the two cables to the corresponding inputs on the receiver/processor. Connect the RCA audio connectors to the RCA inputs labeled Audio 1, 2, 3, and so on. Select the lowest

numbered input that is available. If there is a section on the receiver/processor labeled CD Recorder/Minidisc with two analog RCA inputs, attach the connectors there. Check the connection from the CD or minidisc recorder to the receiver/processor; make sure that Left matches Left, and Right matches Right. Make sure that the connector is on tightly and cannot slide off with light pressure.

Now that your digital recorder is ready, let's move on to the next source device.

Connecting Your Tuner

One component that is optional for most systems is a tuner. You won't need this component if you chose to include a receiver that has a tuner and tuner-related functions built in. However, if you have an integrated amplifier or a processor/pre-amplifier, you will need a tuner.

You can consider a tuner a home theater add-on value. Although you may not think that you will be listening to many radio broadcasts, having the ability to tune in music and even talk shows is something you will grow to really enjoy. Plus, the cost of a tuner is relatively small in the overall expense of your home theater.

In addition, the setup of your tuner is an easy task. So let's get to it.

Antenna Connection

To receive the radio broadcasts, you need to connect some sort of external antenna to the tuner to get AM and FM stations.

In many cases, the tuner package includes an antenna. If so, you must attach this antenna to the proper connector on the back panel of the tuner. Usually, the antenna is a series of two cables running in a *Y*-shaped formation, or a plastic loop with thin wires around the outside. Both of these antennae will have connectors at the end for the wires, including even a coaxial RG-6 connection in some circumstances. The back panel

of the tuner will include a corresponding input connector for the connectors on the antenna. Usually, they will be relatively simple to attach and should get good reception.

In addition, you must find a place to run the antenna for maximum pickup. This usually means that you should raise the antenna as high as possible. One of the most popular and effective locations for the antenna is behind the video monitor so that the antenna remains out of sight, or tucked away behind the component rack.

If you have a circular antenna, it can usually be held in place with a small tack nail or thumbtack at the base of the loop. If you have a *Y*-shaped antenna, it is best to split the two parts of the *Y* as far apart as possible and then tack them to the sides of the wall behind the video monitor or the component rack. The back section of an entertainment centerpiece of furniture also presents an excellent place to connect the antenna.

Finally, experiment with placement of the antenna while tuning in your favorite stations on the tuner. This will at least provide you with a good working location for the antenna.

Alternatively, you may choose to purchase a third-party antenna or use an existing antenna for another device, especially your satellite/DSS dish. In many cases, these powered signal amplification antennae provide you with the best possible reception.

Almost all third-party and DSS add-on antennae connect to the tuner through an RG-6 coaxial cable connector. Check to make sure that you have such a connection type on the back of the tuner so that if you do plan on using a more powerful antenna, you have the proper input. You should insert this cable into the coaxial receptacle and then tighten the cable by screwing the outside metal jacket (which has a hexagonal shape) around the threaded connector. After completing this task, you should receive the radio broadcasts available in your area.

Audio Connection

Only one connection is generally available on consumer tuners today—the good old analog stereo pair. However, as the popularity of digital output sources increases, you will find more and more tuners that function entirely in the digital realm and output via a digital connection. (Some high-end units already use a digital output.)

Until such units become mass-produced goods, we will continue to connect with the analog stereo pair.

A Tuner with Two RCA Stereo Analog Outputs and a Receiver/Processor with Two RCA Stereo Analog Inputs

How Do I Know I've Got It? All tuners on the market today have two RCA outputs to transmit stereo information, usually labeled Left and Right and colored customarily white (left) and red (right). All receivers and processors will have at least one RCA connector stereo pair of audio inputs, also labeled Left and Right and usually in a section called Audio 1, 2, 3, and so on.

Materials You Need: You need two audio interconnect cables with RCA connectors, one colored white or black for the left channel information and one colored red for the right channel information.

1. Attach each of the two RCA connectors to the two connectors on the tuner labeled Stereo Out, Analog Out, or 2-Channel Output. Slide the white or black cable's connector on the white or black output RCA connector on the tuner. Check the connectors for a snug fit.

2. Hook up the two cables already connected to the tuner to the corresponding inputs on the integrated amplifier/processor. Connect the RCA audio connectors to the RCA inputs labeled Audio 1, 2, 3, and so on, selecting the available inputs with the lowest numbers. If the receiver/processor has a section labeled Tuner with

two analog RCA inputs, you should connect to those inputs. Make sure that the cables are wired correctly so that Left on the tuner is connected to Left on the integrated amplifier/processor and that Right is connected to Right. Plus, make sure that the RCA connectors are snugly attached.

Conclusion

The radio is hooked up, so your installation and connection tasks are now complete. It's time for a break for dinner. Then let's fire this theater up!

Remotes, Operating the System, Plus Video and Acoustic Adjustments

- ✪ Remotes
- ✪ Basic home theater operations
- ✪ Video and acoustic adjustments
- ✪ Time to watch some DVDs

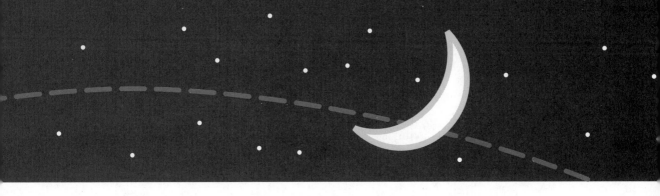

O kay, so now you have everything together. The components are in place and wired up, and the speakers are toed–in. You're now ready to light this candle!

Remotes

Stop. There's something else you need to address. Look down on the coffee table and check out how many remotes you've accumulated. With probably one per component, you should have at least four remotes by now—even for the most basic system (the video monitor, receiver/processor, DVD player, and VCR). You might even have as many as eight to ten!

Let's take a little bit of time to manage all these remote controls so that you and your family can really enjoy your theater without feeling like you're piloting the Space Shuttle.

Using the Standard Remotes

This is the simplest remote management solution, but it's also the most cumbersome and least practical. If you have only dedicated remotes (remotes that will function only with the components that they come with), you don't need to put much effort into your remotes right now. About all you can do is keep the remotes out and well labeled (sometimes a good sticker that says "DVD" works better than the "Toshiba SD-3109 Remote Commander" label already there).

The key to having a well-working home theater system now is education. You will very quickly learn how each remote works and what its capabilities are. However, it is not the same with your family. For them, it is a daunting task for them to learn and even sit down to operate so many remotes.

You need to show them the basic functions and explain how to operate the essential components. For example, you need to explain how to turn on the video monitor with the DSS, how to play the DVD player with the receiver on, and how to select the proper surround sound mode.

However, using only the standard remotes will hamper your family's enjoyment of your home theater. It is especially frustrating to the rest of the family if you are the only one who can truly operate the system, and they need you to do even the most basic tasks.

 NOTE Watch out if you have kids, though; they will start showing you how all this stuff works faster than you can get the remote control out of their grubby little hands.

So, if you are stuck with only the dedicated remotes provided with your equipment, take the time to get the family accustomed to using the remotes and to at least comprehending the basic operations so that they can get the entertainment they want. If you show them what your home theater is capable of, and they see and hear how much fun it is, they will take an interest in learning. Just pick the right movie to use to demonstrate the system, and you will have them hooked. You might even persuade them to contribute toward the purchase of a universal remote.

Universal Remotes

There is no doubt that a universal remote control is the way to go. This option is a big step up from having only the single-function remotes that come with your components.

Ways to Get a Universal Remote

Two ways exist for getting a universal remote. You might find a universal remote included with one of the new components that you purchased, or you can buy a dedicated universal remote from a variety of manufacturers. You should have picked one of these methods based on Friday night's research.

A Universal Remote Included with a Component

Most components today include some form of multiple device remote that operates at least one other device.

Generally, the best choice among such remotes is your receiver or processor's. It will include buttons for its own basic functions and additional buttons for the essential functions of many of your other components. For example, your receiver's remote control will have the functions for volume, surround mode, setup of speakers, and more. It may also have additional buttons for control of your video monitor (including channel and volume), as well as basic DVD, CD, VCR (including play, stop, fast forward, and rewind), and sometimes even DSS receiver functions.

In addition, you might have purchased another component with a universal remote, such as the video monitor or DVD player. However, these remotes will have even less functionality than the receiver/processor remote, and generally are limited to assisting with only components that are somewhat related to the remote's piece of equipment. The video monitor's remote will often have the basic VCR controls, whereas the minidisc or CD recorder's remote will have the basic CD functions for directly recording CD songs.

It is important to note that your overall goal here is to reduce the number of remotes to the minimum possible while still retaining enough sophistication to run most aspects of your home theater. You will never get a remote in this class that will perform every single function of the component's original remote. But by integrating as many functions as possible, you can at least keep most of the remotes off the table until you need a very specialized function.

A Dedicated Universal Remote That You Purchase

A host of these remotes are available today. As we discussed on Friday night, your decision of what kind to purchase comes down to cost, duplication of buttons and functions, and ergonomics and layout.

The best things about a dedicated universal remote are an increase in overall functions, a more updated command set, and improved interfaces and layouts. These remotes tend to be much better than those that come with your components. Often you can find new and updated codes to use on the dedicated universal remote for various manufacturers and equipment on the Internet, and the overall number of compatible components tends to be much larger than a universal remote that comes with any of your components.

However, universal remotes are an accessory that you must buy, and after plunking down several hundred dollars, tacking on a remote to run all the stuff may seem frustrating. But as you know, this remote may be the most important purchase that you make for your home theater.

Types of Remotes

The remote that is included with one of your components and the dedicated universal remote will be one of two types: preprogrammed or learning. This section goes through the basic setup of these two types of remotes. However, it is critical to note that this section describes the most common type of setup operation. Each remote control is as unique as the manufacturer that produced it. Always consult the manual for the specifics of setup and operation.

Preprogrammed Remote Controls

This type of remote control has the infrared functions for a wide variety of products already stored on a chip inside the remote. All it requires is the proper numeric code to trigger the remote to send these functions when you press a button.

The first part of the input process is to check the instruction book for the codes that you need to input. The book will organize the codes by component type first, and then by manufacturer. Normally, each manufacturer will have multiple codes, and you will need to try them all to find the right one to control your component. Some of these codes simply operate a smaller subset of functions than others, so this process involves a little trial and error. The idea is to get as many functions as you can. The better remotes always include a chart for which specialty functions correspond with which buttons (for example these specialty functions include the more complicated activities such as resetting the counter on your VCR to zero).

Usually this process next requires that you press the Learn button on the remote control. This alerts the remote that a code is on its way. Next, you press the Selector button on the remote to identify the component that you are going to activate (the CD player, DVD player, VCR, TV, and so on). Next, you enter the code on the numeric keypad to tell the remote which piece of equipment is available. Finally you may press the Enter button to tell the remote that the transaction is complete.

Now try out the remote to determine whether you have entered the correct code. Often you start by turning the component on and off. Start by pressing the Selector button to tell the remote which component you are about to operate. Then you can start playing with the buttons to see what happens. If nothing happens, move on to the next code until you have entered all the possible codes and at least one works the basic functions. If more than one code works, use whichever code operates the component with the most functions accessible on the remote that you want.

For example, suppose that you bought a Pioneer receiver that came with a universal preprogrammed remote. You also bought a Toshiba SD-2109 DVD player. You would look in the small codebook or instructions that come with the receiver to find out the numeric code that tells the remote control that it will need to send out infrared commands for the Toshiba SD-2109. To find this code, look in the codebook's "DVD Players" section for "Toshiba"; under "Toshiba," you should find a list of several four-digit codes. Try them all and see which does best.

Learning Remote Controls

The other type of remote control is a huge step up in sophistication for your home theater. As mentioned in Friday night's research, this type of remote is capable of actually "learning" the infrared signals from another remote.

This greatly increases the abilities of the remote control to adapt to all the rest of your equipment. Instead of being limited by the functions that a preprogrammed remote control already has in its memory, you are free to input any function that you want to use on the remote.

The only issue with a learning remote is the labeling of the buttons on the learning remote. It is only natural that you label a button for the function that it performs. This is the limiting factor for any remote of this nature. The sheer number of all the potential functions on all the components that exist, which range in complexity from simple to highly component-specific, is staggering. The remote will have labeled buttons for essential functions, but you will probably not be able to replace every button on each component's remote control with one on the learning remote. The remote just won't have enough buttons or the right labels.

To teach a learning remote the signals that you want it to reproduce, you must follow several steps.

Step 1: Switch to Learn Mode

The first part of the learning remote setup process is to set the mode of the remote to learn mode so that the remote is ready to accept a new infrared code. This generally involves pressing a certain button or moving a small switch into the learn mode.

Step 2: Set the Mode for the Device That You Want to Control

Suppose that you are setting up the DVD player's remote control. You have to identify that the DVD player is the component that you want the learning remote to control. When you want to control a particular piece of equipment, such as the DVD player, you will switch the remote to that control mode. Then the universal remote knows to send only the codes for that particular component.

So, simply press the appropriate identifying device button (they are usually grouped together on the top or bottom, and often are indicated with a different color) and you're ready to learn some commands.

Step 3: Point the Remote at the Learning Remote's Infrared (IR) Receiver

You need to set the learning remote physically ready to receive commands from your original remote.

Check out the learning remote. Usually on its bottom you will see a clear, dark plastic cover for the IR receiver. Now set your learning remote down on a table. Next, point your original remote directly at the learning remote's back IR receiver. They should be about 2 inches from each other, and the learning remote's IR receiver should align directly with the original remote's IR transmitter.

Step 4: Press the Button That You Want to Teach

Now press the learning remote control button that you are planning to teach. For example, if you want to teach the Play button on your universal remote the Play command for your CD player, you first press the Play button on the learning remote.

Step 5: Press the Button on the Original Remote

Now press and hold down the button on the original remote that you are teaching. If a red light on your remote goes off when you press a button, wait until this light blinks once. That means that the command has been issued.

It is important to note that for some buttons that have a "hold down" function, such as scanning on your DVD player, you may need to hold down the original remote's button until the universal remote acknowledges the code. This allows the universal remote to send out multiple signals when you press and hold down the button. Not all remotes have this level of sophistication, so you will need to experiment with the buttons to see whether a repetitive command works properly.

Step 6: Check Whether the Remote Accepted the Command

The learning remote will generate a beep, a flashing light, or some other sort of signal that it received and acknowledged the command. If the command was not properly received, the learning remote will display some sort of error message or emanate a tone. Therefore, you will have to try again, starting from Step 4. The learning remote will not switch out of the learn mode, so you can continue with Steps 4 through 6 until the remote learns all your commands.

Step 7: Switch Out of the Learn Mode

After performing this process for all the buttons that you want to replace, you need to switch out of learn mode so that you can actually use the remote. To do so, you press the same key that you pressed to get into learn mode, or you change a switch to the "use" mode and out of the "learn" mode.

Step 8: Give It a Try

As you would with a new car, take the remote out for a test spin by attempting to press all the buttons and activate the corresponding functions on the component. If some don't work right, just go back into learn mode and repeat the steps to input them until you have a final command set for that remote. Then move on to the next remote until you have replaced as many functions on as many remotes as possible and assigned button labels that make logical sense. (In other words, don't teach the button labeled Play to be the command Stop.)

Macros

Macros are single buttons on a few learning universal remotes that can learn and transmit more than just one command. For example, suppose that you want to perform the following sequence of steps:

1. Turn on the video monitor.
2. Turn on the receiver.
3. Tune the video monitor to Video 1.
4. Switch the receiver to Dolby Digital.
5. Turn on the DVD player.
6. Open the DVD disc drawer to await your movie choice.

You can program a single macro button to repeat all these codes to your home theater, which would then carry out all the steps.

Programming a macro on a learning remote is a highly specific task, and the required steps vary widely from remote to remote. Therefore, you should consult your remote control's manual to achieve this level of sophistication. However, we do have a few tips for creating macros.

First, plan out your macro. Run through the steps on a piece of paper and factor in the activities of all your components when the macro starts producing commands one after another. Switch and operate each component (a run-through) as if you were actually pressing each individual key to map the macro out.

Also, beware of the problem of scrolling commands. These commands scroll through a list of settings or inputs. For example, if your video monitor has a single TV/Video button to switch between four video inputs (Video 1, Video 2, Component Video, and S-Video, for example), what if you press the macro while the video monitor is on Video 1 rather than Video 2? If your DVD Play macro says to jump ahead two TV/Video commands, you would hit the Component Video correctly from Video 1, but if you start the macro running from Video 2, you would jump to the S-video input, which might be the DSS! Unfortunately, the only solution is a very expensive remote control system that can transmit to the components with special commands. These systems are quite complex and beyond the scope of this section. For now, it is best to press any scrolling buttons yourself, outside your macro's activity.

In addition, create your macros only after you have finished programming every button for every remote that you intend to replace. Some macro programming remotes will allow you to plug in your sequence only from commands that the remote has already learned.

Keep your macros relatively simple. Big, long, elaborate macros tend to cause all kinds of havoc on a system if one element that your macro expects is out of place or different. Reproduce only the essential functions in the macro, and teach your family how they work and when to use them.

Finally, watch the memory on the remote control. The more commands that you put in the sequence, the more memory it will take up, leaving little for the actual learning of commands from your remotes.

Computer-Based Universal Remotes

The newest remote controls to enter the home theater arena are remotes that are based on a computer platform for interfacing and learning. These remote controls plug into your home computer and allow you to download command sets, button names, screen designs, and even low-resolution pictures for use on the small liquid crystal display (LCD) screen on the remotes.

The two players in this new remote class are the Philips Pronto and the Marantz RC5000 (generally the same remote, with different manufacturers) and the Harman/Kardon and Microsoft Take Control. The Philips Pronto is clearly the leader among home theater enthusiasts because it is incredibly fun to use and program through its powerful computer interface. We have used the Pronto extensively and cannot do without it in our home theater experience. It mimics all our remote controls' functions and has a really cool graphic interface that we designed. Plus, with the ability to put small low-resolution pictures on the touch screen panel, you can impress all your friends with your home theater system's personalized remote control.

Both these remotes are incredibly complex and powerful. Plus, they bring a huge amount of fun and customization to the home theater experience. But they can be very difficult to teach and operate properly, so we will not go into them here. They really demand a book of their own. However, if you have computer skills and a basic understanding of remote controls, you should check out these units.

For more information on these remotes and remote controls in general, you can check out the wonderful Web site Remote Central at **www.remotecentral. com**. Also, please see **www.philips.com**, **www.marantz-usa.com**, and **www.harman.com** for additional manufacturer information.

Basic Home Theater Operations

Now that your remote controls are in order and you've optimized the system, let's turn everything on and go through the home theater's basic operations so that you can get right to the entertainment.

Watching a DVD Movie

Let's start with something that you will be doing a lot of—watching DVD movies.

1. Turn on your video monitor.
2. Turn on your receiver or your processor and amplifiers.
3. Turn on your DVD player.
4. Switch the receiver/processor into the DVD mode. To do so, press the button on your remote or the receiver/processor's front panel to trigger it to accept the audio and video signals for the DVD player. The button will probably be labeled DVD or be one of the Video

buttons (such as Video 2). For example, if you have the DVD player connected to the Video 1 input on your receiver, by pressing Video 1 on the receiver's remote or front panel, you will be able to hear and see the DVD player's output on your home theater.

5. This next step is required only if you are *not* performing your video switching on the receiver/processor. You must switch the video monitor into whichever input the DVD player is connected (that is, which input the video from the DVD player is attached). For example, if you have the DVD player connected to the S-Video input on the video monitor, press the button on your remote labeled Input or TV/Video until the video monitor switches to accept the S-video signal.

   However, if you are using the receiver or processor as your video switcher, you need only make sure that the video monitor is switched to the input to which the receiver or processor's monitor output is connected. If you have the receiver/processor's video monitor output connected with S-video in the Video 2 set of inputs, you must be switched to the Video 2 input section to watch any video signal coming from the receiver. After you press the button on the remote or on the receiver's front panel, the receiver/processor automatically starts sending the video signal to the monitor.

6. Now press the Open/Close button on the DVD remote control so that you can insert a disc. Put the disc in the open tray. Remember to insert the disc with the label side up. If the DVD has two sides, make sure to check which version of the film you want to watch and insert the disc with that side facing up.

NOTE   On a disc with two sides, usually one side of the disc includes the widescreen version and the other is the full-screen version. Sometimes the full-screen side may provide supplemental content.

7. Now press the Open/Close button again to allow the DVD player to begin reading the DVD.

8. After the DVD has been read, the disc menu displays and you can select what you want to do. The key here is to use the arrow keys to navigate through the disc and highlight the Setup menu. *You are now about to do something very important.* On many DVDs (especially those produced at the beginning of DVD's entry into the consumer market), the Dolby surround soundtrack is the default one, not the Dolby Digital soundtrack. This means that when the disc starts playing, your receiver/processor will only be able to read the Dolby Pro Logic soundtrack. Only by going into the Setup menu and selecting the 5.1 soundtrack before you start the disc can you enable your receiver/processor to recognize the signal and lock into the Dolby Digital or DTS soundtrack in full 5.1 channel sound.

NOTE On some DVD players and discs, you can switch the audio signal on-the-fly, while the movie is playing, by pressing the Audio button on your remote control.

You're all set. Have fun!

Watching Your DSS Dish System/Cable Television

Now let's move on to your broadcast television so that you're ready for those reruns of *The A-Team*. The following steps will enable you to watch your DSS dish system or cable television without your VCR or PTVR:

1. Turn on your video monitor (if it's not on already).

2. Turn on your receiver or your processor and amplifiers.

3. Turn on your DSS system or cable box.

4. Switch the receiver/processor to the DSS/cable box input. This requires that you press the button on your remote or the receiver/processor's front panel to trigger the receiver/processor to accept the audio and video signals for the DSS/cable box. The

button will probably be labeled DSS/Cable or be one of the Video buttons (such as Video 2). For example, if you connected the DSS or cable box to the Video 1 input on your receiver, then by pressing Video 1 on the receiver's remote or front panel you will now be able to hear and see both your "local" and "cable" television stations on your home theater.

5. The next step is required only if you are video switching through the video monitor. Remember that in this configuration, you are switching both the receiver/processor and the video monitor to the proper input for viewing. Therefore, press the button on your remote labeled Input or TV/Video until the video monitor switches to accept whichever signal the DSS/cable box is sending directly to your video monitor. But, if the receiver or processor is handling the video switching chores, you must switch the video monitor to the input to which the receiver or processor's monitor output is connected. If you connected the receiver/processor's video monitor output to Composite Video in the Video 1 set of inputs, you must switch to the Video 1 input section to watch the composite video signal coming from the receiver. After you press the button on the remote or the receiver's front panel, the receiver/processor automatically starts sending out the video signal to the video monitor. You just have to switch the video monitor to the input that receives this signal.

6. After properly starting your video and audio, feel free to change the channel and adjust the volume on the home theater. Sound will be coming from the speaker system. Also, you can adjust the speaker volume through the receiver/processor for a better entertainment experience. You may also want to watch the television programming using a sound mode from the receiver/processor. As we have discussed, television signals almost always play in stereo or Dolby Pro Logic. Therefore, you can press the button labeled Sound Mode or Sound Field on the receiver/processor or remote control, and then select which sound processing type you want. You can also take advantage of the ambiance sound programs on your

receiver/processor, like Hall or Church, that can add to your enjoyment of the material. For example, the surround mode labeled Stadium can be terrific for sports such as football and baseball.

NOTE You can also watch television without the home theater in operation. You can do this through your standard coaxial cable connection input on the video monitor. Just switch the video monitor to the Antenna or Cable input and you will get both video and audio. Then run the system with your cable box or DSS receiver remote.

The A-Team is on in a few minutes…better hurry.

Watching Your Regular Broadcast Channels Through a PTVR

If you are fortunate enough to have a PTVR, you will definitely want to watch your broadcast channels through this remarkable device.

1. Turn on the video monitor.
2. Turn on your receiver or your processor and amplifiers.
3. Turn on your PTVR.
4. If you are running one, turn on your DSS system/cable box (which is going to provide the broadcast channels to the PTVR).
5. Switch the receiver/processor to the PTVR input. This requires that you press the button on your remote or the receiver/processor's front panel to get the receiver/processor to accept the audio and video signals from the PTVR. The button on the remote or on the front panel of the receiver/processor will be labeled DSS/Cable or be one of the Video buttons (such as Video 2). For example, if you have a TiVo PTVR unit connected to the Video 3 input on your receiver, by pressing Video 3 or Cable/DSS on the receiver's remote or front panel, you will be able to hear and see your local broadcast and cable television stations on your home theater.

6. The next step is required only if you are video switching through the video monitor. Remember that if you are switching through the video monitor, you must change the input for both the receiver/processor and the video monitor. So, press the button labeled Video, Input, or TV/Video on your remote until the video monitor switches to accept whichever signal the DSS/cable box is sending directly to your video monitor. But, if the receiver or processor is handling the video switching chores, the video monitor must also be switched to the input to which the receiver or processor's monitor output is connected. If you have the receiver/processor's video monitor output connected to Composite Video in the Video 1 set of inputs, you must switch to the Video 1 input section to watch the composite video signal coming from the receiver. After you press the button on the remote or on the receiver's front panel, the receiver/processor automatically starts sending the video signal to the video monitor.

7. After configuring your video and audio, feel free to operate the PTVR in its normal functions of recording, displaying, and managing your television experience. Remember that sound will be coming from the speaker system in this type of configuration. Also, you can adjust the speaker volume through the receiver/processor for a better entertainment experience. You may also want to watch the television programming using a specific sound mode from the receiver/processor. Remember that television signals can record and play only stereo or Dolby Pro Logic information. By pressing the button labeled Sound Mode or Sound Field on the receiver/processor or remote control, you can select which sound processing mode you want. You can also take advantage of bonus sound programs on your receiver/processor, such as Hall or Church, that can add to your enjoyment of the material.

You can also watch television without the home theater in operation. Just switch the video monitor to the Antenna or Cable input and you will get both video and audio because a signal is still coming from the PTVR to the video monitor from your setup. Run the system without the home theater on and with your PTVR remote, and sound will come only from the video monitor's speakers.

That's it.

Watching Your Regular Broadcast Channels Through a VCR

This option is available for television viewing when you do not have a device such as a PTVR or a DSS or cable box. It is a simple connection and a simple operation.

1. Turn on the video monitor.

2. Turn on your receiver or your processor and amplifiers.

3. Turn on the VCR.

4. Switch the receiver/processor to the VCR input. You must press the button on your remote or the receiver/processor's front panel to get it to accept the audio and video signals from the VCR. The button on the remote or on the front panel of the receiver/processor will be labeled VCR or be one of the Video buttons (such as Video 4). For example, if you have a VCR connected to the Video 4 input on your receiver, by pressing Video 4 or VCR on the receiver's remote or front panel, you will be able to hear and see your regular television stations on your home theater.

5. The next step is required only if you are video switching through the video monitor. Remember that if you are switching through the video monitor, the input for both the receiver/processor and the video monitor must be switched to receive the audio *and* video signals. Press the button labeled Video, Input, or TV/Video on your remote until the video monitor switches to accept the input

that the VCR is using to send its output to your video monitor. However, if the receiver or processor is handling the video switching chores, the video monitor must be switched to the input to which the receiver or processor's *monitor output* is connected. If you have the receiver/processor's video monitor output connected with composite video in the Video 2 set of inputs, you must switch to the Video 2 input section to watch the composite video signal coming from the receiver from your VCR or any other composite device. After you press the button on the remote or on the receiver's front panel, the receiver/processor automatically starts sending the video signal to the video monitor.

6. After the video monitor and receiver have their respective signals, you are all set and can begin watching television. You will use the VCR remote to change channels. Also, you can adjust the speaker volume through the receiver/processor for a better entertainment experience. You may also want to watch television programming using a specific sound mode from the receiver/processor. Television signals can record and play only stereo or Dolby Pro Logic information. You can press the button labeled Sound Mode or Sound Field on the receiver/processor or remote control and select which sound processing you want. You can also take advantage of the ambiance sound programs on your receiver/processor, such as Hall or Church, that can add to your enjoyment of the material.

NOTE You can also watch television without the home theater in operation. Just switch the video monitor to the Antenna or Cable input and you will get both video and audio because a signal is still coming from the PTVR to the video monitor from your setup. Run the system with your PTVR remote and without the home theater on, and sound will only come from the video monitor's speakers.

You are all done with this operation. The next operation enables you to watch television through the VCR.

Watching a VCR Tape

The good old VCR tape is still in operation in millions of homes in America. Chances are that if you have younger kids, you have some tapes that have been watched so many times that even you can recite the words to the songs. (Note: *Pokemon* can be hazardous to your health.)

1. Turn on the video monitor.

2. Turn on your receiver or processor and amplifiers.

3. Turn on the VCR.

4. Switch the receiver/processor to the VCR input to watch the video-tape. You need to press the button on your remote or the receiver/processor's front panel to get it to accept the audio and video signals from the VCR. The button on the remote or on the front panel of the receiver/processor will be labeled VCR or be one of the Video buttons (such as Video 2). For example, if you have the VCR connected to the Video 2 input on your receiver, by pressing Video 2 or VCR on the receiver's remote or front panel, you will be able to hear and see your videotape.

5. You should perform this step only if you are video switching through the video monitor. Remember that if you are switching through the video monitor, the input on both the receiver/processor and the video monitor must be switched to receive both the audio *and* video signals. Press the button labeled Video, Input, or TV/Video on your remote until the video monitor switches to accept whichever input the VCR is using. However, if the receiver or processor is handling the video switching chores, the video monitor must be switched to the input to which the receiver or processor's *monitor output* is connected. If you have the receiver/processor's video monitor output connected with S-video in the single S-Video input, you must switch to the S-Video input section to watch the VCR or any other S-video device. After you press the button on the remote or receiver's front panel, the receiver/processor automatically starts sending the VCR's video signal to the video monitor.

6. After setting the video monitor and receiver, insert the tape into the VCR.

7. Press Play on the VCR. You may adjust volume on the receiver/processor and fast-forward as needed.

8. You may also want to play the videotape with a specific sound mode from the receiver/processor. Remember that VCRs can record and play only stereo or Dolby Pro Logic information. You can press the button labeled Sound Mode or Sound Field on the receiver/processor or remote control and select the sound processing that you want. You can also take advantage of the additional special sound programs, such as Hall or Church, that can add to your enjoyment of the material.

That's it for playing a VCR tape.

Playing a Compact Disc

Let's move to something a little simpler. Playing a compact disc is a relatively simple task.

1. Turn on your receiver or processor and amplifiers.

2. Turn on your CD player.

3. Switch your receiver/processor to the CD player input. You can do so by pressing the CD player button on the front panel or on the remote control. Sometimes you might need to switch the audio to a digital input. For example, if your CD player is connected to the Toslink/optical input, you will need to switch to the input labeled Optical 1.

4. Now switch the audio processing on the receiver/processor to the desired mode. Usually with compact discs you will want to switch to the stereo processing mode. You can do so by pressing the Sound Mode button on the receiver/processor to scroll through the available modes (such as Dolby Digital and DTS). Some receivers and processors have a dedicated button labeled Stereo to switch directly to playing only the left and right speakers.

5. Press Open on the CD player and then load a disc into the waiting tray. Then press the Close button. If you have a CD changer with multiple discs, you will also need to decide which disc you are going to play. Often this requires that you input the number of the disc on the remote control either using specific buttons labeled Disc 1, 2, 3, and so on, or using the numeric keypad on the remote after pressing a button labeled Disc Select, Jump To Disc, or Disc # to tell the CD player that you are about to enter the number of the disc that you want to play.

6. Press Play on the CD player and it begins playing the disc.

Listening to the Radio

The radio on your home theater functions almost identically to the car radio that you are so accustomed to operating.

1. Turn on your receiver or processor and amplifier combination.

2. Turn on your tuner. Remember that if you have a receiver, you already have a tuner and do not need to turn it on too.

3. Switch your receiver/processor to the tuner input. To do so, press the Tuner button either on the front panel or on the remote.

4. Switch the audio processing on the receiver/processor to the desired mode. Radio stations are almost always best in stereo mode, with only the left and right speakers playing (two channels of information). Just press the Sound Mode button on the receiver/processor to scroll through the available modes (such as Dolby Digital and DTS). Some receivers and processors have a dedicated button labeled Stereo to switch directly to playing only the left and right speakers.

5. Switch the tuner to the station to which you want to listen. First select whether you want to listen to FM or AM, and then press the appropriate button on the tuner.

6. Use the buttons for tuning up and down the frequency range until you reach the station to which you want to listen.

Playing a Minidisc

Finally, you can play a minidisc through your home theater.

1. Turn on your receiver or processor and amplifiers.
2. Turn on your CD player.
3. Switch your receiver/processor to the minidisc input. You can do so by pressing the MD button on the front panel or on the remote control. Sometimes you will need to switch the audio specifically to a digital input. For example, if your minidisc player is connected to the Toslink/optical input, you must switch to the input labeled Optical 1.
4. Switch the audio processing on the receiver/processor to the desired mode. Usually with minidiscs you will want to switch into the stereo processing mode. Press the Sound Mode button on the receiver/processor and scroll through the available sound modes (such as Dolby Digital and DTS). Some receivers and processors have a dedicated button labeled Stereo to switch directly to playing only the left and right speakers.
5. Press Open on the minidisc player, and then load a disc into the waiting tray. Then press the Close button. (Sometimes the Open and Close buttons are the same.)
6. Press Play on the minidisc player, and it begins playing the disc.

Video and Acoustic Adjustments

Before your system is totally ready for action, but now that you know how to perform the next basic operations tasks coming up, we will spend a few minutes on some very effective adjustments that you can make to instantly upgrade your home theater's performance.

Video Monitor Adjustments
Using a Video Calibration DVD

In most cases, your video monitor is configured "from the factory" with settings that are designed to sell the monitor (often the brightness is turned up and the picture is set for maximum impact), but that do not provide an image as close to the NTSC standards for video monitors, which were used to make all the recordings you will be watching on your home theater.

The best method for obtaining a properly calibrated video monitor is to use a calibration DVD that is designed to optimize the audio and video of home theaters. Currently, two such discs are available—called Avia's Guide to Home Theater (from Ovation Software) and Video Essentials (from Joe Kane Productions).

These DVDs are full of a variety of testing and setting activities for both the video and audio parts of your system. In addition, the Video Essentials disc is sponsored by the Imaging Science Foundation, which is the trade organization that is responsible for proper calibration of video monitors. When you have run through the Video Essentials disc, you are assured of a high level of quality in your monitor's presentation. However, the Video Essentials disc is hard to navigate through, and tends to be low on instructions so that some calibration tasks can be very difficult and time-consuming.

The Avia disc, however, is newer and features an interface that can be moved through very quickly and with minimal effort. This DVD includes most of the same measurements and setting tasks as Video Essentials, but without as much depth to the information provided. It does have a wonderful home theater system overview that is an excellent complement to this book.

Therefore, Video Essentials is a little more A/V Professional oriented, whereas the Avia Guide to Home Theater is more consumer-directed toward the rest of us. Our preference tends to be the Avia disc. Regardless of what level your home theater expertise is, getting one of these discs is now a critical part of your home theater setup experience. It is impossible to force you to buy one, but if we could, we would. To perform the video calibration, jump to the sections on DVD called "Basic Video Adjustments." In this section, you will adjust and LEARN about setting the contrast, brightness, sharpness, color, and tint on your video monitor. Go step by step through the exercises until you have completed all the adjustments you can possibly make on your video monitor.

NOTE It is important to note that your video monitor's performance enhancement is directly related to how much control is offered by your video monitor in its menu. For example, you will probably have the ability to adjust brightness and contrast, but on many monitors, there is no user adjustment of color temperature (which should be set to 6500 degrees Kelvin). Therefore, check out the setting controls on your video monitor to see what you can do.

Also, you should never attempt to make adjustments to the monitor that are outside of the consumer accessible ones. Most video monitors have a "service mode" that allows trained technicians to access certain aspects of the video monitor. Playing with these settings yourself can be very dangerous to your monitor. If you feel that your image is still not satisfactory after calibration, you should consult the Imaging Science Foundation for a licensed video display professional in your area.

The goal of both the Avia and Video Essentials DVDs is to obtain an image that is as close to the NTSC reference monitors used in making the DVDs, VCR tapes, and broadcast television programs you will watch on your system. By going through one of these discs, you can obtain a fabulous picture.

Audio Adjustments Using a Calibration DVD

Like the video calibration section of the Avia and Video Essentials DVDs, these test DVDs also have extensive audio testing sections. It cannot be understated how vast the improvements to audio quality can be from engaging in each of the audio setting exercises. In addition to the calibration DVD techniques we will be discussing below, there are additional activities that you can do to improve audio performance.

Channel Check

This is a quick test to make sure that each channel (Left, Center, Right, Left Rear, Right Rear, and Subwoofer) is all connected to its proper inputs and outputs so that sound comes from the proper geographic location in your home theater.

You can do this with a calibration DVD or also with the test tone generator on most receivers/processors on the market today. A signal of pink noise (sounds like static) is emitted from one speaker to the next and the front panel of the receiver/processor states which speaker should be playing. Check that they all match up. If not, you will have to check both your speaker wire runs and your interconnect cables to make sure they correspond to the channel where they are located.

Phase of the Loudspeakers

This refers to checking whether the positive (red) speaker wire is connected to the positive terminals on the speaker and amplifier and that the negative (white or black) wire is also connected to the white or black terminals on the amplifier and loudspeaker. If you have speakers that are not in phase, they can often cancel out the sound produced by each (while one loudspeaker is pushing out, the other speaker is pulling in, creating a wave that is the exact opposite of the other speaker and resulting in cancellation).

Sound Pressure Levels

This is a calibration exercise to make sure that when sound comes to the listener from any speaker in your system, it is at the exact same volume and intensity regardless of which speaker it emanated from. Remember that the closer you sit to a speaker, the louder it will be. By adjusting sound levels on the processor, we can tone down speakers that are too close and increase the sound level of those that are far away—all to obtain an even sound level in the listening position. This allows the original engineer's sound mix to be presented to the listener without any channels sounding overly present or deficient.

To perform this task, you will need a Radio Shack Sound Pressure Level Meter (Model #32250—a required item for home theater owners—don't get the digital one, it is actually less effective). You place the SPL meter at the listening position, pointing the microphone up, setting it to 70dB, C weighting, and slow response. Then, using either the test tones on the DVD or the test tone generator on your receiver/processor, you can determine what sound level each loudspeaker will produce by reading the needle on the meter. Now, using the channel level settings on your receiver or processor, you can adjust these channels + or - to get the same SPL across every channel in your home theater. The Avia disc has an excellent section informing you how to perform this process in greater depth.

Stereo Imaging

As mentioned before, this is an acoustic principle where the left and right speakers combine acoustically to create sound coming directly from the area between the two speakers. This will dramatically improve the realism of the performance.

To maximize the imaging (especially for two-channel music), you will need to use the calibration DVD or another CD with a strong central voice track (Jewel's "Spirit" is a good example). Several other calibration CDs are on the market, the best of them being the *Stereophile* magazine test disc series (**www.stereophile.com**).

When you have one of these discs, play it in the stereo mode on your receiver/processor at the clearest vocal track (usually the least number of other instruments playing). Now, in small increments, you will turn your left and right loudspeakers in toward the listening position until you can hear a strong central voice coming from between them. This whole process is trial and error, but generally, the speakers pointing directly toward the listening position (center seat in couch) is a good place to start. Don't actually move your speakers (we aligned them yesterday afternoon!), just alter their angle in small steps. We call this process toeing-in the speakers.

Rear Loudspeaker Delay

To assure that a complete surround sound environment is created, you must also set the correct delay level for the rear speakers. This adjustment will provide a much more realistic surround sound experience and prevent the entire presentation from creating an echo-like effect, with too much information at once. Instead, a properly set delay will allow the front speaker information to arrive first, followed quickly by the rear information to give a sense of depth to the enveloping sound. Although this appears to be a strange phenomenon, we're actually talking milliseconds here.

The equation for determining rear speaker delay is as follows:

$(f - r) + 15 = d$ where

f = distance from the listening position to front speakers

r = distance from the listening position to the rear surrounds

d = what the delay is between the front and rear surrounds

f and r should be equal distances to the listening position for both the left and right front loudspeakers and also equal for the left and right surround speakers.

After you have determined the delay value, you can go to your receiver or processor and access the delay controls, which allows you to adjust the rear speaker delay. Increase or decrease the delay in milliseconds as needed.

Eliminate First Reflections

When your left and right loudspeaker play their sound, almost all of the auditory information is sent straight ahead from the speaker toward the listener. However, additional sound comes from the speakers at more severe angles that hits the wall closest to the speaker and bounces off toward the direction of the listener. This sound movement principle is called a first reflection.

The problem with first reflections is that the sound reaches the listener AFTER the initial sound comes direct from the face of the speaker. This produces an echo-like effect that draws the sound on for too long.

To combat this problem, it is strongly advised that you place a room object, like a plant, drapes, or even bookcases to diffuse or absorb the first reflection. Instead of hitting a solid straight wall, the sound would either hit an uneven surface and send the sound bouncing off in all directions (but not to your ear at the listening position), or the material is such that it absorbs the sound wave and sends no sound information on to the listener, like a heavy drape. Many special materials are also sold to absorb sound waves, consisting of fabric-covered panels of a foam-like substance, but these can be much more expensive than a strategically placed room object.

The area where your first reflection will most likely come is about 2–feet down the sidewall next to the loudspeaker. This is the ideal placement for your object or panel to eliminate the first reflection. Start with the object or panel in this location and then move to the left and right against the wall to find the spot where the first reflection is destroyed. You can tell because the sound from the left and right speakers will suddenly come into tighter focus and sound much more precise. When you have an optimal location, plant your object or hang your panel.

Subwoofer Final Placement

We discussed subwoofer placement based on relatively general principles on Sunday morning. However, with the aid of one of the audio and video calibration DVDs, we can now factor in acoustic response to our subwoofer placement.

Each calibration DVD will have a series of subwoofer test tones designed to provide a continual bass signal of the same note and intensity. By playing this track repeatedly, you can sit in the listening position and gauge the bass response as you make subtle changes to the subwoofer. These changes include turning the woofer to face a different way, angling the subwoofer in small increments, moving it inches to the left and right, and moving it closer or further from the wall. All these adjustments could have an effect on your subwoofer output. By sitting at the listening position and generating a constant signal such as this, you can determine how much bass is being generated and adjust the subwoofer accordingly.

NOTE You can also determine the SPL reading on the subwoofer from these test tones, to adjust the sound level to match the other five speakers.

Time to Watch Some DVDs

In this section, we suggest 10 of our favorite DVDs that should give your system a workout in a variety of areas so that you can see the full range of your system.

Air Force One is a very fun film with a spectacular aerial combat sequence that will have your subwoofer dropping low and your mains swirling with directional efforts.

With groundbreaking animation and an all-star voice cast, *ANTZ* is a very enjoyable film, but the surround mix is impressive too, with great efforts and some loud and solid bass during action sequences.

A popcorn film on the grandest scale, *Armageddon* will have your speaker system running hot throughout almost the entire movie with the over-the-top action.

The Fifth Element is a visual and auditory feast. This lavish sci-fi production has sound effects to spare, plus lots of action to keep the subwoofer and surrounds active.

LA Confidential is a masterful crime epic. The brilliant cast, script, and direction are brought through in a terrific DVD. There is a great deal of talking, but the moment that things heat up, your speakers will be put to the test.

The Mummy is pure adventure. This supernatural movie has a terrific soundtrack with massive bass, strong surrounds, and a wide, expansive soundstage. This is one of the best workouts you can give your speakers.

Although not exactly demo material due to graphic content, the stunning *Saving Private Ryan* will have you ducking for cover as the bullets whiz past your couch. This DVD demonstrates probably the best use of surround sound on a disc today.

The 1999 sci-fi masterpiece *The Matrix* has gotten excellent treatment on DVD. The audio detail is exceptionally high, as are the strong bass effects, especially in the impressive kung fu fighting sequences.

The Mask of Zorro is another fabulous popcorn movie. The soundtrack to this film is rich in detail, and an excellent speaker system will provide sounds that you probably didn't even hear in the theaters.

Starship Troopers is more over-the-top sci-fi, but a fun and very impressive DVD makes this one a must-hear for your speaker system. The soundtrack features lots of healthy bass, plus action swirling around the listening position.

And as a bonus pick for you AND the kids, don't miss *A Bug's Life,* with some of the most impressive computer generated imagery that will separate the best video monitors from the ones that are just good. The surround mix is equally impressive, boasting wonderful dynamics (uses the whole frequency spectrum), solid surround sound activity, and a wonderful bass track.

The Future of Home Theater

- ✿ High-definition television
- ✿ HD-DVD
- ✿ DVD-Audio and SACD
- ✿ DVD-R and DVD-RW
- ✿ Home theater computer integration
- ✿ Advanced video gaming consoles

Because you currently are or soon will be a home theater owner, we want to give you a brief glimpse of the various new technologies that will become available for your home theater in the coming years. These are cutting-edge products, with new innovations and new state-of-the-art experiences that will make you salivate with excitement.

Remember, however, that tons of components have been hyped and then came and went (anyone remember DIVX?). We are not guaranteeing the success of these technologies, just making you aware of what is on the horizon. Some of these are sure-fire winners that will change the way you use and experience your home theater. Others will make their mark briefly, and then disappear.

It is also important to note that when these devices come out, they are generally *very* expensive and have limited features. As the owners of DVD players in the first two months of the format's existence, we saw our share of problems with hardware and software *and* paid a premium to be two of the first to own the hottest new gadget.

This can be a very fun time to be a home theater enthusiast—out on the cutting edge and a spokesperson for your purchase. We call these people "early adopters." Enthusiasm among early DVD player owners was rabid and zealous to say the least. Get behind the coolest piece of gear by buying it and you're on the edge of the technological wave. Choose the wrong new component to buy and a small investment goes down the drain.

At the point when enough consumers express an interest in the product or purchase it, the component will gradually decrease in price as more and more companies enter the marketplace to produce it. Features increase as companies try to distinguish themselves, and support increases from side markets such as software or repair.

At this point, the component is ready for mass consumption and becomes another part of the standard home theater gear. Keep your eye on the technologies discussed in this appendix. We have a hunch that they'll soon find their way into your component stack.

High-Definition Television

Ladies and gentlemen, the future of television is finally here. Whether you know it or not, we have all been staring at the same television system for the past 50 years (with the only significant change occurring at the transition between black and white and full, lifelike color). This system, called NTSC (National Television Standards Committee), has not changed much in all that time. Even with advances in all sorts of display technology, especially in the computer industry, television has remained its fuzzy and flawed self.

Well, folks, that's about to change. And whether you think so now or not, you *will* be buying a new type of television in the next couple of years. Why? Because the new system, called high-definition television (HDTV), can give you images that are so lifelike that you will swear that you are looking out of a window. This is not some technology that is going to pass people by. It *is* coming. In fact, HDTV broadcast signals are already available over the airwaves and by satellite.

What makes HDTV so superior to our current televisions is the dramatic increase in the number of pixels—the tiny units that make up a picture on the screen. In an HDTV signal, each of these pixels is smaller, and the signal includes more of them. The result is a vastly more lifelike picture with better color and greater detail.

Let's give some figures. Lines of resolution is the measurement of how many pixels exist in a vertical line and a horizontal line across the screen. The current television system is capable of only 720 vertical lines by 486 horizontal lines at the maximum capability. What you get on broadcast television is only about two-thirds of that, with DSS broadcasts close to the maximum resolution. HDTV is capable of as many as 1920 vertical lines by 1080 horizontal lines. That's about 350,000 pixels for NTSC compared to more than 2 million for HDTV. You can see the difference, literally. Razor-sharp images and vivid colors are basic characteristics of HDTV.

The other main difference between HDTV and current television relates to something that we have already touched on when you were selecting a video monitor and a DVD player: interlaced versus progressive scan.

A video image is comprised of horizontal lines of resolution that fit together to seamlessly create a complete picture. Every time an image is on the screen, the horizontal lines of resolution are being consistently updated with the picture information—a process called refreshing. This occurs so fast that your eyes cannot see it happen. Interlacing is a process by which the lines of resolution are refreshed at every other line down the screen so that you receive a full image in basically two pieces. The video monitor refreshes the odd resolution lines first, and then the even lines next. This generally gives you a fluid image that can move very quickly, but is also subject to fuzziness and that weird striped artifacting that you see on your set today when an image has what looks like black and white lines on certain areas of the picture.

A progressive scan picture, as you learned during Friday night's research, abandons the interlacing to instead show the line of pixels at every single line down the image. This yields a sharper and more detailed image without any artifacting. Think of your computer screen's capability to display very small text accurately and without distortion. Your computer monitor can display such a high-quality image because it applies progressive scan technology, which originated in the computer industry.

You are currently watching 480i on your NTSC television.

The "i" after a resolution listing tells whether you are watching an image that is interlaced (i) or progressive (p).

(When you watch a videotape, your resolution is even worse—a VHS tape can produce only a few more than 200 of those lines. A DVD can yield the full 480.) Your current television set is totally incapable of handling such a huge increase in pixels or their new, smaller size. Therefore, you will need to purchase a new television that is HDTV-capable. Luckily, some of these sets are now available, and chances are you can see them demonstrated at your local home electronics retailer.

You will also need a new device to interpret the signals that you want to watch. Most direct-view and rear projection video monitors available today can tune their reception to get each signal (or channel) along the spectrum provided by your DSS or cable system. However, these original tuners will not receive and output HDTV signals. You will need a special HDTV tuner or a special DSS receiver with high-definition capability. Some early HDTV monitors include an internal tuner, but you can purchase an external one to use with the HDTV.

Of course, the moment that new technology is poised to hit the market, especially one that can generate revenue in the billions of dollars, everybody decides to handle it differently. To this end, two different sets of standards have emerged for your broadcast stations. Some stations want to broadcast in 1080 interlaced and some broadcasters want to broadcast in 720 progressive. The debate over which system is better involves far too many variables to discuss here. It is critical that you understand, however, that even though a video monitor claims to produce an HDTV picture, it may not produce the source image in its native resolution—watching a 720p image in a 720p capable video monitor, or a 1080i picture on a 1080i video monitor.

For example, most of today's HD-compatible video monitors are only capable of producing a 1080i picture. If they receive a 720p picture, the video monitor will convert the 720p images to 1080i output. This conversion will occur in the HDTV tuner. The strength of this conversion process will determine how good your picture is. However, you will always get the best picture from an HDTV signal in its native resolution.

It is also important to note that you will not need extra wiring in your house. HDTV signals travel over your standard RG-6 coaxial cable just like your current television signals. It is also critical to realize that you are already familiar with the audio system for HDTV—Dolby Digital. The HDTV tuner will have a digital output (coaxial digital or optical) that will connect directly to your home theater and provide the highest quality sound to match the best picture available.

So keep HDTV in mind when you look at your television today. This technology will change everything.

For more information on HDTV, you can look up the following sites: the Consumer Electronics Manufacturers Association at **www.cemacity.org/ mall/product/video/hdtv.htm**, **www.interfacers.com/CurrentEvents/ HDTV/status.html**, and **www.sinfonia.net/mike/hdtv/**.

HD-DVD

For most of us, the promise of a high-definition DVD is the Holy Grail of the home theater industry. DVD video is already very impressive, but imagine a system that is four times more detailed and clear, with images that go toe to toe with film! Your DVD player would seem absolutely primitive.

The main stumbling block to a high-definition DVD is the storage capacity on the DVD disc. Already we are using compression techniques to fit a full two hours of 480 lines of horizontal resolution and six channels of sound. A current DVD couldn't even store the video alone due to the massive data stream required to produce an HD picture.

Therefore, something new would need to occur first in the world of lasers and in physical storage on the DVD. First you would need a disc with even greater density of data points. These tiny data points would require a laser pickup system that could read the disc's layers of tiny data points.

The development of the necessary laser has been one of the hot topics in storage science and media for the past several years. Specifically, this development has involved attempts to create a laser that is based on the visual spectrum's blue area, and has an even tighter frequency than that of the red laser currently used. Such a laser would allow even more focused reading of the HD-DVD. The stumbling block has been developing a laser that operates at room temperature and for the durations required by a consumer product.

Of all the technologies listed here, HD-DVD is probably the furthest off, but also the most significant. Guesses range from three to five years for the advent of a fully consumer-ready HD-DVD system, but the movie studios would need to resolve copy-protection issues and then release actual content, which they have been very slow to do if DVD is any indication. However, a prototype of such a system was shown at the 1999 Consumer Electronics Show, although it is very far from production.

However, despite these challenges, if you think DVD is impressive now, wait until HD-DVD shows its beautiful face.

For further information on HD-DVD, it is best to check home theater and DVD enthusiast Web sites, including: **www.thebigpicturedvd.com**, **www.thedigitalbits.com**, **www.dvdfile.com**, **www.hometheaterforum.com**, and **www.etown.com**.

DVD-Audio and SACD

The next major advancement in technology comes in the audio department and has much to do with the advanced storage capacity brought to light by DVD.

Every DVD disc has two layers of information. The top layer of the disc is transparent and allows a new type of laser with adjustable focus to read the top layer and then refocus to read the bottom layer. This increased storage capacity is used to get a full two hours of video and audio for a film. However, what if we were to use that increased storage capacity only for audio? The result is a disc that exceeds anything that you've ever heard before. This is the case for DVD-Audio.

SACD, or Super Audio Compact Disc, is a different system, created by Sony and Philips, but built on many of the same principles as DVD-Audio. It incorporates the same physical storage technique as DVD-Audio, but uses a different method for writing to and reading off the disc.

The reason for all this increased storage capacity is to increase the amount of data on a disc (from 16-bit chunks on a current CD to 24-bit chunks on DVD-Audio), and to increase the rate at which the data is sampled (44.1 kHz on a current CD versus 192 kHz on DVD-Audio). This provides a much more lifelike sound on the recording and much greater fidelity when you play it back through your home theater.

Unlike DVD-Audio, though, SACD uses additional proprietary technology, called Direct Stream Digital, to create a digital recording without any data compression. (The technology condenses the 1s and 0s of a digital signal into chunks that the player then expands. The audio on DVD-Video discs works similarly.) This is one of the key differences between the two systems.

Both SACD and DVD-Audio are aimed at two-channel stereo music, but DVD-Audio is also slated to provide 5.1-channel mixes of recordings. This should open up a brand new category of music reproduction called multichannel music. Recording engineers can use this system to record a concert on one disc that, when played back in your home theater system, sounds as if you were in the concert hall, with all the sounds coming from in front of *and* behind you. Many DVD-Video discs are showing up with this type of acoustics, but without the drastically increased fidelity.

Two critical issues may determine the success of these systems. The first is one that has plagued digital media since its inception—copy protection. With such an incredible method of delivering the audio and video of a presentation, the record labels and movie studios do not want very high-quality copies of their properties made. In the case of SACD and DVD-Audio, the concern is that digital reproduction—copying of the 1s and 0s that make up the sound (done on the computer)—will sound identical to the master it was made from, giving both illegal copy professionals and the legitimate owners the capability to make exact copies of the audio on an SACD or a DVD-Audio.

Therefore, digital copy protection issues have led to delays in both these systems, especially DVD-Audio, which has even had its copy protection schemes broken and posted on the Internet. SACD has already resolved this issue, and you can expect DVD-Audio to follow suit with players appearing soon. But this delay for DVD-Audio may give SACD the head start it needs to wipe DVD-Audio out of the consumers' minds.

However, the critical factor in both these new technologies is software. You probably already have a ton of CDs at home. Luckily, every SACD and DVD-Audio player will be backward-compatible with your whole collection of current compact discs. You can play them on both DVD-Audio machines and SACD players. However, to get the sonic benefits of both these components, you will need to purchase a brand new version of your favorite albums, often at a serious premium price. It's time to buy the *White Album* again.

SACD discs and DVD-Audio discs will not play on your current DVD player or CD player unless the production house specifically sets up these alternatives on the disc—but you will not get any additional sonic benefit. Therefore, you must go out and buy a new player to hear the amazing fidelity that these units can produce.

In addition, little has been said about the commitment of the record labels to produce these new discs for all your favorite albums. Sony, which owns Columbia Records, Sony Classical, and a host of others, will put out a large amount of content on SACD. Toshiba, which has led the charge for DVD hardware, is partnered with Warner Music, which owns the rights to many albums. But will the other record labels follow suit?

The entire new media market is driven by software. When DVD burst on the scene, people were hesitant to buy because there were very few movies available. Now, with around 4,000 titles out, they can't keep DVD players on the shelves. Therefore, the increased fidelity of SACD and DVD-Audio will drive the early-adopting consumers to buy these new, more expensive systems with only a small quantity of software. Only with initial hardware and software sales from this early-adopter group, will the studios perceive a market and create even more content to develop new SACD and DVD-Audio consumers. Then mass-market people will buy. Plus, how good can an album sound on high-capacity SACD or DVD-Audio if that album was recorded back in the '60s with outdated recording equipment?

DVD-Audio and SACD are only now coming to the market. SACD players are available from Sony, but they are exceptionally expensive at around $3,000. DVD-Audio players will soon hit the market and be cheaper because of their similarity to DVD-Video players that have already been built. Almost all DVD-Audio players will also be DVD-Video players, which should really factor into the purchase of a DVD player in the next couple of years.

You can see all the potential problems and questions that are brought up by SACD and DVD-Audio. We are moving toward a higher-capacity audio delivery system at some point in the near future—but are we ready now?

For more information on SACD, please see the Sony Web site at **www.sony.com**. For more DVD-Audio information, you can visit the key manufacturer, Panasonic (and one of their brands—Technics), at **www.panasonic.com**.

DVD-R and DVD-RW

One of the principal concerns of early consumers in the rise of DVD is its inability to record video and audio like the VCR that we have used for the past 15 years or more. This has led to the slogan, "Don't throw out your VCR just yet."

Soon to be appearing is the solution to this deficiency, in the form of DVD players and DVD computer drives that can record video and audio onto a special DVD disc for playback later.

Like the CD-ROM drives that we have grown so accustomed to in our computers, DVD discs will eventually come in two forms: DVD-R, which can be written on only once, and DVD-RW, which can be written to repeatedly on a single DVD. Expect DVD-RW later than DVD-R because of the complicated technology needed to create multiple recordings on a single DVD.

These systems are two to three years away from the consumer market, with current users restricted to industrial or computer clients and large corporations that can afford the huge price tag.

The moment that such a system gets close to consumer availability, the legal ramifications of putting a high-capacity, high-quality recording tool in the hands of consumers will need to be resolved. This is a major stumbling block for DVD-R and DVD-RW. The recorded media industry has always treated consumers as a bunch of pirates who will record CDs and DVDs the first chance that they get—and to sell them for a profit not realized by the record company or movie studio. This attitude will not change for DVD-R and DVD-RW, and you can expect the lawyers to cloud the picture tremendously. It does not matter that the serious damage is actually done by highly sophisticated video and audio pirates who have the technology and know-how to make the business profitable. But that's a whole different book in itself.

In addition, consumers will have to determine what it is that they want to record on these DVD discs—and the blank discs will not be cheap.

Being able to dump a two-hour digital camcorder movie of the vacation to Euro Disney makes sense, but you probably wouldn't really want to record your favorite broadcast show on a DVD-R or DVD-RW unless it is something really special like a *Gilligan's Island* reunion. And with the rise of personal television recorders (such as TiVo), would you really want your DVD player to take the place of the VCR? This question has yet to be answered.

The computer industry will probably have greater use for DVD-R and DVD-RW, so it is almost assured that the development process will proceed. However, the extent to which this technology will reach the home theater consumer remains to be seen. Development to consumer purchase level is probably only 2 years off, based on current estimates.

For more information on DVD-R and DVD-RW, it is best to check the DVD enthusiast Web sites, such as **www.thebigpicturedvd.com**, **www.thedigitalbits.com**, **www.dvdfile.com**, and **www.dvdresource.com**.

Home Theater Computer Integration

A home theater processor is nothing more than a very specific computer that does a limited number of functions, but very rapidly and with highly accurate results. So what happens if you integrate all those processes into your home computer and use it as the brains for the home theater? What if your DVD drive were not a separate DVD player, but instead a part of your desktop computer?

These are questions that are just now being posed and answered. As computer prices drop dramatically, the personal computer industry will need to explore other methods for increasing the value of the machines. One of these methods may be the integration of your home theater into a computer interface. With this integration, operations would come from the computer itself, just like playing a DVD in your DVD-ROM drive and having the output appear on a big-screen video monitor with Dolby Digital surround sound.

Already, many HDTV units and front projectors can display a computer image in its native resolution. In this way, you can use your home theater to work with and play on your computer. This is just the tip of the iceberg.

Expect even greater interaction due to the Internet. Surfing the Web is now a legitimate entertainment option, and with the rise of minisurfers, such as Web-TV, the logical move is toward greater integration of this entertainment choice with the home theater. Downloadable movie previews, games, and information services all could be extensive for the home theater. The result is an even more immersive experience that will only increase your entertainment options.

However, the marriage between computers and home theater has yet to reach a level where the average consumer can effectively choose it as an option. Hookup can be complicated and it is expensive to relocate the computer to the home theater room, or buy a whole new unit besides the computer in the office. But as prices continue to drop, buying a second computer with a card inside to output S-video and digital stereo sound will soon become a feasible reality. Plus, as video monitors become increasingly similar to computer monitors (with progressive scan and higher resolution), expect more and more home theater video monitors to offer direct SVGA input to show computer content too.

Keep your eyes and ears open for computer integration with the home theater. Chances are we will see greater convergence of computers and home theater in the next 1–2 years. Like the Internet that has proliferated computer use, computer integration's entertainment possibilities are limited only by the human imagination.

Advanced Video Gaming Consoles

As we have illustrated before, the enjoyment of passively watching a movie often pales in comparison to interacting with a video game on your home theater. The game's every twist and turn can benefit from a good home theater presentation, immersing you in the gaming environment.

Plus, multiple player games are that much more fun with several people trying to blow each other away on a huge video monitor, and the sound of gunfire blaring across the speakers.

So far, the choices have been Nintendo 64, Sony PlayStation, and the new Sega Dreamcast systems. Although these units are certainly fun to integrate into the home theater, they are the equivalent of a VCR in terms of audio and video. Video output is generally composite and audio is stereo, which can be processed into Pro Logic.

However, the next generation of gaming consoles should have dramatically increased capabilities for audio and video. As home theater continues to gain momentum as a staple of modern entertainment options, look for these consoles to increase in resolution and audio performance.

In addition, there is a high probability that these gaming consoles will also function as overall entertainment devices that incorporate several different technologies. For example, the Sony PlayStation 2 will have DVD video capabilities with its standard gaming functions. Because DVD is such a wonderful cross-platform storage device, look for this list of DVD-capable units to expand. Plus, a heavy reliance on Internet connectivity with these consoles also expands their scope. These possibilities only bode well for the home theater industry because they will raise the benchmark for video game audio and video to make the gaming experience that much better on a home theater.

There will also be a proliferation of new options for console types, including the ultimate heavyweight, Microsoft, entering the fray with its X-Box. This will produce lower costs and perhaps greater sophistication.

The only unknown variable involves the topic of the previous section, computer integration. Currently, your computer is without a doubt the most powerful gaming machine that you can purchase. It has an ultrafast processor, Internet connectivity, and massive storage space for instant game access. The degree to which home theaters integrate with your computer in the future will determine the continued impact of the gaming console.

The big advantage these consoles have, however, is price. For what is estimated at roughly $300 to $400, you can get a very powerful game machine on which you can play mind-bending games. Couple this with a wisely constructed home theater, and you have a source device that pays for itself in just a couple of hours of fun.

Contact Details for Home Theater Products/Companies

While writing this book, we had to search high and low to find the right people to talk with, despite the people we already knew. This appendix references where you can find information on companies in the home theater industry, and how to contact them or review their products. The place we referenced time and time again is **www.stereo411.com**. The owner of this Web site has done an incredible job of putting together a list of industry contact information as well as dealers who can provide you with product.

Lovan Racks

www.lovaninc.com

Jerry Bashin, National Sales Manager

Jerryb@lovaninc.com

1610 East Miraloma Avenue
Placentia, CA 92870
Telephone: 714-630-8208
Fax: 714-630-8991

NHT Speakers

www.nhthifi.com

527 Stone Road
Benicia, CA 94510
Customer Service: 1-800-NHT-9993 (648-9993)
Parts and Warranty Support: 1-800-225-9847
Fax: 707-747-1252

TiVo, Inc.

www.tivo.com

Telephone: 1-877-FOR-TIVO (367-8486)

Audio Design Associates (ADA)

www.ada-usa.com

Telephone: 1-800-43-AUDIO (432-8346) or 914-946-9595

Atlantic Technology

www.atlantictechnology.com

Telephone: 1-781-762-6300

Outlaw Audio

www.outlawaudio.com

Outlaw Audio can only be contacted on the Web, so this site is the only place where you can order this company's incredible amplifier!

Sunfire Amplifiers, Processors, and Subwoofers

www.sunfire.com

5210 Bickford Avenue
P.O. Box 1589
Snohomish, WA 98290
Telephone: 425-335-4748
Fax: 425-335-4746

DVD Express, or Express.com

www.dvdexpress.com

www.express.com

Contact DVD Express for all your home theater and DVD needs.

Rane Corporation

www.rane.com

10802 47th Ave. W.
Mukilteo, WA 98275
Telephone: 425-355-6000

Crown Audio Amplifiers

www.crownaudio.com

1718 W. Mishawaka Road
Elkhart, IN 46517
Telephone: 1-800-342-6939 or 219-294-8200

GLOSSARY

4:3 screen ratio: A screen ratio that corresponds to your standard television, where the screen is almost as wide as it is tall. To show widescreen movies, you must use the letterboxing method.

5.1 channel discrete: When a system like DTS or Dolby Digital is recorded onto a CD or DVD, it contains a separate data track for the audio information of all six speakers in the system. Because the data track for the subwoofer is only low bass information, it is represented by the *.1* in *5.1* channel sound, and the other 5 speakers represent the 5.

16:9 screen ratio: A type of video monitor that can display widescreen images without the black bars at the top and bottom (letterboxing) because the monitor is much wider than a normal 4:3 television. This type of monitor will be the standard for HDTV.

A

amplifier: A device that accepts an audio input and transmits it to your speakers in power signals.

analog: A method of transferring audio and video information where the signal sent is an exact reproduction of the signal that generated it.

aspect ratio: The exact ratio of the length of an image to the height of the image in which a film's picture was recorded.

B

banana plug: A kind of connector used to connect speaker wire and an amplifier. The connector has a long banana-shaped connector that inserts into a small hole on the amplifier or the back of the speaker.

binding post: A connector on the back of amplifiers and speakers that allows connection to bare wire, banana plugs, spade lugs, and other types of connections. A binding post looks like a large screw that can be twisted to tighten it down and has a hole in the middle.

C

cable television: A television that accepts a coaxial input, which usually provides shows via your cable television provider.

CD jukebox/carousel/changer: A CD player that holds 5 to 300 CDs all at once.

CD player: A player that accepts a compact disc as its medium and plays tracks back to the receiver or processor.

center speaker: The speaker that sits directly above or below the video monitor and plays the center channel audio information given to it. This is the most active speaker in a home theater presentation because dialog and all central screen activity sounds are played through it.

chrominance: The color value for an individual pixel that makes up a video image.

color temperature: The richer the color, the warmer the color.

component: One of the pieces of electronic equipment that make up your home theater, such as a CD player or an amplifier. They are called components because no single piece performs all functions.

component cables: The three cables that carry the red, green, and blue information for component output. They are labeled Y (green), Cr (red), and Cb (blue) and have RCA terminals.

component output: A distribution method for video information that transfers the amounts of red, green, and blue that define each individual pixel in a video picture. Generally component output is the optimal video distribution type.

composite cable: A cable with RCA connectors on both sides that passes composite video. Often, the RCA connectors are colored yellow.

composite output: The basic distribution method for video, that sends luminance and chrominance information over a single wire.

conditioner: A component that takes the power/current from an electrical outlet and filters out any spikes or fluctuations that might damage your system or cause unwanted noise.

D

digital: A method of audio and video information transfer that codes all information in streams of 1s and 0s, which are then interpreted in a digital-to-analog converter.

digital coaxial cable: An audio cable that transfers digital information. It is terminated with RCA connectors at both sides.

digital input: An input that sends and receives digital signals. Digital inputs are usually either coaxial or fiber-optic.

digital output: A jack that sends out a digital signal through the cable.

digital-to-analog (D/A) converter: A component that performs the task of transferring digital information, such as a compact disc or DVD, into analog signals to be played.

direct view television: A standard television. That is, a television that uses a cathode ray tube (CRT) to display a picture.

Dolby Digital: An audio playback method that uses a left speaker, a right speaker, a center speaker, a right-rear speaker, a left-rear speaker, and a subwoofer for low-frequency information (bass). Therefore, this is a 5.1 channel discrete system, which means that every speaker has its own signal on the playback media. You must have a Dolby Digital decoder to enjoy this sound system.

Dolby Pro Logic/surround: An audio playback method that incorporates a left speaker, a right speaker, a center speaker, and a pair of surround speakers in the rear playing the same signal. This is a four-channel audio system.

driver: The actual part of the speaker that makes the sound. Drivers are generally round and the speaker's face usually includes two or more of them. They come in three basic types: tweeter, midrange, and woofer.

DSS/digital satellite system: A new system by which you can receive different channels of television as well as Internet access.

DTS (digital theater systems): Another 5.1 channel discrete sound system that is the principal competitor of Dolby Digital. It also uses a left speaker, a right speaker, a center speaker, a right-rear speaker, a left-rear speaker, and a subwoofer for low-frequency information (bass). You must have a DTS decoder to enjoy this sound system.

DVD/digital versatile/video disc: The type of discs played in a DVD player. These 5-inch discs can hold more than two hours of audio and video programming on each side.

DVD player: A home theater component that plays 5-inch discs that can contain more than two hours of audio and video programming on each side.

E

entertainment center: A piece of furniture that houses your components and video source (television).

F

full screen: A compromise format for film and television that reproduces a video picture to fill the entire screen of a standard (non-widescreen) television set. Often the full-screen format cuts off the sides of the image to fit into the 4 feet (length) by 3 feet (height) ratio screen.

G

game console: A video game component that connects directly to your television or to your home theater system.

H

HDTV (High Definition Television): The highest-resolution formats of the 18 total DTV (digital television) formats. HDTV is generally considered to be 1,080-line interlaced, 720-line progressive, or 1,080-line progressive.

home theater: A system consisting of five speakers, one subwoofer, a video monitor, a video source (DVD, VCR, or laserdisc player), and a processor power combination to provide the listeners with a movie theater experience, but in one's own home.

I

image washout: A video effect in which the picture looks faded or bleached.

input: A jack that receives a signal.

interconnect cables: Cables with RCA connectors on both ends that are used to transfer analog audio information.

interlaced: A type of video playback that refreshes an image on every other line of pixels, and then goes back and refreshes the lines in between that were skipped. The opposite of *progressive scan*.

L

left-rear speaker: One of the rear speakers that sits behind the listener on the left side. It handles the left-rear channel sounds.

left speaker: The speaker that sits to the left of the video monitor and plays the left channel audio information that is sent to it.

letterbox: A format for showing the correct widescreen aspect ratio on a 4-by-3 full-screen television. Black bars are placed on the top and bottom of the image, which is produced across the width of the video monitor. This format preserves the director's original image size.

loudspeaker stand: A stand that brings the speaker up to listening height and adds aesthetic value to your home theater's physical appearance.

Low Frequency Effects channel (LFE): The .1 channel, which plays the low bass rumblings of explosions and gunshots. A subwoofer usually plays the LFE channel.

luminance: The brightness value for a particular pixel that makes up a video image.

M

midrange: The speaker driver that is responsible for the sounds that are produced across the midsection of the frequency spectrum, such as the human voice. The driver is usually 3.5 to 8 inches in diameter.

minidisc player/recorder: A player/recorder that records and plays off a medium called a minidisc, developed by Sony. The minidisc is a disc-based digital medium for recording and distributing consumer audio.

mono: A type of audio playback in which all the sound comes from a single speaker. Mono was predominantly used in older movies and recordings.

multiple angle: An option on a DVD that allows you to view a scene from another camera angle.

O

optical cable: A fiber-optic audio cable for transferring digital audio information. The connector is an odd-shaped square with a red light in the center. Also known as *Toslink cable.*

output: A jack that transmits a signal.

P

pixel: The individual tiny dots, set in a grid, that make up a video picture. In general, the more pixels, the better looking the picture.

pre-amplifier: A component that accepts audio signals from different components, and then routes those signals, sometimes filtering or decoding them, to the amplifier.

processor: A unit that decodes Dolby Digital or DTS signals and then sends them in six different signals to the respective amplifiers and units. Synonymous with a *pre-amplifier* in most cases.

progressive scan: A type of video playback that refreshes every single line of pixels in a video image one by one. The opposite of *interlaced.*

PTVR (personal television recorder): A new device with embedded technology that makes television viewing more enjoyable, as well as video recording capabilities that enable you to record, pause, fast forward, and rewind your favorite shows during the broadcast or when you are not near your television.

R

RCA connector: The end part of the wire that has a single center shaft and a circular jacket around it. The connector is inserted so that the shaft slides into an RCA input or output and the jacket grabs around it.

rear projection television: Models generally over 36 inches in size are "rear projection" models. Imagine a movie theater where the image is projected from behind a transparent screen, and you'll have a good picture of how a rear projection TV works.

rear speakers: The speakers that sit directly behind the audience, often split into left-rear and right-rear channels. These speakers play sounds designed to come from behind the audience and ambient sounds (such as birds in a jungle) that envelop the listener.

receiver: A component that combines the functions of a pre-amplifier/processor and an amplifier. Components send signals to the receiver, which then transmits power signals to the speakers.

RF coaxial cable: The standard cable used for receiving cable television and for sending audio and video information to other components such as a VCR.

RG-6 cable: The technical name for *RF coaxial cable.*

right-rear speaker: The rear speaker that sits behind the audience on the right side. It handles the right-rear channel sounds.

right speaker: The speaker that sits to the right of the video monitor and plays the right channel audio information that is sent to it.

S

soundstage: The general depth and width of the sound coming from two or more speakers. A wide, expansive soundstage is good for movies, whereas a very specific sound stage called *stereo imaging* is important for stereo music.

spade lugs: A kind of speaker wire connector shaped like a *U.* The connector is inserted around the center of a binding post, and then the post is tightened down to grab the *U*-shaped connector at the bottom.

speaker wire: The wire that transfers power from an amplifier to the speakers. The wire comes in different gauges (diameters) and always comes in a pair consisting of a positive and negative wire.

spring clip: A type of speaker wire connector that you insert by pressing down a small clip. Then, when you release the clip, it pushes back and holds the wire.

stereo: The standard audio playback method for music playback and also widely for film audio. Stereo incorporates two speakers playing sound: one left and one right. The audience should then be positioned between the two speakers for a very realistic listening experience. (See also *stereo imaging.*)

stereo analog cable: Cable with RCA connectors on both ends that come in pairs, left and right, often white and red. They are used to transfer analog audio information and are often called *interconnect cables.*

stereo imaging: A type of soundstage in which the audience is placed directly in the middle of two stereo speakers, and the audio from each speaker hits the left and right ear at exactly the same time and position. Therefore, the audience senses that the sound is coming from the very middle area between the two speakers. This soundstage sounds exceptionally lifelike and is especially good for vocals that come from the direct center of the room.

subwoofer: The speaker that generally handles the .1 or low-frequency effects channel information. It has a large driver that moves large amounts of air to replicate the booming sound that you would hear, for example, from a rocket taking off.

S-VHS/S-VHS VCR: A VCR that records in a higher video grade than a regular VCR.

S-video: This 4-pin connector cable usually provides a sharper, clearer, higher resolution picture by transmitting the chrominance and luminance portions of a video signal separately.

S-video cable: The special cable used for S-video transfer. It has S-video connectors, which have round ends with four wires and a plastic guide at the bottom.

S-video output: A distribution method for video information that transfers the luminance and chrominance on individual wires dedicated for each value. This distribution method improves overall picture quality.

T

Toslink cable: A fiber-optic audio cable for transferring digital audio information. The connector is an odd-shaped square with a red light in the center. Also called an *optical cable.*

tuner: A component that can receive and play radio broadcasts.

tweeter: The speaker driver responsible for high-frequency sounds, such as swords clashing against each other or a triangle. The driver is usually .5 to 2 inches in diameter.

V

VCR (video cassette recorder): A video recording device that uses large cassette tapes as the medium.

VCR tape/videotape: A cassette shaped like a rectangular box and containing two to six hours worth of magnetic tape that you can record on using a VCR.

video monitor: A projection, direct view, rear projection, or HDTV television. Any display that provides you with the picture for your home theater.

W

widescreen: A particular screen type used in filmmaking. A widescreen image has a picture that is longer than it is tall by 1.85 or 2.35 times.

woofer: The speaker driver that is responsible for the low bass sounds, such as an airplane flying overhead or a cello. The driver is usually 6.5 to 18 inches in diameter to move large amounts of air to generate the huge sound waves necessary for bass.

INDEX